Stories in the Summerlands

A pilgrimage through esoteric Avalon

ABOUT THE AUTHOR

Annie Dieu-Le-Veut is a shaman and former national newspaper journalist. She is the author of *The Sacred Sex Rites of Ishtar*, *The Bright World of the Gods*, *The Grail Mysteries* and *Stories in the Stars*. She can be found on her blog, **Annie Dieu-Le-Veut**.

COVER

Glastonbury Night Glow © **Chris Beard Images**. See more of Chris's work at: **fineartamerica.com/profiles/chris-beard.html**. Cover design by **Sam Richardson**.

ILLUSTRATIONS

Sam Richardson, **Gerri McLoughlin** and **Yuri Leitch**.

PUBLISHER

John Board for *The Holistic Works*.

COPYRIGHT

All content in this book, *Stories in the Summerlands*, is copyright *The Holistic Works* © October 2019. All rights reserved. This book or any portion thereof may not be reproduced or used in any manner whatsoever without the express written permission of the publisher, except for the use of brief quotations in a book review.

ISBN: 9781796291704

Acknowledgements

I am enormously appreciative to all my fellow travellers along the Green Roads of the Soul who have helped me, inspired me, informed me, challenged me and entertained me enormously throughout my own pilgrimage, which has now produced this book.

There are too many to name – but I will mention, of course, Yuri Leitch and Alan Royce, whose works have inspired me enormously. I have also been propelled along the lanes and byways of my thoughts by the findings of the dowser Stuart Dow, the Irish mythologist Anthony Murphy and, of course, the late geographer John Michel.

I must acknowledge my fellow traveller Rosemary Taylor for our journeys into the Old Norse tree Yggdrasil to discover the three wells overbrimming with the sweetest of mead, which must surely have also inspired the *awen* of the Celtic bards that runs like sparkling silver streams through their myths.

I'm also grateful to Holly Hazeltree for discovering the connection between the "birds" of the Summer Triangle and the Holy Islands of Iona, Lindisfarne and Glastonbury. And I'm also indebted to Sandi Adams for her excellent companionship in our peregrinations around the sacred landscape, and for helping me to discover the hidden secret of the Dragon Persecutions.

I couldn't produce any of my books without the

help of Sam Richardson, who edits my words, provides illustrations and designs the covers. And as ever, many thanks to John Board of The Holistic Works for continuing to have faith in my writings.

Dedication

To Gwythyr ap Greidawl

Lord of the Land under the Summer Stars

Ruler of the Birds of the Summer Triangle

Opener of the Heart's Door Into Summer

Contents

Acknowledgements v
Dedication vii
Contents ix
Illustrations xi

PART ONE: The Captive 1
Chapter One: The Hidden Door 3
Chapter Two: The Dreamer in the Land 17
Chapter Three: The Mists of Avalon 29
Chapter Four: The Mysteries of the Chalice Orchard ... 61
Chapter Five: The Mystery in Ye Stones 99
Chapter Six: The Desert Mysteries in Avalon 139
Chapter Seven: Guiding Spirits of the Summerlands. 185
Chapter Eight: Hill Lucre and the Philosopher's Stone
.... 237

PART TWO: The Called 277
Chapter Nine: The Quest of Avalon 279
Chapter Ten: Arthur the Pole Star Hero 309
Chapter Eleven: The Exalted Prisoner 335
Chapter Twelve: The Faery Ring of the Perpetual
Choirs 355

PART THREE: The Chosen 383
Chapter Thirteen: The Sovereignty of the Land 385
Epilogue 431

Appendix: The Glastonbury Declaration 437
FURTHER READING... 441

Illustrations

Figure 1 The eight "stations of the cross" 44
Figure 2 The St Michael or Belinus line 76
Figure 3 Water initiation 77
Figure 4 The Hermetic symbol for water 83
Figure 5 Fire and water initiations of the zodiac hero 84
Figure 6 The Greater Initiation of the Fire Mysteries 85
Figure 7 Solomon's Seal 90
Figure 8 Vesica Piscis 104
Figure 9 The Vesica Piscis with mandorla shaded 106
Figure 10 Vesica Piscis birthing shapes 109
Figure 11 Bligh Bond's sketch of St Mary's Chapel 109
Figure 12 A rhomb produced by the Vesica Piscis 110
Figure 13 Six-pointed star and the Lady Chapel 113
Figure 14 Vitruvian man and dimensions of the Lady Chapel 113
Figure 15 Detail of a numerical sequence 119
Figure 16 The Fibonacci sequence 121
Figure 17 Seven processes of the Marriage of the Sun and the Moon 123
Figure 18 Three stages of the Marriage of the Sun and the Moon 124
Figure 19 The eight-sided octagon from the circle and the square 127
Figure 20 The circle squared created with rhombs 127
Figure 21 Five-pointed star 129
Figure 22 The Celtic Cross 132
Figure 23 Monas Hieroglyphica 132
Figure 24 - The two crosses of the zodiac 136
Figure 25 The Mysteries of the Old and New Testaments 148

Figure 26 The zodiac of the Bible 151
Figure 27 The Hermetic year 155
Figure 28 The astrology of the Jesus mysteries 156
Figure 29 The Summer Triangle aligned with three holy islands 218
Figure 30 Planets, metals, qualities and alchemical stage . 221
Figure 31 The cover of St Dunstan's Classbook 226
Figure 32 The astrological journey of Pinocchio 243
Figure 33 Timings for seven stages of alchemical operation 256
Figure 34 The ciphers for the gods and goddesses of the zodiac 258
Figure 35 The Mithraic Rock Birth by Yuri Leitch 259
Figure 36 Symbols on west window of St Dunstan's Church 266
Figure 37 The tetramorph symbols and cross-quarter days 267
Figure 38 Alchemical interpretation of stained glass window 268
Figure 39 The constellations on the Temple of the Stars ... 288
Figure 40 Glastonbury Temple of the Stars looking south. 289
Figure 41 The fixed stars over Park Wood 318
Figure 42 Celtic characters and their astrological roles 337
Figure 43 Classical seven-ring labyrinth 341
Figure 44 The Faery Ring of Avalon 360
Figure 45 Locations and stars of the Faery Ring of Avalon 362
Figure 46 The gestation voyage of the Radiant Child 375
Figure 47 The dance of the black and gold serpents 387
Figure 48 The Somerset Parallelogram 390
Figure 49 The passage of the Sun and the Moon 393
Figure 50 The Michael line 408
Figure 51 The Royal Stars and the tetramorph 411
Figure 52 Alfred's Jewel 416
Figure 53 The Melkart and Michael lines 418

Figure 54 Detail from the Bayeux Tapestry 425
Figure 55 Tammuz and Ningishzida 429

PART ONE: The Captive

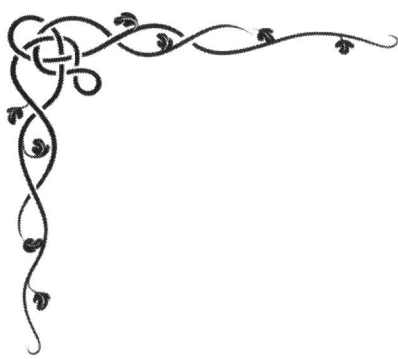

Chapter One: The Hidden Door

> *"... there is a third way to Glastonbury, one of the secret Green Roads of the soul – the Mystic Way that leads through the Hidden Door into a land known only to the eye of vision. This is the Avalon of the Heart for those who love her."* **Dion Fortune, "Glastonbury: Avalon of the Heart"**

I first came to the Summerlands a half-century ago, hoping to gain entrance through the Hidden Door into the Avalon of the Heart.

I was six months pregnant with my daughter as I stood and knocked - just as John Bunyan's hero Christian found himself before the Wicket Gate in his *The Pilgrim's Progress*.

I was among the visitors to the first Glastonbury Festival, a musical event that has since become famous all over the world, although it is now an overblown and commercialised travesty of the small and deeply meaningful gathering it was back then.

Afterwards, we had set up camp among the buttercups on the grass verges of Cinnamon Lane, where I was lucky enough to meet people who thought like me - all intent on digging down into our roots, into our ancestors' understanding about the magical spirits of the land, as we realised that a relationship with those Otherworldly beings was key to our search for the meaning of life.

The term "New Age" had not yet been coined. If it had, it would have sounded strange to us knowing, as we did, that we were immersed in some pretty Old Age philosophies. We had different approaches, as is to be expected from any diverse group of independent thinkers. But one thing that we all agreed on was that if ==humanity could find a way to see through its religious brainwashing and attain true spiritual enlightenment, there would be an end to war.==

On one flower-fragrant, midsummer full Moon night, I was taken to a deeply powerful healing ceremony that was being conducted by a local shaman in her cottage on the lower slopes of Glastonbury Tor.

She didn't describe herself as a shaman and she was a million miles from how we might expect such a person to look today. As a trim, well turned out septuagenarian, Christine wouldn't have seemed out of place at a vicar's garden party in that small market town. In those days, the social fabric of Glastonbury was largely dictated by strait-laced Methodists and Quakers who were quite visibly shocked by this sudden influx of "dirty hippies".

Despite her orthodox appearance, soon after Christian and her companion Elsie had gathered us all into a circle, she shapeshifted before our eyes into a Native American elder named White Eagle. Of course, we had never heard of the term "shapeshifting" back then – but that is what happened. Her facial features morphed into a man's and she seemed to be taller and thicker set. And she carried on with her healing work in that fashion for several hours.

Afterwards, she and Elsie got out their best silver teapot and gold-rimmed, bone china plates decorated with delicate pink roses, and they served each of us with tea and fruitcake. It was as if we'd just finished a whist drive and not a profoundly healing event which would change the course of my life.

I returned, the next day, to Canterbury in Kent, where the night-illumined cathedral filled my bedroom window in a large Georgian house that I shared with some art students. Three months later, I gave birth to my daughter.

When she was old enough for me to work, I drifted into journalism and specialised in writing about complementary health techniques – such as meditation and yoga. In that way, I travelled all around the world for many years and received many different forms of spiritual training from a variety of guides, gurus, swamis and shamans who all helped me, over several decades, to develop in my evolution around the spinning Wheel of Life.

However, while I was tucked away meditating in an Indian ashram, a new movement was being hatched elsewhere that called itself "postmodernism". By the mid-Nineties, a branch of postmodernism had evolved into a sort of rainbow-coloured, Ecstasy-fuelled, "all you need is love" never-ending party which moved like a travelling circus into Glastonbury to establish its perpetual Vanity Fair.

Some called it the New Age movement. Some called it "spiritual freedom". But it seemed a far cry from Dion Fortune's more organic and deeper Green Road of the Soul and it has been a waking nightmare ever since for the locals who have had to watch their neighbourhood being slowly taken over by loud-mouthed drunks and drug addicts who are seen at all hours of the day and night hanging around the High Street.

So it was a painful awakening to discover the dystopian Slough of Despond that Glastonbury had been reduced to after I was unexpectedly pulled back here, like Dorothy of Kansas in a tornado, about 10 years ago.

My daughter had grown up and given birth to a young girl herself and the family had settled nearby. Thus, four decades after such a powerful shamanic healing, the child in my womb been attracted back to the Summerlands. She brought with her a babe that only the stars knew then would be born into our family line. So here we all are now, living around Glastonbury Tor as the archetypal Maiden, Mother and Crone – or, as Christine might have perceived us back then, as three Russian dolls of Mandelbrotian self-similarity, nesting one inside the other.

I had barely finished my training in shamanism when I came to live here. So you can imagine my surprise to be asked by spirit of the Holy Thorn on Wearyall Hill to perform a shamanic soul retrieval for the town of Glastonbury.

The purpose of a shamanic soul retrieval is to

mend the fragmentation of the personality that can occur after a traumatic event. I had carried out such healings for people before but never for a place. I didn't know what I was doing, so I decided to just follow my nose and do my best. And what the whole experience gave me was the key that would unlock the Hidden Door into my own pilgrimage into the Summerlands of Avalon, the fruits of which I will be sharing with you as we go along.

Glastonbury and Avalon

Over the past decade, I have watched in quiet wonder at so many genuine-hearted seekers making their way to Glastonbury. Some are like sleepwalkers whose knowing feet have instinctively led them to this small community of red roofed houses that nestles at the foot of emerald green hills too perfectly formed to have been produced solely by the hand of Nature.

They are often following nothing more substantial than their own intuition which, like Jiminy Cricket, is telling them there is treasure buried in this land. They are quite right; there is and it is life-changing. But it is not what it seems. And so, without a properly qualified guide to lead them, they are easily swallowed up in a whirling sluice of tarot card readers and purveyors of crystals, joss sticks and broomsticks whose sole magical trick is to part them from their money faster than they could say "abracadabra".

In many respects, what purports to be of spiritual or esoteric interest in Glastonbury is just the congealed cognitive detritus of stories that have been chucked, without ceremony, into the remainder bin of history.

All the outcomes of the religious narratives that

have been spun by various priesthoods over time in order to control the subjects of their empires, and that have passed their sell-by-dates, eventually fetch up here like wandering, hungry ghosts intent on ensnaring new followers to fuel their ever-declining existence.

Thus, in our pilgrimage of the heart, we will have to initially feel our way through a choking fog of what is, in effect, a multi-layered pseudo-history to discover the gold of the real Holy Grail that being guarded by the Pen Dragon in the Celestial City beyond.

Even the name of Avalon started off as one of those constructs. It was borrowed from the hill-top town of Avallon, near Vezelay in northern France, which in the early medieval period was the destination of many a long pilgrimage from these isles to visit the bones of Mary Magdalene.

The touring around relics was a hugely lucrative commercial enterprise in medieval times. At one time, there were more than 15 phalluses of Jesus Christ on display across the continent!

But the aim of real spiritual pilgrimage is about finding the meaning and purpose of one's life. So, by setting off down the road with just a virtual knapsack on our back, we are giving ourselves over to the fates in the hopes that they will deal kindly with us, and show us the way to open the heart's door.

The idea of a long walk that offers a meditative retreat from civilisation is currently experiencing a renaissance. With the failure of the main modern religions to capture hearts and minds, all sorts of people – even atheists - are turning to the timeless tradition of pilgrimage as a means of finding themselves and gaining enlightenment.

Many who come to Glastonbury are secretly hoping to catch the will-o-wisp, the *ignis fatuus* or Fool's Fire that is hinted at in William Blake's poem:

And did those feet in ancient times,

Walk upon England's mountains green?

And was the Holy Lamb of God,

On England's pleasant pastures seen?

Others arrive intent on discovering the grave of King Arthur, or on solving the mystery of Merlin, the Holy Grail and the Knights of the Round Table.

Well, they have all come to right place – even, and perhaps especially, the Fools. These Mysteries (with a capital 'M') are here to be solved. However, when there are just as many false prophets practising their dark arts as there are seekers of enlightenment, how does one find the true way forward?

If you approach this book in the hallowed tradition of pilgrimage, it will honour your heart's desire. It will guide you in your search for the meaning of the Holy Grail, the grave of Arthur Pendragon and the red and white fluids contained in the vials of Joseph of Arimathea - but in a way that you might not to expect.

As a visitor to the Summerlands, you can use this book as a guide. But it can be equally employed as an inner pyschopomp wherever you are in the world, to explore the mysteries of the inner Avalon of the Heart.

That other paradigm of Paradise

In her book *Glastonbury: Avalon of the Heart*, local 20th century esoteric author Dion Fortune wrote of a trio of ways to enter into these Mysteries: the high road of history, the upland path of legend or the secret Green Way – the Mystic Way.

Our peregrinations will wind around all three of her routes, because we have to explore the high road of history and upland path of legend in order to sort out fact from fiction. This, in the end, will bring us to the Green Way of the Soul.

It is a long and serpentine route, lined with stoutly built ecclesiastical and political institutions that seem as if they have existed for ever. However, once we examine them more carefully, they dissolve into mirages because their cognitive foundations were built on the shifting sands of Time rather than on the straight and true tracks of the Sun god that the Druids laid out across this land. We will eventually come out of the mists and on to these bright and shining paths that run down to the green banks of a silvery, tumbling river. Once there, you will have to jump in and swim as best as you can, because only total immersion and submersion in the subject matter will give you the gnosis[1] you require.

As we go along, you will soon realise that the ecumenical buildings of magical Avalon were constructed by those who had a very different understanding of the received narratives we hear today. We have been taught to view these stories through a specific lens. But I will be giving you another glass to look through – a more prismatic, multifaceted crystal that will take us over the rainbow.

You will still keep hold of your own spectacles, though, as we fly over that burning Bifrost bridge. After all, you may decide, in the end, that you prefer the view of reality that they give you. But you will only need to suspend your current beliefs temporarily until we are safely through the Mirkwoods. After that, it's all up to you.

Much of the art and architecture of the Summerlands of Somerset reflects that other paradigm of Paradise. Once you learn the meta-language, you will be able to see the messages encoded into the paintings, decorations and architectural proportions of the churches that supplanted the earthworks and rings of standing stones, and thus benefit from a story that our earliest known ancestors have left to us, which contains deep wisdom about who we are and why we are here on this Earth.

So, I hope you will find it all quite simple and easy to understand as we proceed. There is a lot to learn but I promise to guide your steps with simple teachings which build upon each other to cement a foundational knowledge that will enrich your mind with this ancient wisdom, and this will help to propel you along the spinning Wheel of spiritual transformation.

I will be requiring you to gain a basic understanding of some simple mathematics, astronomy and astrology, plus a tiny smattering of alchemy. But don't worry if, like me, you were completely hopeless at maths in school. It also doesn't matter if you have no faith in horoscopes and can't even recognise one end of a Bunsen burner from another. We will be bypassing all that paraphernalia as I explain everything in the plainest English. Then, once you've got a few basic principles tucked away in your rucksack, you will be fully equipped whenever you visit any ancient sacred site – whether Magdalenian, megalithic or medieval, and in this land or any other - to comprehend a lot more about what some have called "sermons in the stones".

You will then hopefully also realise the deep debt of gratitude we owe to the Grail Keepers: succeeding generations of wise men and women who have managed to preserve the secret knowledge by encoding it into the measurements and alignments of the land and within the artwork and architecture of the churches.

The Masons – notably, in Somerset, those of the Holy Royal Arch - inherited this secret gnosis from the Rosicrucians. The Rosicrucians had gained it from the Knights Templars, whose preceptory was at Templecombe, near Cadbury Castle, during the 12th century. Those warrior knights originally learned the esoteric lore from a branch of the Pythagorean[2] priesthood, otherwise known as the Druids, who taught a complex system of natural philosophy as old as the mathematics found on the Vedic fire altars of India, which were built more than 5,000 years ago.

As Hippolytus of Rome wrote in the third century:

> *The Celtic Druids investigated to the very highest point the Pythagorean philosophy ... from calculations and numbers to the Pythagorean art.*

Love of the Land

You are about to discover that the real secret so many pilgrims to Glastonbury seek is actually found in the hills and vales that surrounds the town for miles around. Then you will understand that the ==process of self-realisation has always been instigated by the spirits of the land and that it generates a great love==, which may sound strange at first but perhaps won't seem so odd once you've heard the other side of the story.

The 20th century author Vita Sackville-West expended thousands of words in her great, rapturous, lyrical poem *The Land* in trying to express her love for the seasonally changing landscapes of the Garden of England, the county of Kent. Even then, she probably felt that she had fallen short, just as I always do.

It is unfortunate that even the most lyrical of words turn out to be such clumsy tools when it comes to trying to convey the sense of wonder and joy one feels when watching the golden apricot sunrises and red magenta sunsets of the changing seasons over these Summerlands. Then there is the lightning bolt to the heart upon spying a huge murmuration of chattering starlings flying overhead on cold, icy winter days, and when the creamy white curds of May blossoms and violet-blue ceanothus blooms burst through the lime green at spring.

I wish I could describe the late summer aromas of the lanes and the ridings, and the autumnal parting aromas of the golden leaves as they lay dying... so pungent, dusky and enticing as the days shorten into longer nights, and we slip into dreams of another time... a time we only half-recollect because it has been long forgotten.

==And yet, the land remembers. It always remembers. It remembers us and those who walked here before us.== And when we walk through the meadows and fields, we hear those ancestors calling to us, reminding us of the old stories that contain the wisdom teachings.

We perceive their voices when we eat the golden grain that has been harvested from the soil that has been fertilised from their bones, and we hear their songs when we drink the water from silvery streams that reach us only after running through the deep, dark caverns of their blessed burial grounds.

Those utterances from across the sands of time generate such a genuine love for the land, the land of our fathers, that it brings tears when it arises in our hearts.

This is the true Avalon of the heart that beats out its throbbing pulse across the whole of the Blessed Isles of Britain along energetic "dragon" lines, which have forged straight tracks that are protected by the Sun and the Moon.

The melodic rhythm of this steady heartbeat, which criss-crosses the whole country, comes from the love of the guiding ancestral spirits, the Grail Keepers and the gatekeepers of old. Thus, it is a deeply visceral, organic and spiritual experience.

The Mystery Plays

We are the most fortunate of beings in that those who came before us dedicated their lives to expressing this love and gratitude by creating a colossal theatre of earthworks so that the drama we need to learn will play out for as long as this Earth exists.

One of their dramatic characters was Arthur Pendragon, who, it has been sung, is buried in the land of Avalon and will rise from his grave when the Blessed Isles are threatened and in the direst peril. Even today, memories of the Once and Future King slide silently into our dreams from rhymes that we heard while still in the cradle, which were developed from bardic poems of long, long ago.

The deeper significance of these esoteric dramas on the land is only visible to those with the eyes to see, of whom there are few today. Yet they are still faithfully acted out in Avalon every night, by colossal giants of turf and earth who fight dragons to woo and win the hands of fair maidens on a massive stage lit by stars that shine down into an oft-flooded, cauldron-shaped landscape reminiscent of the Holy Grail.

These mythic Mystery Plays are as rich and fertile as the black peat that was laid down in the soil of the salt marshes and the moss-sweet meadows we will soon be ambling across, because they are threaded through with deep spiritual teachings that come from gentler, slower days… ==when both treasure and pleasure were measured by meaning.== It was a time when a man's dreams were valued more than gold and a real song could birth new worlds from old. When you learn how to sing that song, your life will be revolutionised as much as White Eagle's healing gift transformed mine.

As I write this book, I can hear Christine and Elsie cheering me on. Perhaps they knew it would be my destiny to return to Avalon, to guide pilgrims as they progressed through this enchanted landscape?

Thanks to them, I have learned from my own challenges about how to dislodge oneself from the Slough of Despond and how to resist the lure of the silver mine of Hill Lucre. However seductive the attraction, it cannot compare with our destination. So I will unflaggingly encourage your footsteps as we toil up

Hill Difficulty and inspire you with courage as we traverse the Valley of the Shadow of Death until we reach House Beautiful, the Delectable Mountains and the Celestial City of greater enlightenment.

However, before setting out on our path, we should ask for the blessings of the ancestors. It is necessary to go back in time so that we can tune in to the road maps of those who left us their messages in the underlying meanings of myths and fairytales, some of which are thousands of years old. Once you are familiar with this other, more ancient, way of comprehending the pilgrimage of life, it will hopefully inspire and fire your own footsteps. So, let us all gather now to hear one of the oldest stories in the land.

---

[1] Gnostic knowledge differs from modern scientific knowledge in that it is based upon subjective experience as well as objective evidence.

[2] Pythagoras is said to have lived during the 6th century BCE, in other words, thousands of years after the construction of Vedic altars which exhibit what we, and Hippolytus of Rome, express as Pythagorean proportions.

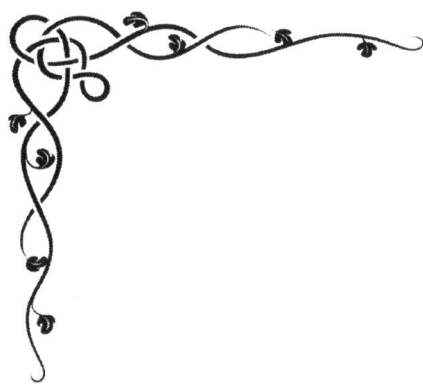

Chapter Two: The Dreamer in the Land

As he followed behind the trods of the great herds of reindeer, Kroy-Khasis always looked forward to the time of year when the stars of the beautiful goddess fell on to the waving seas of burnished grass. He'd noticed, at such times, that the deer would be friskier than usual and starting to rut in a season that was heralded by red-and-white mushrooms poking up their heads through the golden leaves that lay scattered and dying on the ground.

He would keep his steely grey eyes on the winding path ahead as they progressed along but from time to time, he would raise his gaze aloft to admire her graceful form, which was draped in a dark, flowing lapis-lazuli robe studded with platinum-white gems. As the largest constellation in the night sky next to the Dragon's, her sparkling diamonds illuminated the shining blue-white of the snow-frosted mountain peaks below.

Kroy's tribe had been following the herds for several weeks now, since leaving the celebrations that were presided over by the Great Lion. It had been a festival when all the various tribes came together to trade their wares with one another. It was also a good opportunity for the young men and women to meet one another, with a view to finding a suitable match for the handfastings that would take place the following May. The long walk had given him plenty of time to think about one he had met. The more he thought about her, the more his heart began to throb with mounting passion. He began to wonder whether lying in her arms would elicit the same love that he felt for his Beloved above, who he would soon come to below.

As they crossed the mountain's pass, they all stopped to gaze down in wonder, for the first time in a year, at her curvaceous form sprawled across the corn-coloured valley below.

"She's like a great goddess who has fallen from the heavens," he thought to himself.

The fulsome breasts and smoothly rounded belly of this gigantic land effigy were formed by mossy-green hills, and between her slim, elegant legs, mirrored in the Furrow stars above, were long barrows running under a dark, tangled forest, and which were lined inside with glistening-damp stones and the white bones of the ancestors.

The herds then started to head for the lush, fertile valley between her legs.

Once they'd all arrived and set up the camp, the tribe's Dreamers gathered to light their clay pipes and slowly sup tea made from the water of the reindeer that had eaten the red-and-white mushrooms. As evening drew in, they retreated into the velvety blackness of the underground chamber to commune with the spirits of those who had passed on many Moons ago. These journeys could last for many days and nights as the tribe waited patiently for the stars to line themselves up ready to floodlight the drummed rituals, dances and plays that would be staged to honor the Autumn Equinox.

As a child, Kroy had no inkling about the significance of this great Beauty that had been carved out of the land – nor of any of the other great earthworks they visited regularly during the turning of the spinning Wheel of the Year. He just knew that they were like colossal, towering spirit guardians who protected the progress of their passage, like way markers, across the waving seas of grass of the Steppes.

He also knew that, when the Autumn Equinox festivities were done, it would be time to move on again, through their sacred landscape, and they would continue to follow the trods and the stars until they spied a huge Eagle over their heads: This was Aquila, the harbinger of Samhain.

Then, when the ceremonies of Samhain were over, they would decamp yet again, and move swiftly in lantern-lit sleighs pulled by reindeer, in order to be in the right place at the right time for the Winter Solstice. The bells around the necks of the reindeer would be jingling merrily as the white, frozen lake came into view, mirroring the peacock-blue aurora borealis above and silhouetted against it, the black craggy rocks that made up the form of the enormous White Stag. Then the Dreamers would hang their newly gathered red-and-white mushrooms on the great conifer trees to dry out.

As Spring approached, the Rivers of Blood would begin singing in Kroy's sinews again when he saw that the trees' boughs were heavily pregnant and laden with red and white blossoms. He knew then that they must be nearing the time for the manhood rites that were always held on the immense horned effigy of the Great Bull. It must be so, he would think, because now he could see the three birds of Summer Triangle singing over their heads.

And so, the Wheel of the Year would always spin…

However, this autumn, the Elders had decided that Kroy had matured enough to join the work parties of the older men in their continual upkeeping of these enormous giants on the landscape. And so that was how he came to be taught that each one marked out exactly where the constellations fell to the Earth, making this whole vast territory of towering snowy mountains, thick conifer forests, high cliffs, craggy gorges, silvery rivers, glacier-blue lakes and soft green grassy plains a living temple of the stars.

Once the men got used to him, they began to tell him the secrets of their nomadic ways, which were not just random wanderings but had rhyme and reason. They revealed that the Moon provided the rhyme, the rhythm, the tides, and the Sun the reason, the logic, the logos. Thus, these people were always under the protection of these all-powerful heavenly deities as they progressed along paths that had been bequeathed to them and which were now worn down almost to ruts by the footsteps of those who had gone before them.

In this way, he learned about all 13 of these giant

effigies that mirrored the stars. But still, the beautiful goddess remained his first and only love, and so he was intrigued when he heard the men one day refer to her as the Dreamer in the Land.

She certainly seemed to be asleep, he thought to himself. Her oval eyes of dark green moss were closed as she lay peacefully at rest. Her hair was long and tangled and russet-gold, made up as it was of the tall, sun-bronzed wild grasses that were now ready to be gathered in. Her arms were outstretched as if she was holding out and presenting a much-valued object. It was marked by a wheat sheaf but it looked like a cup. He wondered if it could be the same chalice the hero won for his outstanding courage, the one told about by Tabiti in her sing-song sagas around the campfire.

His mind went back to tribe's storyteller, who would cut an imposing figure as she stood and told her stories under the stars. Her tall wooden headdress, embossed with eight carved and gilded golden cats, would glitter in the firelight. Her red and yellow silk-and-wool robes flowed over thigh-high white felt leggings. These were all signs of the high status in which Tabiti was held as an enchantress and storyteller within the tribe.

Kroy remembered how he once plucked up the courage to ask her to tell them more about the goddess carved in the land. Her facial expression visibly shifted as she reached back in her memory to produce what she knew from the ancient stories that had been handed down orally from grandmother to grandmother over untold thousands of years:

"Her name is Satana," Tabiti then informed her assembled audience. "She was born to her dead mother in an Underworld tomb at the bottom of the sea. But she managed to escape her watery captivity to grow into an extraordinarily wise and beautiful woman who eventually became the Oracle of the Narts – the 12 heroic warrior gods of the Scythians who fought for the hero, Batraz.

"You will know her as the raiser of the magical, faery-forged sword from the depths of the lake - the sword wielded by Batraz that always found its mark. Satana is also the bestower of a white-and-gold apple which grants immortality and everlasting youth to anyone lucky enough to taste its juices."

So, remembering this description of her, he turned to question one of the men beside him as they worked to restore the eroded grassy banks of the meandering river that outlined her left hip.

"Tabiti said that her name is Satana," he said. "So why do you call her the Dreamer in the Land?"

"You should ask Maya," was the quick reply.

Kroy was surprised to be referred to the tribe's most august shaman and navigator. To say that Maya was an Elder was an understatement. He was so old that there was no-one now alive who could remember his birth and his ancient mind resembled a vast library of all the lore that had been passed down the Rivers of Blood of a family line extending back to time immemorial.

The Evening Star was just rising on the horizon and so the men started packing up for the day. Kroy decided he would go to look for Maya.

He found the aged wisdom-keeper just as he was settling back against the trunk of a pine tree to enjoy a smoke.

Kroy sat down respectfully beside the Elder and waited for Maya's nod to give him permission to speak.

Then he posed his question.

"Sir, do you know why Satana is called the Dreamer in the Land?"

Maya put down his clay pipe. Then he turned towards Kroy, his leathery, crinkled eyes searched those of the earnest young man carefully. He quickly surmised that the petitioner before him was as advanced in his intelligence as any of his contemporaries – which wasn't very far, he had to admit.

"But perhaps far enough," he thought to himself and so when he replied, it was softly.

"She's dreaming us all into existence," he said.

Kroy-Khasis was stunned.

He thought he'd misheard.

"I don't understand," he said.

"Well, let's try to go back and unravel what you've always assumed to be reality up until now," the old man said kindly, picking up his pipe and taking a long slow drag on it and then passing it to Kroy.

"We can begin with the meaning of my name," he went on. "Maya. It means illusion. My mother named me Maya so that I would never forget that we all live in *maya*, in illusion. The whole of creation is just a dream – a dream of Satana. When she awakens, it will be the end of the world, the finish of this creation, for all of us. Until then, everything you see around you, including your own body, has been visioned into existence by this Sleeping Beauty, the Dreamer in the Land."

"How can that be?" Kroy-Khasis asked,

scratching his head. "I mean..." he stuttered, "surely the leaves turn golden and brown and fall from the trees naturally, at autumn? And don't the grasses burnish automatically over their own accord...?"

Even as he asked these questions, he heard them falling to the ground like pieces of slate. It was a flat sound, as if the spirit of his voice couldn't be bothered to resonate words that were so redundant in their ignorance.

"I see," Kroy said, humbly.

The old man heard the newly birthed realisation in the young adept's voice and so he knew that it was safe to continue.

"It's natural to conflate the words 'naturally' and 'automatically'," Maya chuckled at his own word play, "but that's just because of your automatic assumptions!"

His belly shook as he roared with laughter at his own joke. It took a while before he calmed down to gain enough breath to continue.

"In a dream, all death is an illusion," Maya eventually said, as he banged out his spent pipe on a stone, as if to hammer home his words.

"Birth is just death to another world, the one we are leaving as we come forth from the womb. We are all actors here in the great play that continually cycles through birth, death and rebirth. The trick to playing our part comes from learning the rules of the game."

"Is that why we are here?" asked a stunned Kroy.

Maya deliberately misunderstood his question. He didn't want to overwhelm the young man with a welter of philosophical ideas his tender mind was not yet prepared to deal with. He still had a few more foundational blocks to build.

So he went on: "All our festivals celebrate an aspect of this cycle of birth, death and rebirth as the Wheel of the Year spins. We are here, during this equinoctial fortnight, to honour Satana because she will soon become pregnant again, at Samhain, under the next Moon in the season of the Eagle, and this will be the most fertile time of the year."

Kroy-Khasis opened his mouth in surprise but then quickly thought better of uttering any more words.

Maya sighed knowingly.

"I know," he went on. "You're wondering how it is that we are entering upon such a fecund period when the branches on the trees will soon be as bare and white as the bones of a cadaver?"

"Well, yes," Kroy replied, a little hesitantly. "I'd always assumed that Spring must be the most fertile time with all the fresh green saplings sprouting up from the ground?"

"Just more *maya*," grinned Maya. "The seeds have already germinated and found their way to the surface by then, just as Satana escaped her watery birth in the submarine depths to grow into such a beauty. All seeds – whether plant or animal - need the darkness to gestate, to cultivate their inner fire. Autumn is when the Underworld smith begins to fire up his forge."

Kroy instantly experienced a shudder of recognition. Now he was on firmer ground. He remembered Tabiti telling them a story about Satana, a shepherd and a smith that she'd said was so old that its genesis was lost in the mists of time.

The shepherd was actually one of the 12 Nart warrior heroes who were led by Batraz. When he wasn't being called upon to fight fiends or to overcome ogres, he would get to enjoy a pastoral peace, herding his flocks by the river. And this is how it came about that one day he saw Satana, who was standing on a rock by the river. She had gone there to wash her clothes and she was naked.

The shepherd warrior was so overcome by her beauty that he couldn't move.

And as Tabiti sagely pointed out: "You know what can happen to a warrior once something has settled into his heart."

True enough, the Nart's passion for Satana arose like a banked-up, smouldering fire suddenly flares into life from a kiss of the wind. The flaming force rushed up within him like a fiery sword so straight, so direct and so quickly, it took him unawares. He gasped. Suddenly, he found himself ejaculating a long silver stream that jetted powerfully on to the stone that Satana was standing upon.

She was furious and she sent him away with harsh words.

He turned to obey her but then he threw these words back over his shoulder:

"Satana! You have never given birth to anybody. Perhaps now this stone could one day be helpful to the Narts. Don't leave the stone here. Take it with you."

She hesitated at first. But then she decided to take the stone home with her. She hid it under her bed in the dark.

Nine months later, she started wondering about it, so she pulled it out into the light to find that it had grown into a huge boulder. She didn't know what to do with it, so she thought she should take it to her friend, the blacksmith Tlepshw.

Tlepshw told her he could open it with his hammer. But it turned out to be too blunt a weapon; in the end, he had prise it open with his awl. Even then, it took him a full day and a full night but when it finally cracked apart, and to the astonishment of all present, a tiny baby boy was revealed, nestled within.

They named the child Sosruquo, which meant "offspring of the hit of the fiery sword".

Tabiti had then told them that Sosruquo had eventually grown up to become a small but powerful member of the Narts who relied on guile and trickery to overcome his enemies.

The shadow of night had silently crept into the skies while the old man and young man had been talking. Maya raised his arm and pointed skywards, first at the stars of the Furrow and then towards a kite-shaped constellation which was next to it. That, he told Kroy, was the warrior shepherd holding his son Sosruquo on his lap.

Many thousands of years later, and long after massive flooding caused by the melting glaciers that forced the Scythian tribes down from the Steppes, and then to fan out across Europe and Scandinavia, these two constellations became known, respectively, as Virgo and Bootes, which contains the bright star Arcturos.

But from that day on, Kroy's earthly existence was transformed. He no longer took his human span for granted. Instead, he realised that Tabiti's stories were not just for his evening's entertainment but were stones that hid deep, hidden meanings which, when prised open by the awl of the blacksmith, could reveal so much more about who he was and how he fitted into the cosmos.

The young man now listened more carefully to her tales and thought about them for long into the night afterwards, digging down deep into his subconscious mind to unravel the symbols and metaphors that slowly threaded their ways like golden pathways through her narratives. In that way, he slowly began to discover the rhyme and the reason for why his ancestors had bequeathed him a life that was just a dream.

Chapter Three: The Mists of Avalon

I hope that meeting with Kroy-Khasis, Tabiti and Maya enabled you to gain a clearer idea about how our earliest ancestors perceived themselves and their place in the cosmos. In this chapter, I'd like us to spend a little more time going deeper into that archaic mindset because, as we proceed through Avalon, we will be visiting the creations of those who thought in a similar way, and it will help us to understand the messages that they have left for us.

Our early ancestors were not unscientific in their approach to Nature and the universe; it is a science of a different kind. Some call it "metaphysics": it is an organised and disciplined way of perceiving reality that is based on observable natural cycles – but not as if we are separate from them. It is a philosophy which acknowledges that as much as the planets and stars orbit above, so do their mirrored counterparts cycle and impact on our inner fields.

It is a more holistic comprehension that differs from modern cosmology in that it cognises and encompasses an appreciation for the gargantuan processes of an ever-revolving universe of millions of remote galaxies while, at the same time, allowing the small human being to pursue a sense of meaning, significance and purpose for his path and his destiny within it. It is, if you like, how he maintains his integrity and purpose.

If all that sounds frighteningly complex, please don't worry. Right now, our group is walking through the early morning mists of Avalon and it might all be looking a little blurry. Please be careful. Strange-looking apparitions can suddenly materialise out of the vapours and first instinct may panic us into believing it is an evil demon when it is really just a friendly white-horned cow. So do bear with me as we proceed slowly forward, one small step after another. And as you gradually learn more and more you will soon be able to work out for yourself what's real and therefore of value to you on your path, and what are just worthless tourist-trade trinkets.

Our first challenge has already come, from Maya, who told us about one of the great paradoxes of life. It does seem ironic that we do not believe the visionary messages we receive from our ancestors while sleeping, which we call "dreams", to be real. However, the visionary lessons we receive as we wander from classroom to classroom in that "night school" are teaching us – if only we could understand them - that it is actually our daytime waking life, which we call reality, that is really the *maya* or illusion.

Even modern science is catching up with the ancient Vedic wisdom about the unreality of so-called "reality". Physicists are now reaching a consensus that most of the universe consists of an invisible substance which interpenetrates everything, including us, but which cannot be perceived by any of the five senses. They call it "dark matter" or "dark energy"- it doesn't matter which. Ever since Einstein came up with his famous theorem, matter and energy has been considered to be just differently presenting aspects of the same substance. Matter and energy, we are told, are not only interchangeable but are continually flowing in and out into each other and transforming one another all the time.

So even the most respected of authorities agree that nothing we can see, touch, smell, taste or feel in our waking lives has any reality, other than that which our perceptions bestow upon it. We then share our perceptions and views with each other, broadcasting them through stories, dramas and song, and thus the message becomes the media of ideas that gradually blend into a compromise or an agreed compact that becomes our "consensual reality".

I should quickly add that just because we live in unreality, it doesn't then naturally follow that life has no meaning. To my way of seeing, it is actually the reverse. Life is only meaningless to those who don't know the purpose of their life - what it is for. Once we start to remember and begin to find a way to understand our nocturnal studies, then waking life takes on more meaning than ever before.

Imagine for a moment that our daytime reality is a motorcar – say, a souped-up, turbo-charged, gleaming Porsche. Before we are enlightened, it's as if we've never had a single driving lesson, let alone read the *Highway Code*. So, the vehicle just sits rusting in the garage. We do occasionally wonder about it, and we might feel tempted to take it out for a spin. But even in our relative ignorance, we sense that it is a pretty powerful beast, so we hesitate in our realisation that we have no skills in controlling it; we don't want our life to spin out of control. However, once we've learned the rules and passed our driving test, we can't wait to get it out on the road!

Our life experiences are customised to fit our individual destinies, which were chosen by us before our birth. This means that there is no blanket, one-size-fits-all purpose or meaning to human life, and it is why religions based on absolute dictums cannot help us in our search, even though many will try to. The most important decisions about what we are experiencing right now were taken in the Other Worlds of the shaman and the stars lined up at our births to give us the required "road trip".

The primordial carpet

The stories of old are tales about the pilgrimage of human life that progresses around the spinning wheel of life, death and rebirth. The starring hero keeps going through thick and thin, challenge after challenge, until he attains enough wisdom to act as a key to open the door for the evolution of the soul.

It is this same hidden allegorical meaning which threads its way through the myth about Prometheus, who "stole the fire" of enlightenment from the gods of Mount Olympus. The ancient Greeks, whose story this was, were just another branch of Kroy-Khasis's descendants, although their stories had more of a Phoenician twist. A similar tale is found in the Norse

Edda, in which Odin turns himself into a bird of prey to steal the nectar of the gods. It is also recounted in the Indian Srimad Bhagavatham, in which there is a tug-of-war of the *devas* and *daemons*, to churn the ocean of milk in order to release the elixir of life which, when it finally surfaces, is stolen by the eagle Garuda.

When we dig down deep enough, underneath the rotting story mats of the wandering troubadours and taletellers of old, what emerges is not just another muddy, tattered rug but a richly woven carpet depicting remarkably similar tales and sagas, with just small local differences. This narrative that used to give human life meaning was spread, many ages ago, all over the northern hemisphere where everyone looked up to the same stars to describe the same universal processes.

I call this deepest underlayer the "primordial carpet".

Of course, there are slight variations in the patterns of the carpet, depending upon the location. Some are more in the style of a classical Persian rug, or a tightly woven Balkan kilim or an Indian jute dhurri; other parts of the carpet are of spun Chinese silk, or Irish linen, or Indonesian ikat tie-dye, or embroidered like the Bayeux Tapestry.

However, whatever their stylistic variations, these stories are woven into a worldwide carpet designed to depict remarkably similar stories that are derived from similarly viewed star fields. Thus, all over the world, at one time, those who lived here before us carved out epic adventure plays in the constellations and planets of the night skies that contained, in their deeper layers, esoteric keys and codes. Then they "brought down" that illumination from the gods to the

Earth by geoengineering huge earthwork effigies of the giants, birds, beasts, men and women who starred in them.

In this way, our forebears created pilgrimages that were mapped around Earthly power points. The path to Santiago de Compostella, which meant "field of the stars", following as it does the Milky Way, is one of the few remaining ways. The scallop shell that those pilgrims carry is the sign of Venus, which is why Botticelli painted her standing on one in the waves, and it shows the pre-Christian antecedents of that particular route.

The word *zodiac* comes from the ancient Greek, and it meant "circle of animals", like the bull that is used to symbolise the house of Taurus, the lion of Leo and even the men that symbolise Gemini and Aquarius, because humans and animals are closely related.

These giant earthwork circles give us a clue to the meaning of the following riddle, found in the 6th century alchemical text, the Tabula Smaragdina.

Heaven above, heaven below

Stars above, stars below

All that is over, under shall show,

Happy thou who the riddle readest.

However, rich in wisdom though that verse is, it only gives us only half the story – or I should say, two-thirds. The ancient dramas and orally transmitted stories, like the one about Prometheus, are set not merely in one flat plane of objects above shining down upon another flat plane of objects below. It is about the intertwining of worlds, in which the planes interpenetrate one another and there is also a further world, a third realm, known as the Underworld.

The plots in the myths of the Celts – by which I mean the ancestors of the Scots, Irish, Welsh, Manx, Cornish and Bretons – are also set in these Three Worlds. There is a smith of the Underworld, called Gofannon, whose spinning, spiralling Spindle of Light penetrates up through the Middle World to bore a place for the pole star in the Upper World of the heavens.

The language of the Celts divides into Gaelic and Brythonic. However, both come under the Indo-European umbrella, as does Anglo-Saxon English. Therefore, linguistically, one can often spot poetic resonances that associate certain words and terms at their roots in a much older seedbed of an oral tradition that stretches back to the Caucasus Mountains of the last major Ice Age.

In the earlier centuries of the Common Era, the multi-levelled Mystery teachings were first recorded in secret priestly languages that were derived from Indo-European - Latin and Sanskrit – and this was how "those in the know" communicated all over the northern hemisphere.

It was only much later, after the Norman Conquest, that these stories were transcribed by monks who were so entrained into Judaeo-Christian thinking that the message was almost lost in translation. It was as if these priestly scribes hammered down the three-dimensional stage scenery into a flat pancake. Then they broke off a few static tableaux and mixed them up to forge a jerky, nonsensical narrative to try to justify the current political imperative. Luckily, though, the trained eye can still see what our earlier ancestors were trying to convey – albeit sometimes demanding a bit of peering!

So, you are hopefully now realising that a true pilgrimage is as much about Time as it is about Space or the distance travelled. It is perhaps the source of the saying "the journey is the destination".

A long pilgrimage of days and weeks allows enough leeway for Space and Time to intersect and interact with the pilgrim in a meaningful way, in order for lessons to be learned that will create true transformation. It should take at least a month – or one full cycle of the Moon. This will make more sense to you perhaps, later on. The plays and stories that you will hear about as we walk along contain deep and profound wisdom teachings about Space and Time which reflect the real value of pilgrimage - before it was reduced and traduced to just a walk around the decaying bones of Catholic saints.

The Three Worlds that interpenetrate one another in the ancient myths were inspired by a shamanic mindset, because they represent the other realms that are visited by the shaman in trance.

So, in some contexts, the use of the term "the land" or the word "landscape" does not always necessarily mean the rolling hills and vales of the outer world. While we're looking about and enjoying the views, our inner landscapes will also be sparked into life at the portals where the Three Worlds intersect.

The sagas, tales, poems and plays that make up these wisdom teachings also reveal themselves through the inward eye that the poet Wordsworth described as "the bliss of solitude". They come in the same way people sometimes say "I think the Universe is telling me..." such and such. You will discover that when the "Universe" speaks, it is sometimes in the form of a question or an option. It is up to us then to speak back to the "Universe", to reply in whichever way we see fit, to express our needs. There is no right or wrong answer. The "Universe" is not a jealous, judgemental Jehovah god just waiting for us to slip up. We are in a duality of two – we and the "Universe" – and therefore a dialogue is required to establish a connection and fruitful relationship.

This conversation is being continually carried out by those who are skilled in interacting with the "Universe" or "the land", who were known in older cultures as shamans.

Understanding shamanism

"Shaman" is a Siberian word but it has slipped into more universal usage more recently. A shaman is a person who goes into trance in order to journey to the three extra-dimensional worlds, in order to meet with the guiding spirits who inhabit them. It is while there that they gain guidance on all number of issues and bring the advice back to their tribe or community. Shamans are known by many different names in different cultures. This list, which is by no means complete, will give you some idea of how widespread the practice once was:

      Andean (Quecha) shaman — P'ago
      Arab shaman (pre-Islam) — Baksylvk

Australian shamanism — Wulla-mullung
Australian spirit — Budian
Bedouin form of shamanism — Fugara
Celtic shaman – Druid or Dreamer – Awenwyddion
Chinese shaman —Tang-ki
Hawaiian form of shamanism — Huna Kane
Indian Vedic shaman — Rishi
Indonesian shaman — Dukun
Inuit shaman — Angakok
Jewish shaman — Baal Shem
Korean female shaman — Mondang
Korean shamanic initiation — Nae-Rim-Kut
Lakota spirits — Wakan Tanka
Meso American shaman — Nagual
Mongolian shaman – Boo
Nigerian shaman — Babalawo
Norse female shaman — Voelva/Volva/Vala/Seidhkona
Peruvian shaman —Sheripiari
Siberian shaman – Shaman
Tibetan shaman — Pa'wo
Tibetan shamanism — Bonpo
Turkish shaman — Sahir-þairl
Ukrainian female shaman — Znakharka
Voodoo female shaman — Mambo
West African spirits — Kontomblé

The Celts who used to inhabit Avalon had a name for the spirits of the land; they called them the Sidhe (pronounced *shay*), which morphed over time into the Fae or the faeries. These Otherworldly beings are of a higher evolutionary order to us and their role is to help to steer our destinies, which were written in the stars at our birth.

Before we meet with the Fae, we are unable to gain their guidance. The best we can hope for is just to try to go with the flow. But only dead fish go with the flow, whereas the Salmon of Wisdom swims determinedly upstream, even up high waterfalls, to spawn. So, we might end up flowing over Niagara Falls if we don't learn how to reply to the "Universe" when it speaks, to establish what we want. The secret is to gain the guidance of the genius loci of the land – otherwise known as the power of place - and we will be learning how to do that as we go on.

In the early 20th century, Dion Fortune was writing about the power of place from her cottage at the foot of the Tor. She considered that that serpentine-shaped earthen mound, along with other locations in Avalon, was a potent portal that is activated at key times of the year. She believed that honouring those locations on those specific occasions provoked an optimal response from the Other Dimensions. But how does one honour a place, you may be asking?

I often receive teachings from the local spirits in my dreams, after walking in their sacred gardens at auspicious times. Their teachings are revealed to me in songs and poems and stories.

Then, once I've written and published them[1], I read them back at the same place where they came through to me. This may seem an odd pastime, but to me it's a similar practice to those our ancestors of the Steppes enjoyed through folk-tales, sacred drama and bardic verse.

One Thousand and One Nights

Real storytellers, like Tabiti, were revered by the tribes of old for their ability to cunningly weave the golden threads of their yarns in such a way as to interpenetrate the Otherworldy portals and thus reinforce the Sovereignty of the domain.

Perhaps another way of putting it would be that while her enraptured audience was largely unaware, the elves, pixies, gnomes and dwarves would also join the throng around the campfire and they became so enamoured by her tales they would come into her dreams, to embroider them.

We find the essence of this idea in the framing narrative of a collection of Persian folktales entitled *One Thousand and One Nights*.

The story goes that once upon a time, a proud Persian monarch named Shahryar found out that his wife had been unfaithful to him. He had her beheaded. Then he resolved to spend every night with a different woman and have her decapitated the next day, before she could betray him with another lover.

This plan worked out well for him, for many years. Every night, he would lie with a new woman and, on the following morning, she would be executed. But all that was before he met the beautiful daughter of the vizier, Scheherazade.

Sir Richard Burton described Scheherazade thus in his translation of the work:

> *Scheherazade had perused the books, annals, and legends of preceding Kings, and the stories, examples, and instances of bygone men and things; indeed it was said that she had collected a thousand books of*

histories relating to antique races and departed rulers. She had perused the works of the poets and knew them by heart; she had studied philosophy and the sciences, arts, and accomplishments; and she was pleasant and polite, wise and witty, well read and well bred.

On their first night together, Scheherazade began to tell Shahryar such a cunningly woven story that he was utterly enchanted and enthralled by it. However, her tale was so long and involved that she was unable to finish it. But she promised that she would reach the conclusion the next time she came to his chambers – so the king waved away the executioners.

The following evening, when Scheherazade came to lay with Shahryar again, she continued with her saga, and it was so colourful and interesting, Shahryar was even more fascinated than the night before. But she was unable to reach the end of it on that occasion either.

The king was utterly enraptured by now. He could hardly bear to wait to hear the next instalment, so he was forced to postpone the beheading again and thus it went on, for night after night… one thousand and one nights, to be precise.

On the one thousandth and one night, Scheherazade finally concluded her story. However, by then, the king had fallen so deeply in love with her that he gave her her life. He promised Scheherazade his undying devotion and married her.

So, I find *One Thousand and One Nights* to be the perfect metaphor for shedding light on the practice of telling our stories to the land, and why "the land", in the form of the spirits of the land, tells its stories back to us, and on and on it goes.

The name Scheherazade is an Arabic form of the Persian name Čehrāzād, which is made up of *čehr*, meaning "lineage", and *āzād*, meaning "noble" and "exalted". The word "noble" is often misunderstood. The aristocratic and Oxford-educated translators of the British Raj that colonised India in the 19th century made a similar mistake in believing that the "nobles" they found in the texts of the Vedas meant barons and earls. However, in this context, a noble and exalted person referred to a *rishi*, in other words, an Indian shaman. The Indian caste system, even today, puts Brahmins (the spiritual) ahead of kings (Earthly rulers), and I believe this to be the only surviving remnant of a pecking order that used to be much more universal.

The noble and exalted lineage that Scheherazade carried in her name was a clue to the shamanic spirit of Sovereignty that ran through her Rivers of Blood or DNA. She was in the line of the exalted storytellers of old, who were usually women. Tabiti could have one of her ancestors. And just as she kept herself alive by spinning her enthralling tales, so shamans today keep the Sovereignty of the land alive in an interdimensional conversation which affords ongoing protection for future generations. The stories are woven and shared as offerings, through the portals, and in this way, we form a relationship with the land that ensures our spiritual claim to it.

In other words, we draw out our territory with the help and cooperation of the *genii locurum* or nature spirits, who are known as the spirits of the place. Indigenous folktales, whichever land they derive from, are a natural expression of the knowledge about the power of place and our role in a wider cosmological hierarchy within a creation that was forged out of a love deeper than the night skies.

The greatest of grandmothers who came before us developed that love and wisdom in their young people from the lullabies they sang to them in the cradle through to plays, musicals and dances that were threaded through with archetypal plotlines.

They were performed in huge outdoor theatres that were structured according to the mathematical, astrological and alchemical knowledge of the time – which was vast. And as we learned when we met Kroy-Khasis, they used these great geoglyphs to honour the story of the Sun hero as he passed through each of the eight major "stations of the cross" – the four festivals of the cross of solstices and equinoxes and the four cross-quarter festivals of the saltire cross, as shown below in **Figure 1**.

In this way, the ancestors were able to conceptualise both Time and Space; the 360 degrees of the circle encompassed both. The Scottish word for "church", kirk, comes from the Greek for "circle", which was kirkos or kuklos, and it also meant "ruler" and "to measure". The word "temple" also derives from the Latin *tempus*, meaning "time".

More enlightened scientists might call that sort of interdimensional connectivity "quantum entanglement". But it is a vital part of the role of the shaman and is only now being rediscovered again. The very act of reaching out in this way reawakens the relationship between Man and the Fae. In connecting with these helpful Otherworldy beings, we gain their guidance and protection. It is only when that interdimensional relationship is in place and thriving that an indigenous people have the right to claim the Sovereignty of the land.

Figure 1 The eight "stations of the cross"

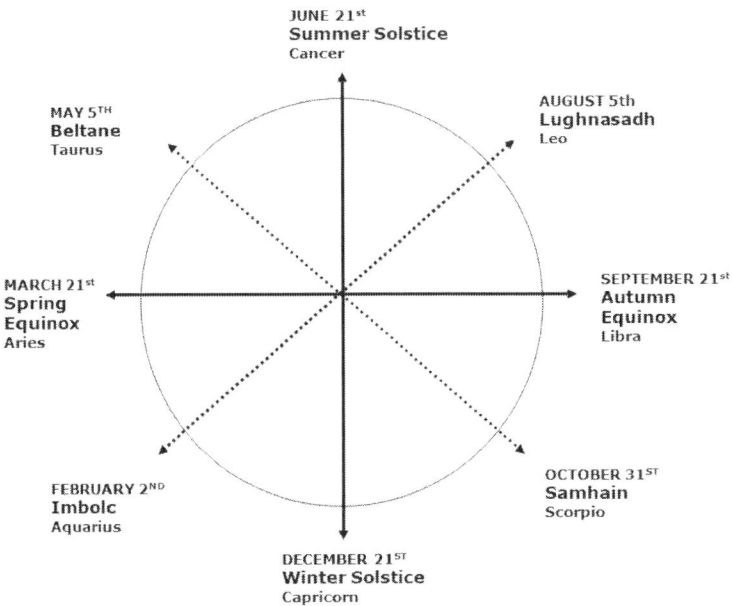

Contacting the Spirits of the Land

I first learned how to practice working with the land, as a shaman, when I was living at the foot of the North Downs in Kent.

Before then, I had been just like everybody else in the commuter-belt town of Sevenoaks, too busy rushing for the train in the morning to even notice the oaks and the lime trees graciously lining the avenues to the station, or too exhausted upon returning home in the evening to appreciate the extraordinary beauty of the huge red Sun slowly bidding goodnight as it slowly slid into the white chalk downs.

I was under the extraordinary pressure, at the time, that is typical of the journalist – going into dangerous situations and then often having to meet impossible deadlines in noisy, smoke-filled newsrooms. I had been coping by wearing virtual horse blinders.

However, once I started training in shamanic practices, those guards to my vision dropped away. The doors of perception opened and, almost overnight, I started to see spirits everywhere.

The trees lining the avenues now began to appear as kindly and courtly elders who had much to teach me – if only if I could find the time to stop and listen. So, I gradually began to learn to slow down and engage with them – although only when no-one else could see me. But I remember once putting my hand on the trunk of one of the oak trees and asking it to heal me of some deep seated pain I hadn't yet managed to process. Within seconds, it pulled it up through my torso and along my arm into its trunk… and it was gone!

One day, I looked up at the hills to see that they looked like a sleeping giant. Then I found that the Sun began to play with me, in a game of peek-a-boo, and the clouds would form themselves into animals and other shapes.I'm talking about a known effect that scientists have labelled "simulacra" or "pareidolea". I'm sure you've experienced it too. But I had been blind to this way of seeing until the spirits started to rebalance my visioning faculties.

Ever after that, the curvaceous, chalky North Downs became my spiritual mother, who had been feeding me from birth with the white, milky water She had so lovingly filtered through her underground calcium deposits.

In other words, I began to relate to Nature as a Being, alive and buzzing with an interdimensional life-force.

A few days before I left that part of the world to move to Glastonbury, I looked out of my window to find all the trees waving goodbye. I was so moved that I cried. Of course, a rationalist would say it was just a very windy day… but I was no longer a rationalist and had no intention of becoming one ever again.

However, upon moving to Avalon, there was much more for me to discover. I found that the spirits of the land here are different. I eventually realised there are innumerable faery races that change as you travel throughout the world. I suppose it shouldn't have come as a surprise. We already know a pine tree cannot thrive in a desert and a palm tree would never survive outdoors in Iceland. So, in the same way, there are variegated and diverse races of nature beings who are adapted to their environment. It is not just created by the flora and fauna of that environment. It's about the stories too. The heroes and heroines of local myths often remain and inhabit the morphogenetic fields long after the people who told stories about them have departed.

So, I had to get to know my new friends and guides in this part of Britain, and it is they who, over many years, taught me the importance of Sovereignty and identity of nationhood. In a similar adage to "you are what you eat", they have shown me that "you are where you live", particularly when we are eating the food and drinking the water of the land in which our ancestors are buried.

I hope the idea of working with the spirits of the

land doesn't sound complicated. It is far simpler than it sounds. The best way is to just get out there and do it. You can just start talking to them, even when you're not sure whether they can hear you. They will soon reply; if not immediately, then they will come in your dreams at night. If you sleep on the land of Avalon, Merlin might come to you, or Morgan the Fae, or Gwyn ap Nudd - and you won't be sure whether or not it is a dream. I'll be explaining to you more about why those guardian spirits are still here later on.

Sometimes, I take large groups of people out on to the land for shamanic ceremonies; at other times, I just go with a friend or two. But more often, I am alone because it is easier to journey into trance and make contact with the spirits, to receive whatever information they want to give me.

During the past decade, my work has been centred on birthing the Radiant Child of Sovereignty through the auspices of the Alchemical Marriage, otherwise known as the Marriage of the Sun and the Moon. I will tell you more about that as we go along.

I am being guided in this work by the spirit beings who are the intelligences of the Cosmos itself Above and of Nature Below. When we stand at the crossroads, otherwise known as the stations of the cross, where those two great forces intersect and interact holographically, at a certain time, we sense the presence of these genii locurum and can interact with them.

What do I mean by "holographically"?

A holographic image is like an ordinary photograph except that it is made with the light of a laser. One can use the light of a laser to take a photograph of a landscape, and when the result is examined under ordinary light, it just looks like lots of meaningless squiggles. However, once a laser is shone on it, suddenly the picture appears in 3D and not only that but on closer examination, every little pixel contains the whole of the panorama in a phenomenon called "the microcosm within the macrocosm". It is this kind of laser-like perception that allows man's mind to explore the whole universe while keeping his own wholeness, integrity and sense of purpose within his ever-expanding understanding.

You might say that practising shamanism – through dreaming, trance, journeying, ritual theatre and ceremony - is equivalent to shining a laser beam within our own inner landscapes to light up the whole.

Shamanic ceremonies on the land

I hope all of that explanation renders it now unnecessary for me to point out that shamanic ceremonies are definitely not Satanic. It is unfortunate that the two words - shamanism and Satanism - sound so similar when their meanings are light years apart. Please rest assured that there are no human or animal sacrifices at shamanic ceremonies or conjuring up of Beelzebub. In fact, these events tend to be quite friendly and relaxed affairs that are very much infused with a sense of theatre, going back as they do, when they were the only entertainment. The whole tribe would turn out on high days and holy days to enjoy them – children, dogs and all.

I often light a small fire or burn incense or herbs in a bowl with some charcoal. We call this form of purification "smudging". My favourite smudging herb is mugwort – also known as artemisia. Old

Grandmother Mugwort seems to be a wise old crone who always knows just what to do and prefers you to let her get on with it without any fuss.

Bonfires are useful when part of the purpose of the event is to purify and purge from the morphic fields all that no longer serves the highest interests of those present. It is an immensely satisfying and powerful way to get closure on any recurring issues. You can just write it on a piece of paper and throw it into the flames.

Once everyone is gathered into a circle, the spirits are drummed in. Drumming helps to build a sort of vibrational architecture of sound, which are the virtual walls of the sacred space or temple. Then we put on various forms of drama – poems, plays, dances, music and singing – and especially what are known as "power songs".

To hear a power song is a sign of great good fortune; we are blessed with a unique sonar healing gift from the spirits in the Other Worlds. They are formed out of musical sounds and words that are completely spontaneous and beautifully melodic. Often, the notes and words will tumble out of our mouths in such a way as to create a fleeting memory of a memory of a memory that we can't quite put our fingers on.

We may sense we've heard the tune before, at an intersection of Time and Space when we were happy and contented; we just can't remember when or where that was. And that is how power songs heal; they reset our energetic emotional and mental state in a way that goes beyond logic and rational thought, by re-minding us. Voicing them works both ways, because the spirits regard power songs as a kind of offering that is nutritious and beneficial to them too.

Poems are also the perfect offering at such occasions; the spirits love to hear words that resonate and ring with rhythm and rhyme. They often communicate back in the same fashion. They really appreciate it when we go to the effort to craft our communication to them in such a way, so much so that they inspire the process of the creation of the poem itself.

The magical power of an ode is carried in the vibrational thrust of the rhythm (the beat) as well as the force of the meaning of the words. Their shamans were known as *awenyddions*, which I know, at first glance, can seem terrifyingly unpronounceable, but not so much when you break it down to awen, wydd and dion.

Awen is the Celtic term for the spiralling silvery stream of inspiration that flows in and out of the portals or gateways of the Fae, known otherwise as the "gods" or the *dion*.

Shamans are inspired by the *awen* at the *dions'* wells of *wydd* or wisdom and wit, which feed, in Old Norse myths, the material reality of the web of the Wyrd.

It used to be the role of the bards, the wandering minstrels and the storytellers of rhythmic and mellifluous prose, to act as bridges between the worlds in order to channel and translate into human language the serpentine silver flows of the awen-imbued wisdom and wit.

The Irish mythologist WB Yeats attested to the magical potency of the *awen*-inspired rhyme when he wrote in his *Mythologies* of the power of the ancient poets of Ireland, which could be used for good or evil.

The bards were the most powerful influence in the land, and all manner of superstitious reverence environed them round. No gift they demanded might be refused them. ... A poem and an incantation were almost the same. A satire could fill a whole countryside with famine. Something of the same feeling still survives, perhaps, in the extreme dread of being 'rhymed up' by some local maker of unkindly verses....

When the shaman wants to bring the *awen* into the ceremony, he or she has to be able to craft the event with great attention to detail because offerings need to be given in the language that the Fae understand and appreciate.

It is the same in our own masterpieces by the great Renaissance painters, once we learn to interpret their symbols and metaphors. To this great Elder race, there is no such thing as a stripped down, built-for-purpose, utilitarian object.

In their rustic settlements in the Underworld no piece of wood, no mere plank or beam, goes untwisted, uncarved or unpainted. And the flourishes and furls are not just for decoration. Everyday objects are engraved and embossed with meaningful symbols, or woven and plaited into so-called Celtic knots that, once understood, reveal important principles of sacred geometry.

Perhaps it is possible to forge a habitat that is a living and breathing work of art when Time runs differently to how it does for us on Earth. It does seem, to me, to process much more slowly in their world.

Time, as we know it, is part of the illusory nature of our realms. It is not absolute or fixed at a certain pace but will expand or contract according to how we feel. You know how it is when you're really enjoying a holiday, how quickly the week or fortnight rushes by? And do you remember how much more slowly a day took the pass when you were a child?

If we need further evidence of Time being part of the illusion of *maya*, we only need to remember the hype that surrounded the invention of the internet. We were promised the so-called superfast information highway would be such a fantastic labour-saving device, which would free us up for much more leisure time. However, we soon realised that in trying to "save time", the sands of Time seemed to slip through our tightly grasping fists even faster.

It's the same with trying to save Space. When we take high-speed trains, boats and planes, we are trying to fold up and concertina the amount of distance travelled into a more manageable time. It is equally illusory. We can get from London to New York in about seven hours now but then we have to spend a whole night and day, at least, waiting for the rest of our lagging selves to catch up.

All of this is to explain why, in performing shamanic ceremonies to contact the Fae, we try to act from their perspective rather than one based on human thinking about the nature of reality. The whole event is an expression of a loving exchange been us and the genius loci or the Fae, and it is that love which causes the awen to flow in and out of the ceremonial circle.

If we think it's all a waste of Time, we need to think again. Our walking reality may be acted out in *maya* or illusion, but what does have real resonance in quantum reality are our thoughts.

In this context, all thoughts are things that have value and meaning, and all thoughts are heard. No properly intended pronouncement or request is ever wasted and not least when it comes to loving and grateful exchanges through the liminal walls. It is the original meaning of Thanksgiving.

In Earth Mysteries circles, the *genius loci* of a certain location is often referred to as the power of a place. The connection with the power of a place was once considered to be key to the fertility of the land.

In pre-Christian times, these spirits were the focus of what are now called harvest festivals. You may have seen them in religious iconography - carved gods and goddesses that hold overflowing cornucopias which represent the harvest, libation bowls that symbolise offerings and a snake that embodies the Underworld serpents of regeneration.

As we go through our pilgrimage, you will learn how to establish your own connection with the *genius loci* and then you will be able to take that skill back to your own land and bring it alive again.

Medieval writers referred to Avalon as the small mound of land that used to poke up through the inland seas, found between Hart Lake to the north-east and Wirrall (Wearyall) Hill to the south-west. It is the paradisiacal isle described here by the 13th century Breton monk, William of Rennes.

> *This wondrous island is girded by the ocean; it lacks no good things; no thief, no reiver nor enemy lurks in ambush there. No snow falls; neither summer not winter rages uncontrollably, but unbroken peace and harmony and the gentle warmth of eternal spring. Not*

a flower is lacking, neither lilies, rose nor violet; the apple-tree bears flowers and fruit together on one bough. Youth and maiden live together in that place without blot of shame. Old age is unknown; there is neither sickness nor suffering – everything is full of joy. No-one selfishly keep anything to himself; here everything is shared. A royal virgin is the guardian of this place and everything in it; a nymph of surpassing beauty, attended by the fairest maidens, graceful of feature, sprung of noble ancestors, potent of counsel, renowned for her healing skills.[2]

However, the Avalon you will discover on this pilgrimage is a much bigger and more multi-dimensional space that was known to William of Rennes and his fellows. That is why we have had to spend a little time learning about how the ancestors of much earlier times contacted the spirits of the land through the portals. Through their seeding work, you will be able to discover many of those portals as we go along, spread out at various locations over more than 100 square miles of liminal saltmarsh terrain that was once largely under an inland sea.

These days, the terrain is largely recovered sea moor and marshland lined with water willows that overhang rivers which snake like quicksilver streams of *awen* through green valleys of buttercup meadows and apple orchards that lie between high, terraced hills and earthworks.

As we travel into it, I will be showing you how we know that vital shamanic work to bolster the Sovereignty of the Blessed Isles of Britain has been carried out here, in the spiritual heart of the nation, for thousands of years.

The Dreaming Seed

First of all, though, we will need to let go of what modern science has taught us about the morphology of the universe. That is not to say what is taught in the universities is not true – it is just that the truth about the meaning and purpose of the human pilgrim's journey within such vast and possibly infinite starry fields cannot be found in an absolute dictum based merely upon a sort of circular thinking.

So much of what cosmologists believe about the universe is based upon a series of unproven theories. It's rather like a chain of uncashed cheques, all supporting each other. However, the first cheque has not yet made its way to the bank, so its value is unproven and it may bounce.

Instead, let us tune into a far more holistic vision that belongs, even today, to peoples who have found great meaning to their lives through bringing the stars down to the land.

The Australian Aborigines refer to the seed of the philosophy that underpins that of the power of place as a Dreaming Seed that is buried in the Earth.

In the Aborginal view, every meaningful activity, event or life process, that occurs at a particular place leaves behind a vibrational residue in the Earth, as plants leave an image of themselves as seeds. The shape of the land … echoes the events that brought the land into creation. As with a seed, the potency of an Earthly location is wedded to the memory of its origin. The Aborigines call this potency the "Dreaming" of a place. [3]

The ancient Chinese carved their own stories in

the land as part of an esoteric system of geomancy that they called feng shui. Much of it still visible today in certain parts of China. They have geo-engineered beautifully harmonious rolling landscapes that date at least as far back as 1000 BCE – but probably are much older.

These beautifully manicured shapes represent different planetary rulers and associated elements. For instance, the Chinese attribute a hill carved into a pyramid shape to the genius loci or god of Mars and fire. The Pythagorean symbol for fire is an upright triangle. Interestingly, Glastonbury Tor in Somerset looks, from some angles, as if it could have been pyramid-shaped before it was rendered into its current, more staggered form by an earthquake in the 12th century, and its *genius loci* is called, by some, the fire bird or phoenix.

The Chinese would construct horizons of long wavy ridges, like the knobbly, zig-zagged tails of dragons, and these they attributed to the element of water. Thus, the old myths which contain metaphors for dragons and serpents that refer to the serpentine-shaped constellations above are re-staged and re-enacted in the green mantle of the land below. Draco was associated with Saturn.

A smoothly rounded hill would be seen as a full breast or a pregnant belly and associated with copper and Venus. Steep-sided plateaus were linked to the element of earth, while flattened-off peaks were connected to wood.

However, these genius locii were part of a much wider system:

The five elements are seen as by-products of the interplay of two great forces – opposed but complementary – known as Yin [female] and Yang [male], and symbolised by the White Tiger and the Blue Dragon respectively. In addition to being seen in terms of the elements, the hills are also seen in terms of these two animals. Dragons are everywhere; a long ridge may be a dragon, and so may a cluster of hills with a high mountain. Wherever there is a true dragon, there must also be a tiger; they are inseparable... [4]

We do find dragons in the landscape of Avalon and I look forward to introducing you to several of them! I haven't yet discovered a tiger. But there is a huge landscape effigy of a lion – and not far away from it, there is unicorn.

The royal seal of the Lion and the Unicorn represents, magically, the yin and yang, or the alchemical Marriage of the Sun (Lion) and Moon (Unicorn) that is marking the royal territory. I will tell you all about this practice of kings that goes back to at least the times of King Alfred the Great, who once lived in Avalon, later on.

Since Dion Fortune was writing in the 1930s, much more has been discovered in the mystical landscape of Avalon and it all supports the thinking of Earth Mysteries researchers that our ancestors had very advanced cosmological and esoteric knowledge.

For instance, a map dating back to early medieval times has been discovered, and it shows water nymphs (female, yin) as the spirits of the rivers, wells and springs of Avalon. At the same time, gods in red costumes (male, yang) are depicted standing on the tops of the hills. And what used to be considered Iron Age military hill forts, like Cadbury Castle and Oliver's Fort, are now seen by some as serpent mounds.

Dowsers have discovered an absolute plethora of energy lines crossing and criss-crossing the landscape, although few yet fully understand their purpose. Tom Graves, in his excellent book *Needles of Stones*, makes a good case that one of the purposes of Megalithic-era standing stones organised along these energy lines is to perform the same balancing and revitalising function that acupuncture needles do on the body.

Graves found that many of these stones transmit and receive energetic impulses via the quartz crystals embedded in them. I have confirmed this phenomenon myself, at the three stone circles of Stanton Drew in Wiltshire. Even though much of the original arrangement of the circles has been destroyed, there is a permanent, inter-dimensional conversation still going on there – in other words, informational energies chatting away with one another across the cosmos for reasons we can only wonder at.

We owe much to the Freemasons for their preservation of highly valuable esoteric knowledge in the art and decoration of churches, like St Dunstan's in Baltonsborough and St Peter's in Hornblotton – which is a virtual art gallery of imagery rich in the symbols of the esoteric branch of Royal Arch masonry.

Among their members we find the early 20th century sculptor Katharine Maltwood, who helped to identify a Beltane (May Day) solar alignment. This finding was augmented by John Michel, Paul Broadhurst and Hamish Miller and it is now known as the St Michael line, which traverses the south of the British Isles, from St Michael's Mount in Cornwall to the east coast of Norfolk.

There will be much more about those alignments later on and we will also be visiting a newly identified ley line that has been found by local illustrator and author Yuri Leitch, which he believes is pivotal to the story of the Sovereignty of this land.

But Maltwood's most important discovery was a great landscape temple that is made up of 13 earthwork effigies, which reflect the constellations above. The Irish shaman Coleston Brown has progressed that work even further in showing that it mirrors the faery characters found in Celtic myths. Later on, I will be guiding you through this three-world faery ring that is a virtual stellar-lit stage for the indigenous dramas of 5,000 years ago, which were eventually re-told and re-spun into Norman Arthurian myths.

So, these are just a few of the discoveries I will be sharing with you as we follow the way markers of our pilgrimage through the hills and vales of esoteric Avalon.

There is a lot to take in and I don't want you to feel weighed down and overburdened from having too much unprocessed material in your rucksack. But there is no rush. This is going to be a journey of a lifetime.

[1] These stories, so inspired, can be found in my books *The Bright World of the Gods* and *The Grail Mysteries*.
[2] *Gesta Regnum Brittaniae* (c. 13th century) attributed to Breton monk, William of Rennes.
[3] *Dreamtime Stories of the Australian Aboriginals* by Anon.
[4] *Needles of Stone* by Tom Graves.

Chapter Four: The Mysteries of the Chalice Orchard

Back along, we learned that the spiritual leaders of the ancient tribes, like Tabiti and Maya, had what is called a "shamanic worldview". This is one which is more multi-dimensional and holographic in nature than the pancake-flat perceived single world we live in today. And that it was one in which the gods or spirits played a pivotal role in transmitting wisdom to humans from their "wells" in realms which are eternal in that they are ever-present, unlike the one in which we spend our waking lives, which is governed by the tick-tocking grandfather clock of Time.

We don't know when this cosmological vision of life was first formulated. It could be millions of years old. We are aware, though, from their myths and from the artwork found in their graves and caves, that this was science that gave great meaning and purpose to those who lived during the last major Ice Age.

The ice was it thickest and most extensive during the Last Glacial Maximum (known as the LGM), which was about 22,000 years ago. In those days, ice sheets covered most of the northern hemisphere and some were a mile thick. The world only started to warm again in the 9000s BCE.

However, even during the LGM, there were a few small habitable areas and one of those was in the seas of grass of the Circassian Steppes. And as you know, it was here that the tribes of our ancestors followed their herds of migrating reindeer in a yearly circular passage that was overlooked by giant earthwork effigies reflecting their mirror images in the stars above and the stars of the inner landscapes of those treading the way forward below.

We also learned about the silver streams of *awen* that flow between the two great species who are the custodians of planet Earth. And we heard that the role of *awenwyddion* is to be the bridge between those channels, to translate the dreams of the gods to humanity, who then feed back their understanding in a back-and-forth, two-way dialogue via artworks, stories, dramas, poems, songs and dances that mirror the cosmological symbolism imbibed from the wisdom imbibed from those Otherworldly wells.

We should be able to tune into this *awen* stream because the inner life of a tribe in those days was no different to the inner life of an individual today. We are all on the same pilgrimage of human existence that our ancestors followed. In a way, it's a kind of divine game or *lila*. So now it's time to start to learn the rules of this game, which are based on certain indestructible laws and without which we cannot proceed to our destiny.

We need to discover why the human being is born into a dimension governed by the ticking clock of Time. We also must find out how the human being can pursue his or her destiny, which gives life meaning. And we need to know if the two quests are linked.

Part of the role of the *awenwyddion* over many millennia has been to receive the key that unlocks these great mysteries from the Elder race of the Fae.

We are born into Time and then our lives are made up of a series events which are chronologically organised and make up a map of a path through the Space of our life. Those who can read the stars, like astrologers, can guide the human being, as can those who practice alchemy. This is because they recognise the symbolic language of the way markers – or challenges – that are customised and laid out along the camino, which are spun into being according to how the stars are lined up at their births.

So, this is why mages of old were skilled in astronomy and astrology – actually, they didn't separate those two disciplines. In addition, they observed natural processes very closely to discover how the universe regenerates itself over and over again and they found it grew, thrived and died in repeating patterns which are governed by numbers. The wise men were called natural philosophers and their holistic teachings have come down to us broken up into the separate silos of astrology, alchemy and sacred geometry.

The whole system is sometimes referred to as the

Hermetic Arts, because it is governed by Hermes, the Greek version of Mercury, the catalyst without which no alchemical process can be successful. Thus, thousands of years before the scientists of CERN in Switzerland began to search for the "god particle", the natural philosophers found a practical way to express how a god, like the Indian Vishnu, could generate, maintain and ultimately destroy the creation.

The Vedas tells us about Vishnu, who is sleeping on the coils of a huge serpent which is floating on the Garbodharka Ocean, otherwise known as the Ocean of Milk or the Milky Way. He is dreaming the creation into existence, and when he wakes up, it will be the end of the world. The Rainbow Serpent and the Dreamtime of the Australian aborigines comes from a similar mythological seedbed.

The Hermetic Arts were developed from the same cosmological science that Kroy learned from Tabiti and Maya, in what is termed "the cradle of civilisation" or the Fertile Crescent, which stretched between Jerusalem and Babylon. The Scythian tribes had settled in this rich, lush green land that was irrigated by the rivers of the Tigris and the Euphrates after the melting glaciers forced them out of the Steppes, and submerged their giant landscape gods under great lakes, like the Caspian Sea, which formed almost overnight.

But this being the Fertile Crescent, you can imagine how often and how fervently that territory was fought over. To cut a very long and blood-stained story short, Alexander the Great's Macedonian Greek armies eventually conquered much of the area in 331 BCE and they – there's no other word for it – stole all the esoteric lore of the Babylonians and set about codifying it. Thus, the blueprint of the Hermetic Arts was just a more formal way of organising the information previously taught in the Steppes and it was based upon the notion of hierarchy, which originally meant "spiritual governance", or coming from the rule of the gods that inhabit the arc of the Milky Way.

Actually, "hierarchy" is a good example of the sorts of words Tabiti chose for her campfire stories and songs – words that were like seeds which implanted themselves in the subconscious mind, only to sprout later on. It is no different today. We love to tell our children the same tales we were told on our mothers' laps and so it goes on and on. We may not realise those nursery tales have double meanings but by the time we finish this pilgrimage, you will be an expert at decoding them!

The clue, as with Scheherazade, is often found in the name. Take, for instance, Cinderella, who has to spend all day in the cellar sweeping the ashes of the hearth. The first part of her name, "Cinder", is an allegorical marker for the first burning stage of the alchemical Great Work, known as calcination, during which the material to be transformed is first incinerated to ashes. The "elle" or "ela" suffix derives from *Il* or *El*, which is one of the oldest Babylonian/Hebrew words for a god or goddess.

Today, we are no longer taught how to interpret the meanings of these magical words. We don't realise why the word "spell" is shorthand for "incantation". But we need to know the morphologies of the words of power – in other words, how to spell them - in order to be able to impregnate our own works with the oratory powers of a storyteller like Tabiti. Of course, one can always "kick against the pricks"[1]. But the more we rebel against this stellar hierarchy that was identified and put into practical form by the natural philosophers who knew how Nature worked, the more the pricks are driven into our flesh. We can complain, fall into depression and become a professional victim. Or we can learn the rules of the game and start to play it.

The earliest mythological pilgrim known to us was the Babylonian Gilgamesh, who trod the rim of the spinning Wheel of the constellations around the pole star in order to face his adversaries in adventures that would eventually turn him into a king fit to lead his people.

The Greeks took the *Epic of Gilgamesh* and mapped on their own hero Hercules, who has to undertake a challenging labour at each of the 12 Sun signs on the zodiac.

Dante Alighieri maintained the circular nature of that journey and the Three Worlds of the shaman in his *Divine Comedy*. But in John Bunyan's *The Pilgrim's Progress*, the circle of stars has completely disappeared and his champion, Christian, has to meet his trials and tribulations by resisting temptation along the straight and narrow road of King's Highway.

So, if we find it difficult to understand the messages contained in our ancestors' myths, or struggle to find meaning in our lives, it is largely because the stories upon which we base our consensual reality have lost their circular framework. We imagine our progress along the pilgrimage of life to be a straight line from A to B and thus we keep hitting brick walls.

Humans may be born into Time but a clock face is round and viewed in 3D across the Three Worlds, a circle is a spiral. Nature doesn't use straight lines. You may have noticed, if you have ever watched speeded-up film of a flower growing, that it rises up from the ground like a spiralling snake doing a hula hoop dance; even a tree has rings.

So, we will now be going back to the Fertile Crescent to learn what the older and wiser ones have to teach us about the pilgrimage of life.

The Mysteries of Eleusis

The Hermetic Arts were taught through a structured, layered and secret system of teaching called the Mysteries in which adepts learned about how the hierarchy of the cosmos was governed by mathematical, alchemical and astrological principles, and they were shown how to abide by them in order to lead a fruitful and meaningful life.

According to Plato:

> ...the ultimate design of the Mysteries ... was to lead us back to the principles from which we descended, ... a perfect enjoyment of intellectual [spiritual] good.

Initiations into these Mysteries were given in outdoor groves and at one time they would have taken place all over the Middle East. However, successive Roman emperors, determined to install Christianity, had all the groves destroyed, apart from one. And so the only Mystery grove left to us today is at a place called Eleusis, which is in Greece.

The Eleusinian Mystery teachings were traditionally conducted in two stages.

The first of these rites, the Lesser Mysteries, was always held on the Spring Equinox, which today is around March 21st. The second one, the Greater Mysteries, took place on the Autumn Equinox, which is around September 21st.

The call for candidates to become adepts to the Lesser Mysteries was broadcast widely and enormous groups of people would travel long distances to attend them. But most were just intent on enjoying themselves as spectators to the colourful dramas, stories and songs staged in lavishly costumed productions.

One of the plays was based on an ancient Greek myth. It was about an Earth goddess named Demeter and her cool, pale Moon goddess daughter, Persephone.

Demeter was responsible for ensuring that the grains and fruits ripened each year and she also oversaw the laws of the land. But one day, Persephone was stolen by Hades, the dark god of the Underworld. The mother was instantly propelled into a long period of mourning for her lost daughter and the Earth fell barren.

Eventually, though, she went down to the Underworld to confront Persephone's abductor and managed to persuade Hades to strike a deal with her. He agreed to keep Persephone in his realm for just three months annually but after that, she could return and spend the next nine months with her mother.

There was another popular drama, which was usually performed as a sort of finale. It was about the miraculous adventures of a Sun god who had 12 devoted followers. At the end of the drama, the Sun god is gruesomely murdered by his enemies, who nailed him to a pole erected on a mound. Then he was reborn three days later.

There were so many different gods and

goddesses in these Mystery Plays that it got to the point where people needed some help to remember them all, so the images of Demeter, Persephone, Hades and the Sun god were moulded into figurines, ornaments and statues, and their likenesses were also reproduced and painted on pottery.

At the conclusion of the Lesser Mysteries, there would be a mass baptism, which was the water initiation.

That would be the end of the experience for most. Only a few were called back, six months later, to take the 17-mile pilgrimage from Athens to Eleusis at the Autumn Equinox, for the true inner meanings of the stories and plays to be revealed to them within the Greater Mysteries, so that they could achieve full enlightenment.

It was at the Greater Mysteries that they learned the deeper meaning of the drama about Demeter and Persephone. It was about the Moon, which appears to go dark for three days each month, before its rebirth as the New Moon. Likewise, they were told that the play about the death of the Sun god was really about what happened at the Winter Solstice.

Solstice is Latin for "Sun stands still" and this is just what Sun appears to do each year as it reaches its furthest point away from the Earth. It remains – or seems to remain – stationary and there is so little light then that the Earth experiences its shortest day of the year. The Sun starts its journey back towards us again three days later, on Christmas Day, just in time for its rebirth.

They would also be taught that these cosmological cycles in the outer world mirrored the pilgrimage of man below, as he faced what the Celts called the Four Joys and Four Sorrows of the human journey in order to eventually resurrect into their own life.

The Greater Mysteries ended with a fire initiation in honour of the Sun god. Unfortunately, this practice is often misunderstood by historians to be "Sun worship" but that is only because we no longer have the words to mentally pigeon-hole the practice correctly.

It was more nuanced that that; it was about a recognition that the human being is an integral and holographic part of universal processes governed by geometrical principles which rule the orbits of planets above as much as they rule the orbits of the electrons and neutrons in the single cell of the human body on Earth.

The Sun, in this context, is the Son of Chronos who rules Time. The Son marks his father's time around the 360-degree circular vault of the biome above and the circular cellular biome below like hands on a clock. It is what scientists call "circadian rhythms". In other words, the rite was an opportunity to engage with and honour the true nature of the creation that is ruled at every level, microcosm within macrocosm, by Time.

Throughout this Dance of the Spheres, which is ever-present in our inner and outer landscapes, the Sun marks Time to the rhythm of our hearts, which pulse at about 60 beats per minute. When you multiply that 60 by 60 minutes, it comes to 3,600 beats per hour, which comes out to 86,400 heartbeats every 24 hours or a full day. This is the amount of time the Earth takes to travel each day around the Sun - which, coincidentally or not, is 864,000 miles across.

As D.H. Lawrence wrote:

I am part of the Sun as my eye is part of me,

That I am part of the Earth my feet know perfectly

And my blood is part of the Sea.

About time

So, you might be asking yourself: why do we have Time in this dimension, when existence doesn't appear to be measured out, in the same way, in other realms?

In my view, it is because the lessons we need to learn in this dimension require the alchemical container of Time in order to work, to achieve the ultimate act of creation and re-creation otherwise known as the Marriage of the Sun and the Moon.

In other words, the evolution of the soul is a stepped, circadian process around a spinning Wheel or Clock that marks the Time. To the Greeks, the god who measured out Time was the clockmaker, Chronos, and this is where the word "chronology" comes from – in other words, events laid out by the logos ruled by Chronos.

The word "circadian" comes from *circa* (about) and *diem* (a day). The word "ruler" is used for both one who rules from his throne and a measuring rod for good reason. The use of alignments to show who has measured an Earthly domain, and thus who rules it, will make more sense to you later on.

Demeter, the mother of Persephone, who was kidnapped by Hades, was the daughter of Chronos and so she also had a role in meting out the laws of Time. Her name is thought to be linked to the word "diameter", which is the measurement of the width of the clock face wherever it occurs.

Her daughter, the Moon, was responsible for controlling the Tides both above and below and in-between. She oversaw periodical flooding of the Milky Way, which is when the old pole star "submerges" to give way to its successor.

She governs the flux and reflux of the rivers and the seas upon the Earth. She oversees the circadian flows of our inner bodily fluids and the deep, dark, mysterious oceans of our subconscious minds. And not least, as the cool, pale-skinned grand-daughter of Chronos, she governs the ebb and flow of the tides in the hearts and minds of men.

The Latin word for time was *tempus*, and so this is where "temple" comes from. Temples built according to sacred geometrical principles are, in effect, transformers[2]. So, when we are viewing landscape zodiacs and Earth alignments known as ley lines, we are in effect looking at temples on the land within which the cognoscenti practised sacred theatrical rites for the good of the evolution or transformation of their souls.

Initially, these star stories were passed on in the form of verses that were recited orally. This was a more powerful transmission. That which is heard (*śruti*, as the Vedics called it) penetrates a different part of the brain to that which is merely seen as squiggly shapes on a page.

Eventually, though, the scribes began to record their allegorical sagas with ink and red ochre, at first as hieroglyphic images on cave walls, and then later in more stylised ways on papyrus and vellum scrolls. These myths, along with all star charts going back for thousands of years, were stored in huge libraries all over the world, like the one at Alexandria, which was eventually destroyed by the Romans at the beginning of the Common Era.

The destruction, over time, of these great repositories of the Mystery teachings led to a literal Dark Ages in which a small priestly elite were left holding the keys to enlightenment that was buried under the weight of a coded system which, as time went on, they could barely understand themselves.

The Fraternity of Inner Light

So now let's fast forward to the early 20th century. We're going to meet a fascinating group of people who would gather regularly in the Chalice Orchard, on the flanks of Glastonbury Tor.

They were led by the spiritualist Dion Fortune and her magician friend Charles Loveday, whose involvement in the secret society of the Golden Dawn gave them egress to hidden, esoteric materials unavailable to most at that time.

Fortune wanted to bring those teachings to a wider audience and so she decided to establish a school in the Chalice Orchards, on the flanks of Glastonbury Tor. Here, people came from all over the country to attend lectures and plays that would lead them towards initiation into the Mysteries.

On the Spring Equinox of 1928, she and Loveday inaugurated "The Lesser Mysteries of The Fraternity of the Inner Light"[3] to offer teachings that were spread over several months, in order for candidates to learn sufficient esoteric lore to go forwards into the Greater Mysteries of the fire initiation.

Another member of her fraternity was the architect Frederick Bligh Bond. As a former member of the Rosicrucian Order, Bligh Bond had used psychic means to discover the ancient ruins of medieval buildings that were buried under the grounds of Glastonbury Abbey and we will be visiting these later on.

At around the same time, Dion Fortune wrote her novel *The Goat Foot God*, which contains hidden allusions to the landscape geometry of the West Country[4]. These writings show that she knew about an alignment of religious monuments across England that are dedicated to St Michael. So, this sort of "land magic" would have featured in her Mystery teachings, particularly given that she was in a wider movement of theosophists who subscribed to an esoteric era that was dedicated to the serpent-slaying archangel.

This Age of Michael had been inaugurated in 1878. Queen Victoria's husband, Prince Albert, in full masonic regalia, had led a ritual on the embankment of the River Thames in London that had culminated in the erection of the phallic-shaped obelisk of Cleopatra's Needle.

However, this royal launch had been more of a relaunch. It shored up an already existing Christian gloss over the domain of the Celtic Sun god that had been imported from Italy to Avalon in early medieval times by the Benedictine monks of Glastonbury Abbey.

This means that ever since about the 12th century, there has been an alignment of Michael churches and other sacred monuments that would have once honoured the spirit of place of the Celtic Sun god, which stretches across southern England, between Land's End in Cornwall and the east coast of Norfolk. As shown on **Figure 2**, it crosses St Michael's Mount off Penzance, Glastonbury, Avebury and Bury St Edmunds as it follows the rising Sun of the May Day festival of Beltane, which took its name, in pre-Christian times, from Belinus.

Weaving around the male Sun god Belinus, we find another alignment. This one is marked by water courses – springs, streams, rivers and brooks. It is called the St Mary line, who could have been a Benedictine substitute for the Celtic pale-faced Moon goddesses Elen or Don. It doesn't matter which, though, for our purposes. Now that we have dug down underneath the modern glosses, we can see that Michael and Mary are just the more current representatives of the original Sun and the Moon of the Mystery Teachings.

The Sun god and the Moon goddess are the spiritual governors of the two initiations of, respectively, fire and water that interweave, in a sacred fertility dance, around one another.

These two male and female characters are indicators of the same initiations of fire and water of the hero who traverses the rim of the Wheel of the starry constellations, that Kroy learned about around the campfire millennia ago.

Since the papyrus and vellum scrolls that contained all the astrological, mathematical and alchemical teachings of the Mysteries were incinerated in a series of conflagrations inflicted, over time, upon of the Library of Alexandria by various quasi-religious and political imperatives, we have had to rely on the spirits of the shaman to tutor us in how to reconstitute the secret lore

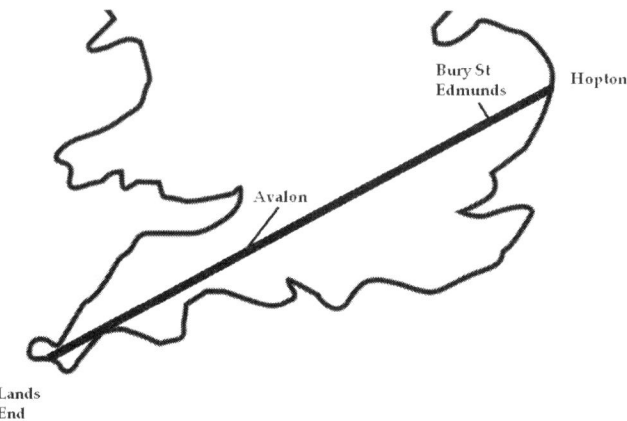

Figure 2 The St Michael or Belinus line

In my experience, it has been a journey in which I've learned how to see what it is hidden in plain sight, around the landscape of Avalon. These are the places where I take my trainees and it is the teaching I will be sharing with you as we proceed.

First, we will explore the initiations of water and then fire in more detail. Afterwards, we can put them together in a magical working so that you will be able to recognise when the land is expressing the same message to help reveal the real meaning and purpose within the journey of the pilgrim.

Water initiation

Lesser Mysteries

Spring Equinox

Colour: White

Governing planet	Gender	Goddess	Zodiac signs	Body parts
The Moon	Female	Satana Persephone Don Bridie Mary the Virgin	Cancer Scorpio Pisces	Lungs Kidneys Feet

Figure 3 Water initiation

So just like its ancient forerunner at Eleusis, the Lesser Mysteries at the Chalice Orchard culminated in a baptism. But the meanings of the stories were only revealed to the chosen few when they were allowed to go forward to the Greater Mysteries, in which the fire of enlightenment is sparked within them.

According to the 19th century Neoplatonist Thomas Taylor:

The dramatic shows of the Lesser Mysteries occultly signified the miseries of the soul while in subjection to the body, so those of the Greater obscurely intimated, by mystic and splendid visions, the felicity of the soul both here and hereafter, when purified from the defilements of a material nature and constantly elevated to the realities of intellectual [spiritual] vision.

At the end of the Lesser Mysteries, after the finale of the baptism, one can imagine the young adept returning home wondering what it was all for. However, if they had read their Bible, they would have got a clue from the gospel story about a famous water initiation that was held on the banks of the river Jordan.

In the *New Testament*'s *Gospel of Luke*, we read the following explanation for how the water initiation fits into the larger framework of the Mysteries by John the Baptist:

> *And as the people were in expectation, and all men mused in their hearts of John, whether he were the Christ, or not; John answered, saying unto them all, I indeed baptise you with water; but one mightier than I cometh, the latchet of whose shoes I am not worthy to unloose: he shall baptize you with the Holy Ghost and with fire: Whose fan is in his hand, and he will thoroughly purge his floor, and will gather the wheat into his garner; but the chaff he will burn with fire unquenchable.*

These waters were also referred to as "the deeps" of the zodiac, which made up the Underworld or the subliminal seas of the mind. So the stories and plays, if composed and staged by shamanically skilled poets and playwrights, would act like seeds in the dark of the subconscious of the initiate, where they would eventually germinate and sprout into grain that would become ripe in time for the harvest of the Autumn Equinox, where the chaff would be burned away in the fire initiation.

The Mystery Teachings of Eleusis were so secret that those who took part were under pain of death not to reveal what they had learned. Similarly - although almost certainly without the threat of murder! - Fortune's adepts never told anyone what they learned at the Lesser Mysteries in the Chalice Orchard.

But there are many clues to be found in her books. It seems that her metaphysical framework would have been based on a mixture of Gnostic Christianity and the Hermetic Qabalah that she transliterated through the lens of the Norman stories of the Arthurian mythos.

So, while the Eleusinian Mysteries had focused on the Moon goddess type of Persephone to embody the element of water, Fortune would have used Arthur's mysterious faery half-sister, Morgan Le Fay, for her Moon goddess, which finds expression in the Qabalistic sephirah (or metaphysical realm) of Yesod.

Geoffrey de Monmouth was the first, in the 12th century, to introduce Morgan le Fay into the Arthur stories[5] and he derived her name from the Welsh *morgen*, which meant "sea-borne" or "water-sprite".

The Fay or Fae part obviously needs no further explanation – she was Morgan of the Fae who, to my mind, sounds very much like the Scythian water-born fertility goddess Satana, who bestows the faery-forged sword on Batraz of the Narts, an earlier prototype for Arthur.

As you know, Satana was born to her dead mother within a tomb in "the Otherworld" beneath the seas. When she grows into adulthood, she is credited as the discoverer of the power of the life-force of water.

And while Morgan the *morgen* ferries the wounded Arthur through the Mists of Avalon to be healed in the land of the Ever Young on the Isle of Apples, Satana discovers a gold and white apple that imparts immortality and everlasting youth to any who should be lucky enough to taste of it.

In my book *Stories in the Stars*, I go into much more detail about how the character of Arthur was derived from star-based myths that are much older than the King Arthur of British history, for which there is scant evidence.[6] The English, Scots, Welsh and Irish also come from Scythian stock, so these stories have been woven into our race memories – otherwise known as the double-helix of our DNA.

Thus, they provide the weft and warp of the tapestry that supports the cognitive fabric known as "The Matter of Britain" and which contributes to the culture of the blessed British Isles their culture and their claim to the Sovereignty of the land.

As Nicholas Mann writes in his book *The Red and White Springs*:

> *The Arthurian material is central to the subject and gains its weight not so much from the elaborations of medieval romancers and other later myth makers but from the fact that it is believed to originate in the ancient, pre-conquest history of the land. The rich vein of lore which constitute "the Matter of Britain" has it roots firmly in the pre-Roman and pre-Christian tradition, and secondly in the renaissance of that native tradition in the period immediately following the Roman withdrawal at the beginning of the 1st century…*

Dion Fortune found a way to embody the *morgen* or water sprite faery of the Matter of Britain in Vivien Le Fay Morgan, her heroine of *The Sea Priestess*. Vivien claims to be a reincarnation of a priestess from Atlantis, which in Plato's myth was itself submerged under the waves.

The novel is set at Brean Down, a high, windswept and bleakly atmospheric promontory which extends off the coast of Somerset into the Bristol Channel.

She goes on to develop the Moon priestess character further in her final book, *Moon Magic*, with the same heroine who has changed her name to Lilith Le Fay Morgan and in which the Bristol Channel is replaced by the River Thames in London.

Towards the end of her life, Dion Fortune recommended her students use her novels as companions to her more theoretical guide, *The Mystical Qabalah*, which had been published three years earlier. In *Moon Magic*, Le Fay Morgan sings that she is a secret queen, Persephone, and that "all tides are mine, and answer to me".

She clarifies that what she means by "all tides" includes the tides of the air, of the inner earth, of death and rebirth and men's soul's and destiny.

So, going by what I've gleaned from her books, I believe that her Lesser Mystery teachings could be synthesised into the following saying: "Time and tide waits for no man."

In other words, the Temple of Time is constructed by Chronos and through it flow the Tidal streams that are governed by his grand-daughter, Persephone the Moon.

At the human level, the walls of this Temple of Time provide the crucible or container through which our lives progress in stages along a long and winding river. Its grassy banks are lined with the chronologically organised landmarks and way markers of our major relationships and life events, which all possess, within them, our own customised challenges and blessings, dictated by the position of the stars at our birth or entry into this Temple.

In learning by way of the Mystery Teachings how to row our boat, we can avoid getting trapped in the watery mire of the Slough of Despond, like John Bunyan's pilgrim character, Christian.[7]

Dion Fortune associated the gently curving, round-shaped, neighbouring Chalice Hill with the element of water and her adepts would journey in trance to a place within it that she called The Sanctuary, thought to be a cavern of blue lias stone that would have held about a dozen people, which lies about 40 feet beneath the turf.

Even in Fortune's day, it was no longer possible to reach the Sanctuary physically, through a tunnel that once led off from where the White Spring is now. The entrance was blocked up more than a century ago. But her students would journey there, in trance.

Chalice Orchard was established atop an embankment in Wellhouse Lane, which runs up beside the Chalice Well Gardens. The two streams that had carved out the Sanctuary emerge here, on either side of the narrow road. They are known as the Red and White Springs – the former being mineral-rich with iron, the latter with calcium.

Hopefully, those names will make more sense

when you read about the fire initiation of the Greater Mysteries and the meaning of the Vesica Piscis. And so, we just need one final piece of information before going on. We need to know the magical symbol for water in the Hermetic system. It is a downward-facing equilateral triangle.

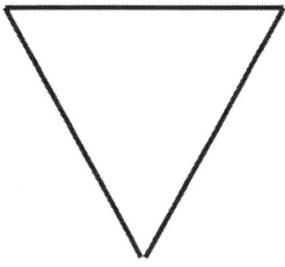

Figure 4 *The Hermetic symbol for water*

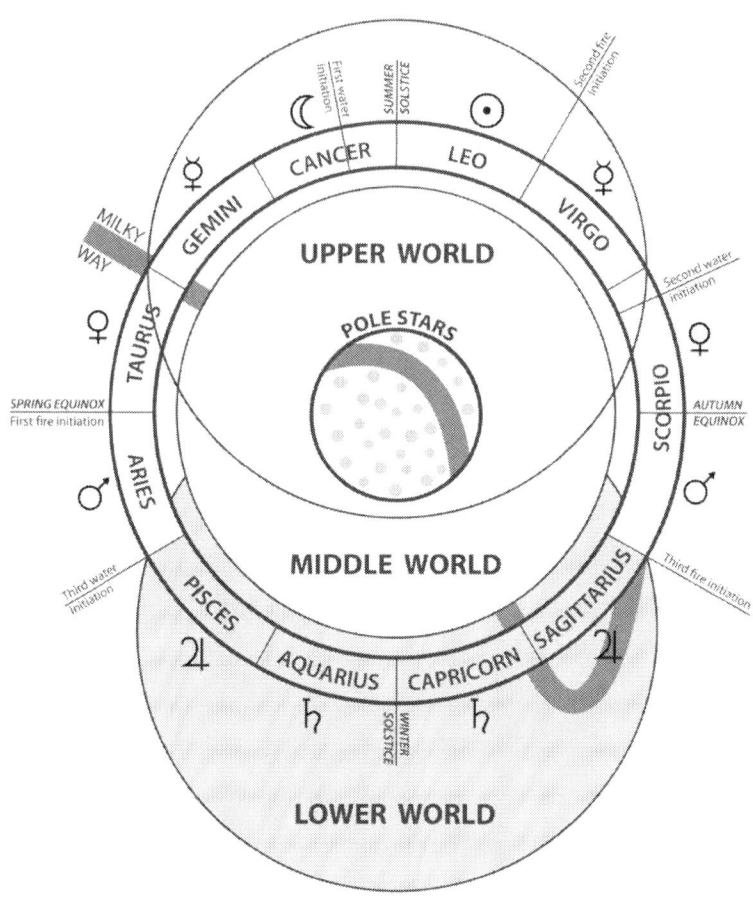

Figure 5 *Fire and water initiations of the zodiac hero*

Fire initiation
Greater Mysteries
Autumn Equinox
Colour: Red

Governing planet	Gender	God/Goddess	Zodiac signs	Body parts
The Sun	Male	Beli Lugh Arthur Michael Jesus Christ	Aries Leo Sagittarius	Head Heart Pelvis

Figure 6 The Greater Initiation of the Fire Mysteries

In **Figure 5** you can see how the three fire and water initiations are organised around the spinning Wheel of the zodiac, which is arranged across three worlds. They each represent different stages of the alchemical process through which Nature continually reinvents Herself. This, as you now know, is called the Marriage of the Sun and the Moon, which leads to the birth of the Child of the Philosopher, or the Philosopher's Stone.

At the Greater Mysteries, the adept was taught the deeper meanings of the allegories hidden in the stories and plays of the Lesser Initiation and so finally they would be enlightened about the workings of the hierarchy within the cosmos. The essence of this teaching might be put as simply as: "The early bird catches the worm."

You may not think much to worms or *wyrms* until you realise that this is early Anglo-Saxon for "dragon" or "serpent", which initiates throughout medieval and Renaissance art and architecture are seen trampling underfoot. This is because there was much more to the Mysteries than a mere science lesson; there was a practical aspect too. At the level of the individual, the multi-layered myths are about sacred sexual practices that lead to such powerful and indelible inner transformation that the effects of it can never be overturned. The change is eternal in the sense that is permanent because the old life has been burned to ashes.

So how does that work, I can hear you asking?

Well, imagine, if you will, that the human body is a parked car that only requires the turning of the right key in the right lock to spark it into life. Turn the ignition and what you'd assumed was just a museum piece turns out to be a gleaming red Ferrari purring and raring to go, as the energetic serpents begin to raise their heads. Then you are suddenly forced backwards with the speed of the "worms" racing up your body like flaming arrows to their goal, the cup-shaped hypothalamus.

Here, they pause for a nanosecond, to rest their heads upon the rim of the "chalice". Then they begin to secrete Red and White drops of nectar that gently fall on to the pineal gland or Third Eye. The drops swirl together to create a catalytic mixture that causes the crown of the head to turn into a "thousand points of light", which, in turn, activate the higher brain centres, thus granting wisdom to the ruler and the right to reign over the land.

It is the equivalent of waking up the court of the Sleeping Beauty. Even though they have all been asleep for a hundred years, once woken they are aware of reality. In Hollywood films, it is the red pill of *The Matrix* – although the food is better!

The Secret Fire of the Alchemists

The fire of the serpents is no ordinary fire. It is a secret fire. The alchemists of old recognised four grades of fire: elementary fire, celestial fire, central fire and secret fire. So let's examine them in detail:

- Elementary fire is the spark that enlivens Nature;
- Celestial fire is star fire
- Central fire is the Word of God vibration at the heart of all matter.

To discover the identity and nature of the secret fire, we need to turn the 18th Benedictine alchemist Antoine-Joseph Pernety.

He writes: [8]

The fire of the Sun could not be this Secret Fire. It is unequal and does not penetrate. The fire of our stoves, which consumes the constituent parts of matter, could not be the one. The Central Fire, which is innate in matter, cannot be that Secret Fire so much praised, because the heat is very different within the three kingdoms; the animals possess it in a much higher degree than the plant.

In allegories and fables, the philosophers have given to this Secret Fire the names sword, lance, arrows, javelin etc. It is the fire which Prometheus stole from the heaven, which Vulcan employed to form the thunderbolts of Jupiter and the golden throne of Zeus.

The poet William Blake was a contemporary of Pernety and once your eyes are opened to the Mysteries, the inner meanings from his paintings and poems leap out. Not least, in this respect, is his poem *And did those feet in ancient time*. Its verses, since being set to such chest-thumpingly patriotic music by Hubert Parry, have been much misunderstood.

In **Figure 5**, we saw how the mythological hero, traversing the zodiac, passes through three fire initiations – at Aries, Leo and Sagittarius. Now, let's examine Blake's great bardic work through the eyes of the enlightened initiate that he surely was.

> **ARIES** (Lamb or Ram)
> And did those feet in ancient time,
> Walk upon England's mountains green:
> And was the holy Lamb of God,
> On England's pleasant pastures seen!
>
> **LEO** (The Sun)
> And did the Countenance Divine,
> Shine forth upon our clouded hills?
> And was Jerusalem builded here,
> Among these dark Satanic Mills?

SAGITTARIUS (The Archer)
Bring me my Bow of burning gold;
Bring me my Arrows of desire:
Bring me my Spear: O clouds unfold!
Bring me my Chariot of fire!

SOVEREIGNTY (the king marries the land)
I will not cease from Mental Fight,
Nor shall my Sword sleep in my hand:
Till we have built Jerusalem,
In England's green and pleasant Land.

Blake's use of the symbols "bow and arrows", "spear" and "sword" are reminiscent of Pernety's description of the secret fire.

The "dark Satanic Mills" are actually the Wheels of the gods that "grind slowly, but they grind exceedingly small"[9] in churning out the granular fate of man. They are operated by our old friend Chronos, this time in the guise of the Grim Reaper, the miller who the Romans called Saturn. This "miller's tale" is as much to do with the secret knowledge or "private parts" of astrologers, and bawdy wenches being grabbed by the "quente", as Geoffrey Chaucer's *Canterbury Tales*. We also know him as Old Father Time through his creation of the parameters of the alchemical container, or meted-out life span, of the human being.

The alchemical symbol for fire is an upright equilateral triangle. **Figure 7** shows them combined with the downward-facing triangle of water, which I've dotted for clarity. This gives us the six-pointed star, also known as Solomon's Seal.

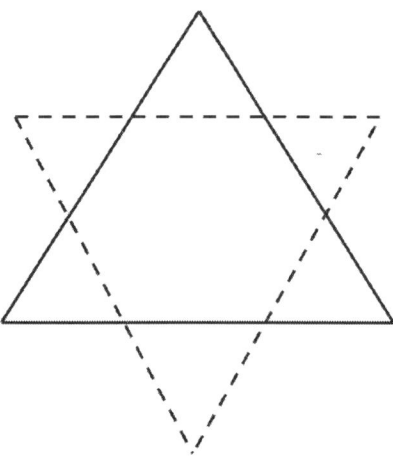

Figure 7 *Solomon's Seal*

Sleeping with the Fishes

In Wells Cathedral, which is only a short drive from Glastonbury, you will find the former bishops and treasurers of England's medieval period "sleeping" over their tombs and wearing headgear resembling open-mouthed fish. These odd-looking mitres are a remnant of the Mysteries and the full initiation of the hero which begins, in ancient myths, with a fire initiation at Aries. He moves around the rim of zodiac, meeting his adventures, until he falls down into the Underworld at Scorpio. Here, he has to face the Dark Night of the Soul before being reborn at Capricorn, on the Winter Solstice, as the Radiant Child. The newborn baby houses a soul that does not reach full maturity until the third and final water initiation at Pisces, as shown in **Figure 5**.

Aries was represented on the human body as the

head and Pisces was symbolised by the feet, which were in the Underworld. So the whole journey along the rim of the Wheel of the mythological hero began, physiologically, at the (conscious) head of Aries and ends at the (unconscious) feet of Pisces.

Thus, when the human's feet (the fish of Pisces) are joined with his head (of Aries), it is to signify that this pilgrim has completed the zodiac full-circle and thus his unconscious has become conscious, allowing him to reincarnate into his own life.

As Carl Jung once said: "Until you make the unconscious conscious, it will direct your life and you will call it fate."

The wearing of fish-shaped headwear used to be the sole preserve of the initiate. It is a version of the Phrygian cap, shown on the heads of many a mythic pilgrim like Perseus, Attis, Aeneas and Ganymede. Whether or not the bishops buried in Wells Cathedral had actually reincarnated into their own lives through practising the Mysteries or were just blindly following tradition in adopting such headgear is open to question.

Four Elemental Hills

It is not the aim of this pilgrimage to teach you how to be an alchemist. But I will need to explain a few basic principles so that you will be able to better read the underlying stories in the land in the places we visit.

In this chapter, we have dealt with the elements of fire and water but we also need to talk a little about air and earth to get the full picture.

In brief, air governs fire. If you have ever used a pair of bellows to feed the flames, or have snuffed out a fire with a blanket, you will understand this principle. Air represents all things gaseous, expansive and vibrational, such as speech and song. Air signs in astrology are Gemini, Libra and Aquarius.

Similarly, earth governs water, in the way that the banks of a river act to contain the flow. The earth is matter - the invisible net of energy that makes up the matrix and is the madron, meaning mother in Welsh, of the creation. Earth signs in astrology are Taurus, Virgo and Capricorn.

Therefore, fire, water, earth and air are the foundational forces that give rise to creation and re-creation, and are known as the four elements. Dion Fortune attributed each of the elements to four hills in the Isle of Avalon as follows:

Glastonbury Tor – Fire, Red

The terraced, conical hill of Glastonbury Tor, we believe, was once more pyramid-shaped, until an earthquake in 1275 gave it a more staggered, elongated summit.

Dion Fortune herself commented, in her *Glastonbury: Avalon of the Heart*, that seen from afar, the Tor is the perfect pyramid.

The word 'pyramid' is derived from the Greek *pyro*, meaning fire. Some see it as a firebird or phoenix.

If you are driving towards Glastonbury from Wells, the Tor first appears on the left just as you are leaving the village of Coxley. It seems to be sailing fast towards you like a great ship, its funnel shaped by the ruined tower on its summit and white, fluffy puffs of steam by the clouds.

When you catch it at sunrise, it is as if it is sailing on a sparkling sea of silver mists and, when silhouetted against skies painted with apricots and marigolds, it could be the Dawn Treader.

For a mile or so, the road turns downwards, and so the Tor disappears from view behind some trees. But then, just as you reach the sign proclaiming Welcome to Glastonbury, this great green serpent mound is there again, standing right before you as if in greeting.

You can walk up the Tor by taking the winding steps that lead off from the right at the start of Wellhouse Lane, as you turn off from Chilkwell Street. There is another entrance, a mile or so up the lane, but parking there is tricky with vigilant traffic wardens around. You can choose to ascend on either side, where stepped, winding paths take you up to the summit.

Dion Fortune called the Tor the "Hill of Vision". The views from it across the Somerset Levels are certainly stunning. On a good day, you can see as far as the Cheddar Caves. However, I wouldn't recommend it as a place of peaceful meditation. It is a popular destination with tourists and even on the hottest and stillest of days, there's usually quite a breeze blowing. I have my own ideas about the permanent breeze. I don't think it's an ordinary wind but an energetic force that that is generated by the geological geometries of the mound.

Those with strong ankles might prefer to follow the spiralling path that is formed by the terraces cut into the hill. The tower on its summit is all that remains, after the earthquake, of a St Michael church that was built by the Benedictine monks of Glastonbury Abbey.

Chalice Hill – Water, White

I'm afraid that you won't be able to visit the round green dome of Chalice Hill because it is now privately owned. But you will be able to enjoy the neighbouring and equally wonderfully enchanted Chalice Well Gardens, which were lovingly created by the early childhood educator Alice Buckton in the early 20th century.

Enter through the gate on Chilkwell Street and you will first notice a grassy area to your right in which there are two old and majestic yew trees. This is a faery portal, and so it's always a good idea to ask for permission first before passing between them.

Follow the pathway through the garden until you reach the covered well. On its lid, you will see a Vesica Piscis that was forged by the aforementioned architect Frederick Bligh Bond. I'll be explaining about the meaning of this symbol in the next chapter.

The well itself is constructed of unusual stones that are not found in the locality, although they are similar to those used to build Stonehenge. The 15-foot shaft leads down to a bed of blue lias gravel, upon which floats a rare iron-laden fungus that turns the water red, giving rise to its name Blood Spring.

I should warn you that all heartfelt and sincere prayers and wishes directed into this faery well are always answered. So be careful what you wish for!

Wirrall Hill – Earth, Brown or Yellow

Wirrall Hill is shaped very much like the steep-sided plateaus the Chinese used to associate with the element of earth. It is on the other side of the town to the Tor and the Chalice Well Gardens. Just go down the

High Street until you reach the Market Square. Then turn left to follow Magdalene Street, which turns into Fisher Hill. At the top of the hill, there is a residential road called Hillhead, which goes off to the right. If you turn up there and continue walking for a few hundred yards, past all the houses, you will eventually come to a gateway in a hedge on the right.

Go through the gate and then follow the winding path up the hill. This will take you past a stump of a thorn tree that is still honoured today, even though it lost its crown to vandals in the winter of 2010 [10]. It has been known as the Holy Thorn for centuries, and, despite all appearances to the contrary, its spirit is still very much alive - so I would recommend having a chat there with the *genius loci*.

Local legend decrees that the Holy Thorn is a descendant of a tree that grew out of the staff of Jesus's uncle, Joseph of Arimathea. He apparently planted it into the ground upon arriving in the Isle of Avalon with his party of tin merchants, which was "weary all" from the long sea voyage – hence Wirrall Hill is dubbed Wearyall Hill.

Native thorns usually bloom on May Day; whether the day is named after the blossoms that this tree bears, or vice-versa, I cannot say. But the Holy Thorn on Wearyall Hill is a species that thrives only in the Middle East and is one that flowers only in winter. Hence, a bouquet of the white flowers from one of its siblings, growing in Glastonbury Abbey, is always sent to Queen Elizabeth on Christmas Day.

It is said Joseph brought with him relics from the crucifixion – a cruet of bottles, one containing a red fluid and the other a white liquid. The story is that the red fluid was Jesus's blood and that the white liquid was either his semen or plasma.

However, after digesting the inner meanings of the stories that made up the mysteries of the marriage of the red Sun and the white Moon that were taught where the Red and White Springs cross, you may be reaching a different conclusion.

Windmill Hill – Air, Blue

Windmill Hill must have been named for its high, airy position above the town – or "Bove Town" as the locals call it. It would have made an ideal spot for a windmill – or for a sacred rite dedicated to a miller? Astro-archaeologists believe it was used for star-watching thousands of years ago.

Windmill Hill was renamed to St Edmund's Hill, probably by St Dunstan, the 10th century abbot of Glastonbury Abbey. It is a good 15 minutes' walk up the steeply ascending Bove Town Road, which you will find at the top of the High Street. Just before Wick Hollow, turn up the Old Wells Road and then, just to your left, you will see a children's playground on a grassy mound. That is Windmill or St Edmund's Hill.

[1] Acts 26:14. "And when we were all fallen to the earth, I heard a voice speaking unto me, and saying in the Hebrew tongue, Saul, Saul, why persecutest thou me? It is hard for thee to kick against the pricks"

[2] Chapter 4, A Holographic Universe of Music, *Stories in the Stars* by Annie Dieu-Le-Veut

[3] The Lesser Mysteries of The Fraternity of the Inner Light was re-named later to The Society of the Inner Light.

[4] Described in *The Terrestrial Alignments of Katharine Maltwood and Dion Fortune* by Yuri Leitch.

[5] *Vita Merlini* by Geoffrey of Monmouth.

[6] Chapter 6, Camelot of the Polar Stars, *Stories in the Stars* by Annie Dieu-Le-Veut.

[7] *The Pilgrim's Progress* by John Bunyan.

[8] *Dictionnaire mytho-hermétique, dans lequel on trouve les allégories fabuleuses des poètes, les métaphores, les énigmes et les termes barbares des philosophes hermétiques expliqués* by Antoine-Joseph Pernety (1758).

[9] Charles A. Beard, American historian. "The mills of God grind slowly, but they grind exceedingly small. The bee fertilises the flower it robs. When it is dark enough, you can see the stars."

[10] As I write, it has been cut down again. You may just find a stump but its spirit is still there.

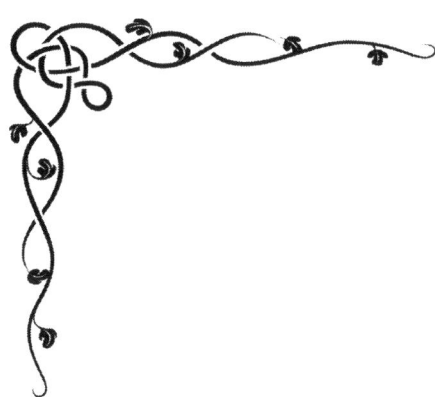

Chapter Five: The Mystery in Ye Stones

Glastonbury is a fine example of multiple overlays placed upon an already potent and enlivening landscape. Every human culture and period places an overlay upon the land, but this is usually more or less unconscious … More rarely, aware individuals or groups will feed ideas and forms into their culture's consciousness in order to harness the power of a place to a specific end. This end can either be benevolent or tyrannical, depending upon the nature of the perpetrators. It can also be long or short lived, stable or unstable, depending on the capabilities of its makers.

Alan Royce, "Avalon" magazine, summer 1998

We are now going to visit one of these overlays or glosses that Alan Royce mentions above. It was deliberately placed upon the land during the sixth century and it is Glastonbury Abbey. We will be making these ruins of blue lias stones the next stop on our camino because the dimensions of what remains of its architecture demonstrate the clearest example of a story that predates it in the land by thousands of years.

But do be careful. As we wind through the town's crowded, narrow streets, you will have to run the gauntlet of swift-mouthed mountebanks and disreputable dissemblers spinning their rainbow-hued yarns. They may try to wind you in with a beguiling story: that the early Christians came to Glastonbury with Joseph of Arimathea, soon after the crucifixion, and it was here that they established the first Christian church in Britain in the form of a round wattle and daub building.

This old canard has been underpinning the tourist industry in Glastonbury since medieval times. The grave of two skeletons was exhumed in the abbey grounds in 1191, whereupon the current abbot and king, along with his retinue, all agreed to agree were the remains of King Arthur and his wife, Guinevere.

However, all the evidence points to it being just a clever piece of theatre for the benefit of the unruly indigenous Britons, who had been threatening to revolt and take back the land stolen from them ever since they had been pushed into the western margins of a country that was named after them.

Now that the royal stamp of approval had been given to the story that the great Celtic war leader, Arthur Pendragon, was well and truly dead, the wordsmiths quickly began to forge a new narrative about Joseph of Arimathea arriving with his tin merchant cohorts on Wearyall Hill with the two vials containing red and white fluids.

It was a clever ploy – and a lucrative one. Claiming to be the site of the first church gave Glastonbury independence from Rome and Canterbury – cities that didn't convert to Christianity until the fourth and sixth centuries, respectively. Thus, this tiny Somerset town went on to equal its ecumenical rivals in influence, splendour and riches... until Henry VIII tore it all down in the 16th century - but more about that later.

It might have been easy to convince people in the 12th century of... well, practically anything. There was no internet then. Now we know that, for a good few centuries after the date attributed to the crucifixion, Christians had been regarded by Rome as little more than terrorists.

And so, at the same time that the relations and followers of Christ were supposed to have been worshipping in the round, wattle and daub church, the imperialist conquerors were actually building one of their famous roads straight through it, along an already existing track that ran between Glastonbury and Stonehenge. All that is left of that thoroughfare today is Dod Lane, which leads up to Bushey Combe.

This anachronism is compounded by the discoveries of archaeologists, in recent years, who have excavated the abbey and found that the earliest evidence of habitation was not until the sixth century. In other words, this was about the same period in which Augustine crossed our shores to establish Roman Christianity in Britain.

Legend has it that this so-called first church went up in flames in the great fire of 878 CE. I have my suspicions about that conflagration, too, but that's another tale for another day.

Anyway, Glastonbury Abbey is easy to find. It takes up half of the town. The entrance is in Magdalene Street, which runs south from the Market Cross at the bottom of the High Street. It is a huge, ornately carved stone archway, which used to be the gatehouse. The last abbot of Glastonbury spent his final night on Earth here before being executed on Glastonbury Tor – but we will get to all that further on.

The lush, emerald green turf of the Abbey grounds has been described as "the holyest erthe in England" and it probably is.

It is sacred ground not because it is home to first church in England, which it isn't, but because ghostly memories still linger in its morphogenetic fields of a great and eternal prayer of exultation dedicated to the glory of God. By God, I don't mean a grey-haired man in the sky. The aim of the pilgrimage of an initiate of the Mysteries is to discover the nature of the godhead hidden in its creation and we will be making a good start on that now as we examine the dimensions of this paradisiacal-inspired architecture.

It is certainly a tonic for flagging spirits to walk under what remains of the towering, arched nave of blue lias stones and its ruined transepts, on ground consecrated by the magico-spiritual communion of buried rulers, relics and ruins dating to Anglo-Saxon times.

At the western end, we find the 12th Century Chapel of St Joseph, otherwise known as the Lady Chapel, which is ornamented with scenes from the nativity, such as the Three Kings, and if you can bear to look, King Herod's men, complete with Norman armour, are spearing babies through with their pikes. At the far end of the nave is the Edgar Chapel, which was excavated by Bligh Bond in the 1920s at the behest of his spirit guides.

We could pour scorn upon such "woo-woo" methods of obtaining information. I do myself, at times. Some so-called "channelling" is at best unhelpful. However, all around in the abbey grounds we find clear evidence of what used to be there. This is solely because Bligh Bond dug at the places where he had been directed to by a spirit medium who claimed to be guided by Otherworldly voices associated with the Benedictine monks of pre-Reformation times, who signed themselves "the Company of Avalon".

It is clear that the architecture of the abbey demonstrates a mish-mash of Druidic influences which derive from both Irish and Welsh traditions.

But what is also obvious to those with the eyes to see is that the builders were proficient in the occult mysteries of the Hermetic system and knew about the vital importance of the Marriage of the Sun and the Moon in any true spiritual endeavour.

As a former Rosicrucian and initiate of Dion Fortune's Mysteries of the Chalice Orchard, Bligh Bond must have recognised these signatures too. It may be why he left a sign on the lid of the Chalice Well in the form of the Vesica Piscis, which is the geometrical expression of the same alchemical principle, as shown on **Figure 8**.

So, you'd think that the Glastonians would have been grateful to Bligh Bond and the Company of Avalon for bringing the Mysteries to light in the stones of the abbey. Hell, no!

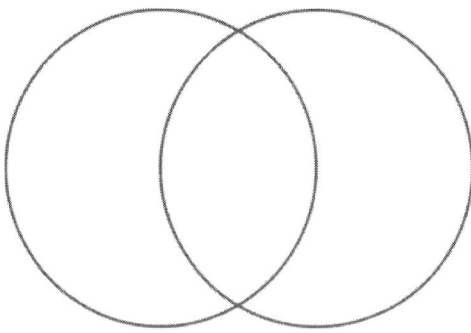

Figure 8 Vesica Piscis

The small-town, narrow-minded gossips quickly got to work in a whispering campaign and it wasn't long before the movers and shakers of the community began to regard his methods to be, at best, highly irregular and, at worst, directed by the Devil. The poor man was run out of town. Thus, the deeper Mysteries of the abbey had to be buried again, in the consensual consciousness, to wait for more enlightened times in which they could be discussed again more openly.

Luckily, the members of the Company of Avalon inhabit an ever-present realm, like a dream that remains in the land. When they visit me in trance, I see them, in my mind's eye, with their cassocks flying as they leap over the medieval abbey's high stone wall, which borders my garden and they probably built themselves.

It is these dear companions who taught me that the Philosopher's Stone is a metaphor for the culmination of the process the soul undergoes through many lives of pilgrimage around the rim of the Wheel, culminating in what they call the transfiguration of Christ consciousness. Today, we call it "spiritual transformation".

They have also shown me how some of these same teachings are hidden in the scriptural stories which, no doubt, some of them transcribed and edited in what I believe was once a huge and influential Scriptorium on the other side of my wall. I'll be sharing much more about that with you in the next chapter.

As we've already discussed, the student of the Hermetic Arts is required to become versed in astrology, alchemy and mathematics. So, I'm afraid that we're now going to have to do a little simple geometry.

Please do bear with me as I know the subject can be a little off-putting, especially to those who were taught mathematics by useless teachers, not to mention those poor souls who had to undergo the tortures of the Common Core system – they have my utmost sympathies. I must say, though, I find it vastly amusing to see the vast amounts of money and effort expended by the film industry in producing dark horror films about bloodthirsty vampires and flesh-eating ghouls. If the aim is to put people off the study of magic, all they needed to do is tell them they'd have to work through a little basic maths first.

Anyway, I promise that you will only be required to absorb the very least you'll need to know about how sacred geometry is used to express alchemical formulas - and in the very simplest of terms. My aim is that this teaching will guide you to make sense of the stories I'll be showing you as we walk through Avalon and to, eventually, be adept at interpreting the tales in the dreams of your own land.

Sacred geometry is the study of the eternal laws that govern the omnipresent, omniscient and omnipotent principles of all life, as Above, So Below. Let's start with the root, the seed, the Vesica Piscis, and then our understanding should flower and fruit naturally from that point outwards.

The Vesica Piscis

The Vesica Piscis is easy. It is just two circles of the same size that intersect to "birth" a third shape in the centre, which you can see shaded in **Figure 9**. The centre is known as the *mandorla*, which is Latin for the "almond" nut that it resembles.

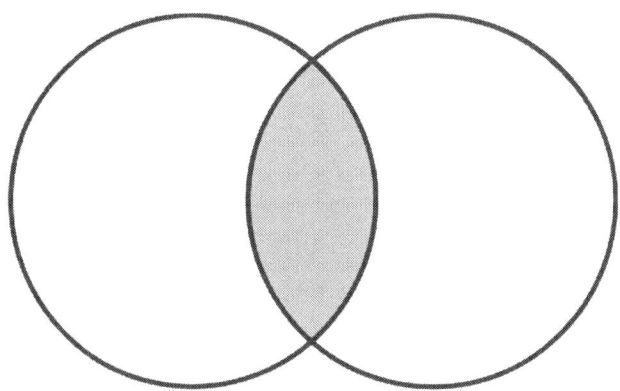

Figure 9 *The Vesica Piscis with mandorla shaded*

The *mandorla* represents the product of the intercourse of the red Sun (fire) with the white Moon (water) that leads to fertility and growth.

It is the epitome of the fruiting of the divine coupling and the inherent geometries produced from it mirror those through which Nature reproduces herself.

The Vesica Piscis is the mathematical answer to one the great Mysteries of life and creation. It is the seed that Mother Nature uses to birth and organise Her matrix, Her matter, Her material.

The walls and borders that are produced from the birth of this divine marriage go on to form the shapes of our physical world. Everything that exists in the material realm is birthed from this womb, this creatrix, this mandorla.

Thus, the Vesica Piscis is the root of sacred geometry.

That is why we find that that the architectural designs for so many sacred buildings – including Glastonbury Abbey, Stonehenge and Wells Cathedral - were generated from these triangles, squares, pentagons, hexagons, octagons, decagons and dodecagons, right up to the icosagon, five of which can be developed into Platonic solids, as shown on **Figure 10**.

We can see these same geometries of light when we close our eyes. They form an eternal dance of myriad universes coming together and then exploding like quasars to create new ones.

Archaeologists have found similar shapes and symbols daubed in red ochre in the deepest, darkest recesses of caves in southern France.

They were painted thousands of years ago by our shamanically-minded ancestors as they journeyed and dreamed in the womb-like darkness of these great Ice Age cathedrals. If you were to hear this inner light show of luminous liquid gold on velvet black, it would sound like a massive generator. Go even nearer and it's as if you are at the centre of a thunderstorm.

Make sure you don't venture too close, though, because it is deafening – which is only to be expected;

after all, it is the Word of God.

Revelations of the Divine

All truly holy buildings – from standing stone circles and Medicine Wheels to temples, mosques and cathedrals - exhibit dimensions that demonstrate they were designed and built by those who understood the laws of sacred geometry that express the music of the "voice" of this vibrational Word of God. Glastonbury Abbey is no exception.

Figure 11 shows one of Bligh Bond's own sketches of the Lady Chapel, which was built in the 12th century after the second fire that consumed the abbey.

There is an expression that speaks of "an idea whose time has come". I have found that unless one can anchor the inspiration from the spirits into a recognisable system based on science and shown in a familiar narrative, the warp and the weft of the consensual reality cannot contain it and it is either rejected in the public sphere, as poor Bligh Bond discovered, or it just dissolves and vanishes.

So, these days we are indebted to more modern specialists in sacred geometry, such as John Michel and Keith Critchlow, for being able to advance in our knowledge about the dimensions of this chapel. They discovered that both Stonehenge and the Lady Chapel were built to the same proportions that are produced from the three rhombs of the Vesica Piscis.

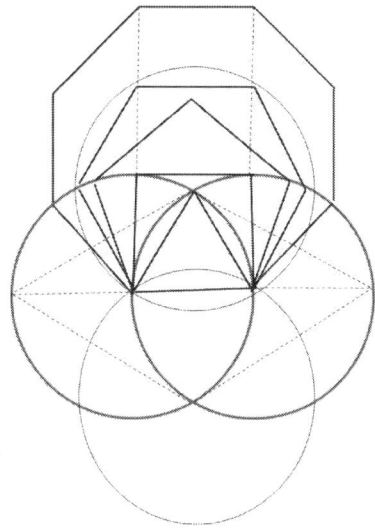

Figure 10 Vesica Piscis birthing shapes

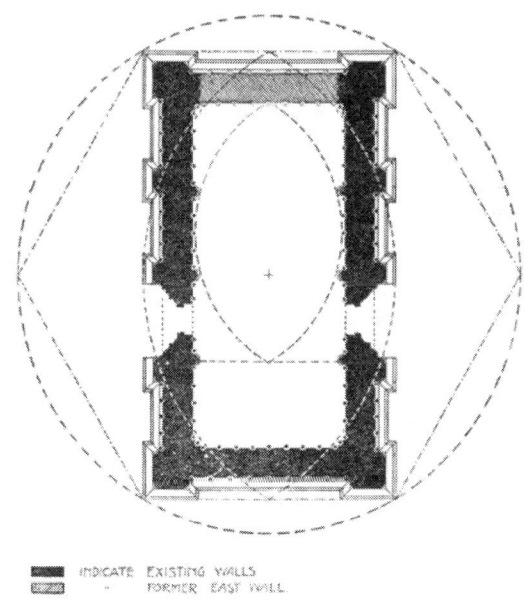

Figure 11 Bligh Bond's sketch of St Mary's Chapel

A rhomb is a "double equilateral triangular parallelogram", which, I know, sounds terrifying. But it's just a sort of kite. I've drawn one below in **Figure 12**, which, when you look at it, you'll see is not such a big deal.

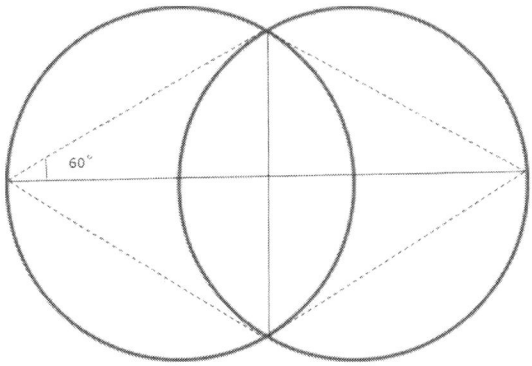

Figure 12 A rhomb produced by the Vesica Piscis

The three rhombs make up the six-pointed star of Fire and Water, which, as we learned in the last chapter, is another symbol for the Marriage of the Sun and the Moon. Thus, turning the chapel in **Figure 11** on its side, we get the result shown in **Figure 13**.

These sacred dimensional proportions were taught to the builder stonemasons of the first century BCE by the Roman architect Vitruvius. The Renaissance polymath Leonardo da Vinci went on to show how the human body was a microcosmic mirror of the macrocosmic whole with his *Vitruvian Man*.

The inner circle of the St Joseph's Chapel is 39.6 feet in diameter and the middle circle is 79.2 feet. Both circles match the dimensions of Stonehenge, where the inner circle also measures 39.6 feet and the outer circle of blue stones measures 79.2 feet in diameter

In **Figure 13** and **Figure 14**, you can see how these numbers map on to both St Joseph's Chapel and the figure of man. You will notice that da Vinci's man is standing with his arms outstretched in the shape of a saltire or St Andrew's Cross to denote the circle, while his alter- image forms a Tau upright cross to show the square. Vitruvius explained his drawing thus:

> *Now the navel is naturally the exact centre of the body. For if a man lies on his back with hands and feet outspread, and the centre of a circle is placed on his navel, his figure and toes will be touched by the circumference. Also a square will be found described within the figure, in the same way as a round figure is produced. For if we measure from the sole of the foot to the top of the head, and apply the measure to the outstretched hands, the breadth will be found equal to the height, just like sites which are squared by rule.*

The square enclosing the middle circle forms what is known as the squared circle which John Michel described as "denoting the reconciliation between all opposite elements in nature, but especially between heaven and earth".[1]

Before Bligh Bond came along, most of what anyone knew about medieval Glastonbury had been gleaned from the writings of one William of Malmesbury. Malmesbury is described as "a gifted historical scholar and an omnivorous reader, impressively well versed in the literature of classical, patristic and earlier medieval times as well as in the writings of his own contemporaries. Indeed, William may well have been the most learned man in 12th-century Western Europe."[2]

However, Malmesbury may not have realised that the earlier monks had felt compelled to disguise the esoteric teachings about alchemy and sacred geometry in their codices, just as the writers of the *Revelation of St John the Divine* had, at the end of the *New Testament*.

> *An angel shows St John a 12-gated city, "the holy Jerusalem descending out of the heaven" (Rev. 21:10) and this angel "carried a golden reed to measure the city, and the gates thereof, and the wall thereof. And the city lieth foursquare, and the length is as large as the breadth; and he measured the city with the reed, 12,000 furlongs. The length and the breadth and the height of it are equal. And he measured the wall thereof, and it was 144 cubits, according to the measure of man, that is, of the angel".* [3]

Of course, Malmesbury may have been an initiate of the Mysteries who was just passing on the Mystery teachings whole.

Nevertheless, he wrote about documentary evidence that he had discovered in the old library – now lost to us – of the earliest monks being granted 12 hides of land, which is obviously a metaphor mirroring the same code found in the *Revelation of St John the Divine*.

As Anthony Roberts writes in *Glastonbury: Ancient Avalon, New Jerusalem*:

THE MYSTERY IN YE STONES

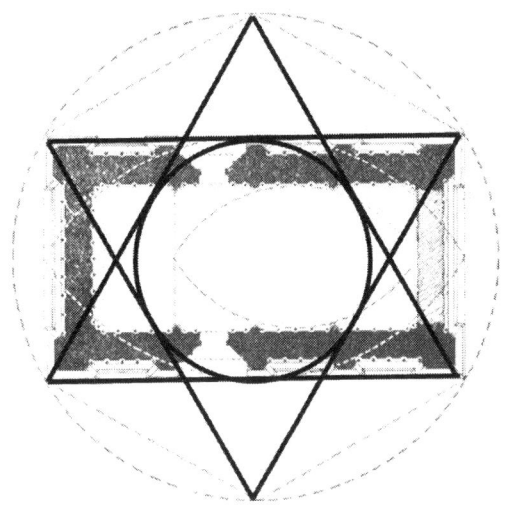

Figure 13 *Six-pointed star and the Lady Chapel*
Figure 14 *Vitruvian man and dimensions of the Lady Chapel*

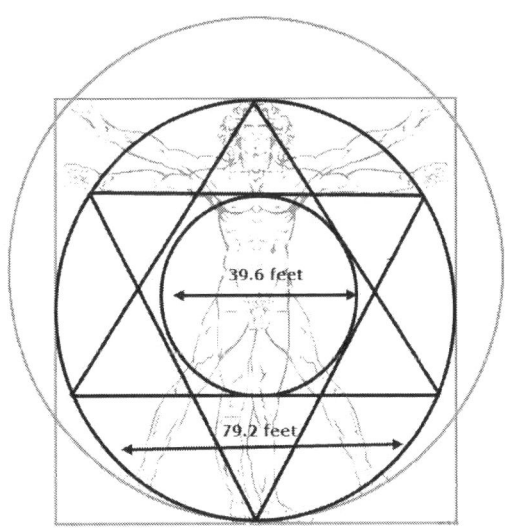

> *In Somerset, a hide of land measures 120 acres. The ancient 12 hides of Glastonbury would have totalled 1440 acres and if this area is reckoned as a square, its sides would have been 12 furlongs in length… the perfect proportional microcosm to its heavenly counterpart.*

Malmesbury's "history" of the abbey, *De Antiquitate Glastoniensis Eclessiae*, is most informative, largely because he was privileged to have had access to documents and scrolls from a monastic library now lost to us. Most of the contents went up in flames during the wholesale pillaging and destruction of the abbey in 1538 by King Henry VIII's men after the murder of the last abbot, Richard Whiting.

And so now it seems that our pilgrimage has brought us to the Valley of the Shadow of Death.

I hope you can find your courage to follow me through. It is necessary if we are to gain a holistic understanding about how the knowledge of magic is like a knife; it can used and abused, depending on who is wielding it – and why.

The story about the murder on the Tor of Abbot Whiting and his two retainers is one of those overlays in the morphogenetic fields, which, although it was woven in the 16th century, still reverberates in the weft and warp of the place, despite decades of dedicated spiritual and shamanic work. It is also known as the Dark Side of Glastonbury.

The Dark Side of Glastonbury

Local writer and researcher Alan Royce composed the following poem entitled "Glastonbury".[4]

The heart of the cauldron is no place of comfort,

The maidens who warm it have breath that can sear.

For a year and a day the companion of poisons,

And where is the drop which will make the way clear?

When the flesh of illusion is softened and fallen,

The fat of assumptions is boiled away,

The bright bones of Spirit, no longer encumbered,

Can leap like a salmon into the new day…

Though the greatest of the gifts,

The attentions of the Powers can be terrifying!

It was one of those bitterly cold and biting windswept days in the November of 1539 when Henry VIII's executioners dragged a horse-drawn hurdle up the High Street, carrying Abbot Richard Whiting and his two assistant clerics, John Thorne and Roger James. The three prisoners were then hauled along the processional path. When they reached the summit, they would have instantly seen the three gibbets already prepared for them and, beside them, a cauldron of boiling tar.

Abbot Whiting was hung with the two monks on gallows either side of him like the two thieves in the crucifixion at Calvary. Then all three were cut down while still alive and thrown into the cauldron of boiling tar. Next, they were taken back down the Tor to Wellhouse Lane, where they were drawn and quartered, so that their red blood flowed through the White Spring.

Finally, what was left of them was brought back down to the town and their heads were hung on the main West gate of the abbey with their genitals stuffed into their mouths, said to be as a warning. But a warning about what?

For a long time, it has been a natural assumption that this grotesque rite, which immediately preceded the destruction of the abbey, was just part of the general mayhem that took place up and down the country during Henry VIII's Dissolution of the Monasteries, which led to the Reformation.

However, better evidence now shows us that was just a post-hoc, anachronistic view. On closer inspection, it appears that, at that time, the wilder and violent excesses that accompanied the infamous destruction of monasteries and abbeys up and down the country were yet to come. Additionally, Sir Thomas Cromwell, Henry's henchman in such matters, had no real excuse to take Glastonbury Abbey, let alone the lives of these three august monks. They had all, to a man, signed their obedience to the Act of Succession, which granted Henry VIII the right to divorce himself from his wife, Catherine of Aragon, and the Church of Rome, and to establish the Church of England.

It seems to me that this gruesome assassination

was no ordinary act of political suppression but a magical or alchemical rite. According to local cultural historian Geoffrey Ashe, it was either "an act of madmen or mystics". He writes:

> *This Glastonbury savagery was no mere terroristic routine. At the time, it was exceptional and startling. The blacker phases of the English religious upheaval were to come later, during the reigns of Henry's three children. When their father ruled, the sustained exterminatory impulse had yet to be unleashed ... To recollect these things on the top of the Tor is to shudder, not so much at the martyrdom itself, as at the mentality of the men who arranged it.*
>
> *One senses a hateful darkness, a memory of witchcraft or Druidical rites. For the task which they undertook was so needlessly burdensome. Look down the slope and imagine driving a horse up it, in the mud of late autumn, with a human body on a hurdle trailing behind it: or carrying up heavy timbers required for the gallows: or performing the work of execution on the tiny platform of level ground by the tower, with a perpetual wind blowing.*
>
> *If the object was to strike terror, the place to do it was in the town. The ascent of the Tor was the act of madmen or mystics ... it would not have been possible to remain unaware (or suppose that the perpetrators remained unaware) of the monstrous irony which the Reformation had reared above Somerset: a gibbet on a hill.* [5]

The aim of this atrocity could not have been merely in order for Henry VIII to accrue more lands and wealth, as Geoffrey Ashe continues in his book *King Arthur's Avalon*:

> *There was no attempt to preserve the Abbey for the King. Pillage was the soul aim ... The King did not keep the property. He needed cash, not estates. Within a few weeks, Abbey lands were being knocked down to those who helped in the business.*

One can just imagine the portly Tudor king, in his classic pose of arms folded over his copious, barreled chest and stout legs planted firmly apart, watching with satisfaction as the abbey burned from the window of the coaching inn of the George and Pilgrim.

Four centuries previously, before William of Malmesbury had gained access to it, the abbey's library had already suffered a fire which destroyed an extensive collection of manuscripts collated by the previous abbot, Henry de Blois, who was the nephew of Henry I. So, by the time Henry I's Tudor namesake arrived on the scene centuries later, intent on arson, the monks had had enough time to rebuild and restock it. Thus, destroying this repository once again, and executing the master mages of the wisdom it contained, would be the perfect way of erasing the power of Glastonbury Abbey for good. Henry VIII may have even got his own Venetian Hermeticists to steal its contents before setting the building ablaze.

Setting fire to libraries is rarely an accident, although the events recounted later often portray it as such. This was a medieval version of the book burnings of modern fascist regimes, with magicians fighting magicians, alchemists fighting alchemists.

There is no difference between magic and alchemy; both work in concert with universal principles to which neutered, impotent science remains oblivious today. Even the word "magic" refers back to the mages of Alexandria, who could easily predict the future because once you know a few universal principles, you can just "zoom out" to see the whole picture.

This sort of pattern recognition enables the wise person to perceive the ultimate outcome of an existing flow to give them power over events. So it might be a good idea to examine an example of such pattern recognition. Look at the detail below in **Figure 15** and see if you can tell what it is.

Those trained in the principles of sacred geometry will be able to recognise this pattern instantly. It's part of a sequence of numbers that follow the laws of the Golden Mean and it is created when the next number in the cycle is the sum of the two preceding ones.

Figure 15 Detail of a numerical sequence

Pattern recognition is about having enough knowledge to be able to "zoom out" enough to see the whole picture, which is shown in **Figure 16**. The numbers that create this sequence are found on Vedic altars that are thousands of years old but they are accredited to a mathematician of the Italian Renaissance named Fibonacci.

The Fibonacci number sequence is what creates much of the natural world and it is instantly apparent in the spiralling nautilus shell. It dictates ratios in its curves that follow immutable laws known to those who study sacred geometry. They know that in order to create that shape, they have to start with the numbers 1, 2, 3, 5 and 8, and then go through 13 and 21 to reach the number 34.

In other words, the ultimate trajectory is pre-determined by the first few numbers and once you set out along that path, there can be only one destination. Like the unicursal path of the labyrinth, there is only one direction and one destination – which you don't to be crystal-gazer to predict.

Most people spend their lives with their noses pressed up against a desire for the number 34. They are continually going down rabbit holes in trying to work out how to achieve certain outcomes or, when that fails, decide to ignore the whole issue as if it never existed – especially if they are told that such knowledge is evil.

After all, in the land of the blind, the one-eyed man is king, while the two-eyed man gets crucified. Dating from as far back as the 10th century at least, Hermeticists were either in the secret service of the king or they were in jail.

Even today, the knowledge of what is called

"magic" – but is really the true science – is still in the hands of the chosen few.

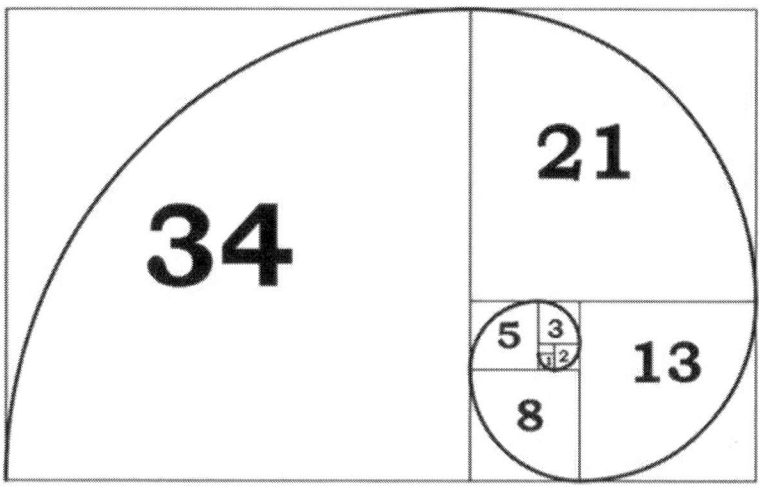

Figure 16 The Fibonacci sequence

A magical rite on the Tor

Once we understand certain alchemical principles that the monks hid in their revisions of the scriptures, we will be able to comprehend the king's real intentions, which were not merely about removing the source of Glastonbury's power which was held by its monkish teachers and its library. It was also to perform a magical act of their own and in decoding it through the Hermetic arts, here's how it breaks down.

As you know, the Vesica Piscis is the symbol for the alchemical work known as the Marriage of the Sun and the Moon. It is also called the Great Work because it is the highest form of alchemy that creates the "birth" the Child of the Philosopher. The Child of the Philosopher is another name for the Philosopher's Stone, which, like King Midas, is said to turn all it touches to gold. I will be explaining what that's all about in a later chapter but for now, I'm going to explain a few basic principles – just enough for you to understand the intentions of King Henry's magical rite on the Tor.

The operation of the Great Work passes through seven processes that are timed with the phases of the zodiac and the planets, and these are shown in **Figure 17**.

A piece of matter – known as the First Matter – is put through these seven processes to achieve its final outcome of the Philosopher's Stone.

The seven steps of the whole operation are divided into the three stages of nigredo (black), albedo (white) and rubedo (red) as shown in **Figure 18**.

Medieval monkish alchemists regarded the three-day period of the murder of Jesus Christ on the hill of Calvary as a metaphor for these three stages of black, white and red.

> *Now from the sixth hour there was darkness over all the land unto the ninth hour.*

The next two stages, white (albedo) and then red (rubedo), are also found in the gospels [6]:

> *But one of the soldiers with a spear pierced his side, and forthwith came there out blood and water.*

Figure 17 Seven processes of the Marriage of the Sun and the Moon

	Stage	Zodiac sign	Ruling planet
1	**Calcination**	Aries	Mars (masculine, fire)
2.	**Dissolution**	Cancer	Moon (feminine, water)
3.	**Separation**	Gemini, Virgo	Mercury (catalyst)
4.	**Conjunction**	Taurus, Libra	Venus (soul love)
5.	**Fermentation**	Scorpio	Mars (transformation)
6.	**Distillation**	Sagittarius, Pisces	Jupiter (exuberance)
7.	**Coagulation**	Capricorn, Aquarius	Saturn (fixation)

Figure 18 **Three stages of the Marriage of the Sun and the Moon**

NIGREDO (black)	**Calcination** The material is burned to white ashes.
	Dissolution The white ashes are dissolved in fluid.
ALBEDO (white)	**Separation** Opposite elements are separated out, one from the other.
	Conjunction Opposite elements are reunited.
	Fermentation The resulting mixture is left in the dark to putrefy.
RUBEDO (red)	**Distillation** The mixture is heated until its essence rises to the surface.
	Coagulation Birth of the Philosopher's Stone.

When Christians celebrate Holy Communion, they consume red wine with a white wafer under the rubric of the saying: "in re-memberance of me". It is a magical ritual.

The red and white foods are taken together

because it symbolises the body of Christ being re-membered, or brought back together again. Thus is the stage of the conjunction, after the separation that had preceded it, during which all the elements were purified and isolated one from the other, and the dross removed.

> *Whose fan is in his hand, and he will thoroughly purge his floor, and gather his wheat into the garner; but he will burn up the chaff with unquenchable fire.*[7]
>
> *The ungodly are not so: but are like the chaff which the wind driveth away.*[8]

The next step, after conjunction, is called fermentation and it is where the re-membered parts are left to putrefy before going through the final two stages of distillation and coagulation.

But there was to be no bringing back the separated parts for Abbot Whiting and his two faithful retainers. After being hung and dismembered while still alive, the various parts of Abbot Whiting's body were divided between four separate abbeys in the area - Wells, Ilchester, Bath and Bridgewater. But why four abbeys?

The number four represents power and dominion on Earth and is symbolised in sacred geometry by the square. When the square is combined with the circle, which represents the Universe, you get an eight-sided figure called an octagon, and this is known as the circle squared, as shown in **Figure 19**.

Figure 20 shows how circle squared is organised on Leonardo da Vinci's Vitruvian man when it is based on the rhombs developed from the Vesica Piscis.

The sacred number 108

If you are familiar with ancient Vedic literature of the Indian rishis, you will know that the numbers 108 (1080) and 432 (432,000) are coded into many of their ancient myths. The number 432 divided by 108 equals the number four.

The diameter of the sarsen stone circle of Stonehenge, which archaeologists believe was built about 4,000 to 5,000 years ago, is 100.8 feet. The classical Greeks must have also put value on that number, because it is found in Homer's Odyssey.

While Odysseus is away on his long, labyrinthine sea voyage that lasted for 10 years, his wife Penelope is told that he is dead and then she is courted by 108 suitors.

Even today, the number 108 is used in fictional plots of films and programmes. In the popular American TV series *Lost*, total disaster could only be prevented by keying the numbers 4, 8, 15, 16, 23 and 42, which total 108, into a computer.

The five-pointed star, shown in **Figure 21**, is a product of 10 angles each of 108 degrees, and later on I'll be showing you how this Christmas star is sparked up across the land all over the world on the Winter Solstice.

According to the Hermetic system, the number four represents worldly power, dominion and sovereignty upon the Earth. So, was the purpose of spreading the dismembered Abbot Whiting's bones across four dioceses to ensure that the power of Rome would never be re-membered again in Avalon in holy communion?

Figure 19 *The eight-sided octagon from the circle and the square*

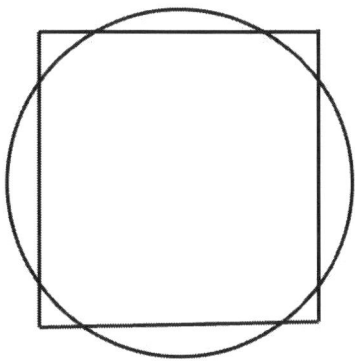

Figure 20 *The circle squared created with rhombs*

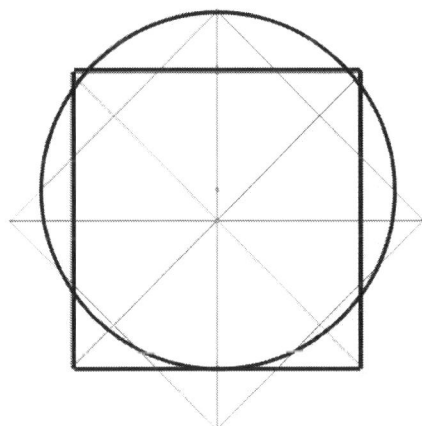

I believe that the murder of these three wise men was a ritual, magical act with the execution by hanging and dismemberment representing the first two steps – calcination and dissolution - of the seven-stepped operation that leads to the birth of the Philosopher's Stone but which was truncated – in other words, the act of creation was broken in half – in order to stifle further growth.

In the years that followed, there was a wholesale destruction and dismantling of more than 900 abbeys, monasteries and friaries up and down the country. They called it the *Dissolution of the Monasteries*. There are so many words that could have been chosen to describe that wholesale act of desecration: demolition, obliteration, annihilation, degradation, ruination to name but a few. But instead, the word "dissolution" was chosen. I rest my case.

Thus, although the murder of these priestly men was a vicious and violent act, it was not a crude, senseless act, as it is sometimes described. There was a method in its madness and it only appears to be meaningless to those whose lack of the correct education renders them blind.

Those who directed this bloody execution would have been initiates of the Mysteries and so knew full well what hanging and dismembering a holy man between two men on a green hill "without the city walls" would mean in ritualistic terms. And those with the eyes to see would read its clear message: that the power of Rome and its alchemists had been permanently broken in this land.

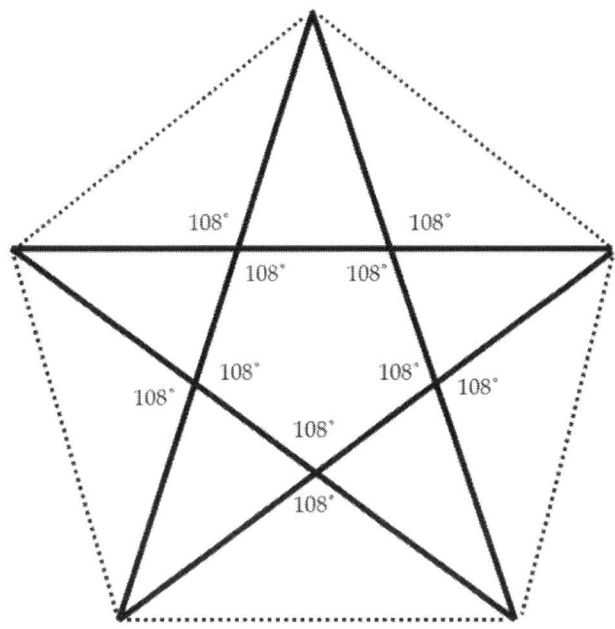

Figure 21 Five-pointed star

Nicholas Mann, in his book *The Isle of Avalon*, agrees that the "Christianity" practised at Glastonbury Abbey in medieval times was a long way from the more Protestant Christianity of today:

> *There are too many influences on the written documents to get to the true story [of how Christianity was practised in Glastonbury in earlier times]. Yet this much is clear – early British Christianity stood apart from the orthodoxy created around Rome and Constantinople.*

The British Christians drew directly upon the old spiritual practices of the Celtic Druids. They leant heavily towards the Celtic concept of communion with the realms of plants and animals. They tended towards Gnostic beliefs. The British were in the company of those who saw the Bible as providing further allegory and teaching on the ancient and universal truths.

The fifth century monk, Pelagius, for example, taught that there was no 'original sin'. He said the creation was sacred and through the practice of the Hermetic arts and the advancement of knowledge, each soul could move towards enlightenment.

Thus, it seems probable that the teachings the wise Benedictine monks of Glastonbury disseminated to the pilgrims who flocked here in their thousands before the Reformation were much more akin to how the Mysteries were taught thousands of years ago.

They may even have trodden the same labyrinthine, spiral walkway of the Tor, up which Abbot Whiting was hauled, because they would have known that the outer act of the camino mirrors the inner journey of the Way.

As we proceed, we are making our own pilgrimage in a conscious and deliberate act which will eventually make us the agency of our own salvation, guided by the spirits of the medieval monks through the process of inner alchemy, to reach the Philosopher's Stone of Christ Consciousness. The metaphor for taking the agency for one's own inward self-enlightenment is found in the distillation stage of the alchemical process, which is the sixth step and precedes the birth of the

Philosopher's Stone.

The distillation stage is often symbolised by a long-beaked pelican feeding her young with the blood that she brings forth by pecking at her own breast.

You can see a carving of this pelican on the gateway of Abbey House on the Wells Road.

Medieval alchemists would use a container called a pelican for the distillation, in the form of a glass retort in which two tubes connected a long neck with the lower part of the apparatus.

> *The result was a reflux or rectification still, in which the mixture was boiled and vapours condensed in the neck and then flowed back into the boiling liquid through the tubes. This inner circulatory process produced a very pure essence from the original mixture.*[9]

The crux of the matter

The monks have given me to understand that the Philosopher's Stone was symbolised in their version of Christianity by the Celtic Cross. We can see the similarity between the Celtic Cross in **Figure 22**, and the Monas Hieroglyphica in **Figure 23**, which was the Elizabethan alchemist John Dee's symbol for the Great Work.

Figure 22 The Celtic Cross

Figure 23 Monas Hieroglyphica

John Dee wrote [1]:

It is therefore clearly confirmed that the whole magistery depends upon the Sun and the Moon. Thrice Greatest Hermes has repeatedly told us this in affirming that the Sun is its father and the Moon is its mother: and we know truly that the Earth ... is nourished by the rays of the Moon and the Sun which exercise a singular influence upon it ...

He who devotes himself sincerely to these Mysteries will see clearly that nothing is able to exist without the virtue of the Hieroglyphic Monad. Whoever does not understand should either learn or be silent.

The word "cross" has many meanings.

The Tau cross is formed by the plane of the equinoxes intersecting the plane of the solstices. There is also the saltire or St Andrew's cross, which occurs when the Milky Way intersects the ecliptic. Both are shown in **Figure 24**.

But we should also note that the Latin for "cross" is *crux* and *crux* was another name that the mages gave to the "cauldron" or "crucible"; both containers that are used by alchemists to achieve the Philosopher's Stone.

William of Malmesbury wrote that the Old Church at Glastonbury had strange geometric shapes engraved on its walls. He didn't know what they meant. But now we need no longer wonder about this mystery when we understand that the Vesica Piscis is capable of producing triangles, squares, pentagons, hexagons,

---

[1] *The Monad*, Theorem XIV, John Dee.

octagons and so on, right up to the 64 Tetrahedron Grid.

And so it was at Glastonbury Abbey in medieval times.

The architects, engineers and masons who constructed the buildings were Hermeticists trained in these universal sacred geometrical principles, who went on to build churches in the same style all over Britain.

Malmesbury also mentions his discovery of ancient documents in the library which recorded that the Old Church of the Abbey had been "prepared by God himself" and that "God's Son distinguished it with greater dignity by dedicating it in honour of the Mother".

Those who understand the deeper meanings of those words – now long gone up in smoke – will recognise what they really meant: That the vibrational resonance of the Word of the Maker of this Universe booms geometries of light from the womb of the Vesica Piscis that erupt into a multitude of different forms to create, and ultimately to destroy, the processes of the heavenly stars Above along with those that are mirrored in the works of Mother Nature Below.

And they would also then understand why the monk magicians built such a huge stone wall around this precious star temple and its precinct to protect "the holiest earthe in England".

The Child Tension Victory

One day, my Otherworldly visitors gave me a teaching for the last stage in the seven-stepped operation that leads to the Philosopher's Stone. They described it as the Child Tension Victory. In this way, I realised that the final stages of distillation and coagulation do not happen automatically. The Philosopher's Stone can only be won by some sort of battle of strength, one worthy of a dragon-slaying hero. If the slightest impurity remains in either of the two opposing elements, it can go wrong to such an extent that all previous efforts are rendered redundant. The whole work has to be jettisoned in order to start again, from the beginning.

Following that teaching, I received an addendum from the Fish Pond, which you can find quite easily if you walk through the wonderfully fragrant herb garden of Glastonbury Abbey and its orchard of old, twisted apple trees.

One warm May Day, many years ago now, when the swallows were swooping overhead and the apple blossoms were in full bloom, a friend was meditating beside the Fish Pond and she was very quickly taken through the Veil.

She saw a "faery door" at the side of the pond and flew towards it, intending to go through this portal. But she was stopped by a stern monk sitting at a desk and writing with a quill.

He tried to shoo her away and so she retreated. But then she turned to look back at the pond and she saw that all the water had disappeared and in its place, on its base, was a huge geometric diagram consisting of a red circle next to a green circle with a Celtic Cross in between the two.

My friend has no knowledge of alchemy or sacred geometry and so she didn't know what the image meant. It was a symbol for the Child Tension Victory and from that the message came to me that the battle between the polar opposite colours of red and green had been won and had produced the Child of the Philosopher – or the Philosopher's Stone.

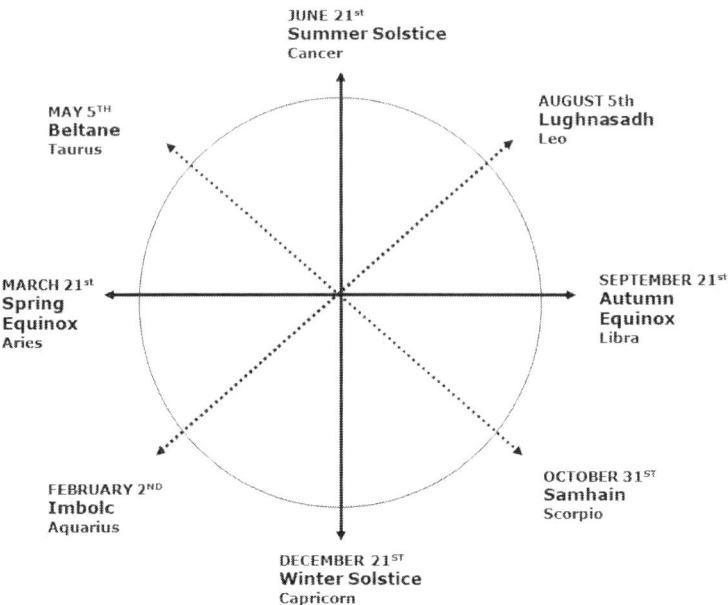

Figure 24 - *The two crosses of the zodiac*

[1] *New Light on the Ancient Mystery of Glastonbury*, by John Michel.
[2] *Henry 1* by C. Warren Hollister.
[3] *Revelation:* 21: 15, 16, 17
[4] Leaves from the Orchard by Alan Royce.
[5] *King Arthur's Avalon by Geoffrey Ashe*
[6] John 19:34
[7] Matthew 3:12
[8] Psalms 1:4
[9] *The Complete Idiot's Guide to Alchemy* by Dennis William Hauck

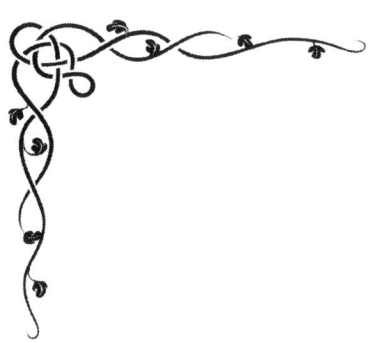

Chapter Six: The Desert Mysteries in Avalon

Astrology is the Word, and written from the beginning ... an exact science, sublime and holy, which has existed longer than we have at present any history, and handed by the great and wise of the past, those builders of the temples of the Sun, or universe, until in its old age its ashes are buried in Roman Catholicism but yet burn in Freemasonry ... The astrology of the ancients is the base of all and every science, either of the past or the future, and ... it was at one time a universal religion, science and language, the remnants of the sign language still held by Masonic bodies, to whom it is as "shining in the darkness and the darkness comprehending it not". [1]

The root etymological source of the words "authority" and "author" is the same in Indo-European languages. So, whoever authors the narrative that eventually becomes accepted into consensual consciousness becomes the authority that gets to rule that territory. To my way of seeing, whatever the "back-story" that has been laid down as "authoritative" in terms of our political history, it is, in large part, just a long and twisting scroll of myth piled upon myth that is stretching towards us from a vanishing point lost deep in the mists of time. And it seems that the more modern the record of the events, the less evidence is evident of the wisdom that was originally buried in those foundational myths of those who came before us.

Even today, each new order of would-be authorities bring their own scribes and authors in tow: PR and marketing agencies, and different forms of media whose role it is to win hearts and minds with whatever idea they are trying to sell – by hook or by crook - as the authentic "truth".

Two millennia ago, the Romans were no different in this respect, hence the saying: "The Romans built a desert and called it 'peace'." That "peace" was sold to the masses by rewriting and repurposing the teachings of the practitioners of the vestiges of Hermeticism during the first few centuries of the Common Era. These hermits are considered to be the fathers of what eventually became Christianity, and so are referred to as the Desert Fathers.

The Desert Fathers were a polymorphous group of mystics who had retreated to meditate in the caves of the arid wilderness of Egypt. Their dreams, which came out of that alien, foreign landscape, were used, centuries later, to weave a narrative about a God of Love that was used to bind together the authority of the new empire.

The cognitive framework of the Desert Fathers was based on the star stories to which Kroy-Khasis had listened in his icy, mountainous homeland, which culminated in the death and resurrection of the son of a god. Even then, those tales were already so old that they went back to a time when the movements of the pole stars were considered to be at least as important as those of the Sun and the Moon.

Thus the champion of these most ancient sagas met his trials by sailing around the precessing pole stars of the flooding firmamental deeps in order to separate the mound from the waters, and to install on its summit the new flag of the age, or pole star. It wasn't until much later, when man entered the agricultural age, that a new overlay began to appear in which the protagonist faced his challenges by treading the rim of the wheel of the 12 astrological Sun signs [2].

These multi-level sagas were based on, and designed to teach about, vast macro-cosmological events and cycles. But they had a double function; they also worked on the microcosmic level in that they contained allegorical meanings that aided the progress of the human pilgrimage of life. So just as the outcome of any camino worth walking is intended to be empowering and ennobling – and ultimately, transformative – so were the passion plays based on these stories, which were staged at the Mysteries.

Another name for the study and practice of Hermeticism during this period is Gnosticism. The Desert Fathers are often referred to as Gnostics, which just means those who are not ignorant of the Mysteries. We know they were knowledgeable from their writings, which were only discovered in 1945 when an Egyptian farmer, Muhammed al-Samman, stumbled upon 13 papyrus codices that had been buried in a jar at a place in the desert called Nag Hammadi. They turned out to be metaphysical scripts written in Coptic and three of them contained wisdom teachings based on the astrological-alchemical codex known as the Corpus Hermeticum.

You might be wondering why these texts were buried in a cave? In one word, I would say "revisionism". During the second century, a cleric named Iraneus, who was in the employ of the Roman authorities, turned the metaphorical stories of the Desert Fathers on their heads in order to author a new narrative. These multi-dimensional Gnostic texts were hammered down flat to produce a story about a real historical flesh-and-blood son of a god who was born in a stable in Bethlehem, and who went on to become a great evangelist with 12 disciples, but who was eventually murdered in Jerusalem at the behest of the Jews.

As the early 20th century Egyptologist Gerald Massey wrote in *The Historical Jesus and the Mythical Christ*:

> *The actual birthplace of the carnalised Christ was neither Bethlehem nor Nazareth but Rome.*

Iraneus went on to devise the canon, which is the four gospels of the present-day New Testament, out of dozens of assorted Gnostic texts. Thus, he composed the books of Matthew, Mark, Luke and John from a mishmash of magical lore that contained allegories for astrological and alchemical Mystery teachings dating back to time immemorial.

The new testament, or story about a poor carpenter whose life was cruelly cut short on the cross of Calvary, became the consensual reality that bound the Roman Emperor Constantine's overweening empire into the shared guilt of Original Sin for almost 2,000 years. The narrative was so effective because it was able to dig down deep to inspire the dreams that flowed in the race memories of the conquered masses. It won over hearts and minds across an imperial dominion so vast that it stretched between Britain in the north, Babylon in the east, Spain in the west and Egypt in the south. This great feat was achieved by plundering already-familiar mythological themes such as the Persian Mithraic nativity, the old Hebrew and Vedic massacre of the innocents and the Egyptian turning of water into wine to name but a few.

All this was possible because Iraneus drew on the mystic seed-bed of the Desert Fathers, the spiritual inheritors of the system designed by the mages and sages of the Cradle of Civilisation in Jerusalem, Antioch and Alexandria.

The ancient Greek philosophers – or at least the ones with whom we're familiar– were largely Gnostics, such as Pythagoras, Plato and Philo, and the historian Pliny is among their ranks. Socrates, who was Plato's teacher, was also one of these natural philosophers who told stories about a familiar stock character that starred in dramas throughout the whole Mediterranean and Middle Eastern region thousands of years "Before Christ". The Virgin Mary character of the Greek Gnostics was called Sophia, and it from her name that the word "philosopher" was developed, meaning "love for Sophia."

The equal-armed Tau cross of the equinoxes and solstices was the blueprint for the wooden cross that was mounted on the Hill of Calvary.

Iraneus then developed the 12 disciples of Jesus

from an astrological metaphor that came from the myths of the Old Testament, that of the 12 tribes of the Children of Israel, which, in itself, was an allegory for the 12 signs of the zodiac.

Historians are pretty much in agreement that the 12 tribes of Israel never existed as such. Even the much-esteemed first century historian Titus Flavius Josephus wrote of Moses's tabernacle as if it was an astrological allegory in his history of the Hebrews: *Antiquities of the Jews*.

> *And when [Moses] ordered twelve loaves to be set on the table, he denoted the year as distinguished into so many months. By branching out the candlestick into 70 parts, he secretly imitated the Decani, or seventy divisions of the planets …*

> *Each of the sardonyxes declares to us the Sun and the Moon; those I mean that were in the nature of buttons on the high priest's shoulders. And for the 12 stones [on the breast plate of the high priest] whether we understand them as months, or whether we understand the number of the signs of that circle which the Greeks call the Zodiac, we shall not be mistaken in their meaning.*

In the minds of those who loved Sophia, Jacob's dream [3] in which he sees 72 angels ascending and descending a ladder that reaches to the heaven symbolised the 72 decans, or thirds of each zodiac sign, that make up the total 360 degrees.

THE DESERT MYSTERIES IN AVALON

Initiation stage	Old Testament	The Gospels
THE CAPTIVE	The slavery of the Children of Israel in Egypt. (**Note 4**)	Straight after his birth in Bethelehem, the family of Jesus escapes into Egypt where they keep the babe hidden from Herod's massacre of the innocents. (**Note 5**)
First fire or light initiation in Aries		
	God appears to Moses as a burning bush and commands him to lead the Children of Israel out of Egypt. (**Note 6**)	The apostles are gathered in the "upper room" when the Holy Spirit descended in tongues of fire and the flames hover of each of their heads. (**Note 7**). This causes them to "speak in tongues" as they lead the new church into the world.
First water initiation in Cancer		
THE CALLED	God's parting of the Red Sea to enable the Children of Israel to cross it, while	On the shores of the River Jordan, John the Baptist tells the crowd he is baptising with water that Jesus will

	the pursuing Egyptians are drowned, just like the old pole star drowns to give way to a new epoch. (**Note 8**)	come and he will baptise them with light. (**Note 9**)
	The Children of Israel spend 40 years wandering around the wilderness where they face a number of trials sent by God. (**Note 10**)	Jesus spends 40 days and nights in the wilderness being tested by the Devil. (**Note 11**)
Second fire or light initiation in Leo		
	Upon Aaron's completion of the altar offerings for the first time and his blessing on the people, a fire springs up from the altar and when everyone sees it, they fall on their faces.	Saul of Tarsus receives a light initiation on the road to Damascus, which temporarily blinds him, and he falls off his donkey. (**Note 13.**) This experience of the divine converts him to Christianity and he

	(Note 12)	changes his name to Paul, in order to lead a new mission for Christ.
Second water initiation in Scorpio		
	Moses turns brackish, bitter water at the oasis of Marah into potable, clean liquid that is fit to drink. (**Note 14**)	The fishermen disciples are out in their boat on the sea near Capernaum and they see Jesus walking on the water. (**Note 15**)
Third fire or light initiation in Sagittarius		
	The Children of Israel are being fatally bitten by serpents sent by God. Moses sets up a bronze serpent on a pole and tells the Children of Israel to look at that image to be saved. (**Note 16**)	Jesus tells Nicodemus that unless a man be born of water and of the Spirit, he cannot enter into the kingdom of God, and goes on: "The Son of Man must be lifted up as the serpent was lifted up by Moses in the wilderness." (**Note 17**)

THE CHOSEN	The Children of Israel follow a pillar of cloud by day and a pillar of fire by night, which leads them to the Promised Land. (**Note 18**)	Jesus is crucified on the Cross of Light to grant his followers the promise of eternal life. (**Note 19**)
Third water initiation at Pisces		
	The Children of Israel are thirsty on reaching Mount Sinai and so Moses strikes a rock with his rod, and water gushes forth. **Note 20**	Jesus turns water in wine at the Marriage at Cana 21 - an alchemical metaphor for the transmutation that is the result of the operation of the Marriage of the Sun and the Moon.

Figure 25 The Mysteries of the Old and New Testaments

New lamps for old

One of the contemporary writers of the Desert Fathers was a Christian saint Justin Martyr [22]. Justin wrote that the philosopher Plato, who lived 500 years before him, must have borrowed the idea of the Son of God being crucified in the Cosmos [23] from the Moses story that features a serpent on a cross. But as you know by now, it's much more likely to be the other way around. These stories of the dying-and-reborn Sun god on the cross of the equinoxes and solstices were spread right across the cradle of civilisation long before the Old Testament was compiled.

For those with the ears to hear, the first books of the *Old Testament* (known as the *Torah*) faithfully replicate these more ancient cosmological teachings in many ways. For instance, there were three different leaders of the Children of Israel. Viewed through the metaphorical lens of the Gnostics, Moses, Aaron and Joseph would have each represented the three precessing astrological ages that change, roughly, every 2,000 years, and which are dictated by a cosmological cycle known as the precession of the equinoxes, which is caused by the tilting of the Earth.

The zodiac ages run backwards, meaning that the shaman-mage Moses would have been the overseer of the Age of Taurus. When it turned into the Age of Aries four thousand years ago, his brother Aaron was anointed as the first high priest of the Israelites. After Aaron came Joseph ben Nun and because nun means "fish" in ancient Aramaic, it seems likely that he was intended to have been the spiritual leader to guide in the Age of Pisces[24] – and would have been if Iraneus had not plundered and reconstituted these Hermetic-based myths into a new narrative about a hero named Jesus.

So, it is no coincidence that Joseph ben Nun appointed the 12 tribes of Israel after crossing the same river Jordan in which Jesus was "later" baptised, and after which he appointed his 12 disciples. In another correspondence, Joseph ben Nun defeated the Amorites at Gibeon by causing the Sun to stand still, while during Christ's "later" crucifixion on the cross, the Sun disappeared.

It seems likely that the character of Jesus was Iraneus's retread for Joseph ben Nun as he authored a narrative that turned the vindictive and jealous Jehovah, based on the worst aspects of the Greek Chronos, into a god who so loved the world, he gave it his only begotten Son. Even 2,000 years later, we are still being enticed into buying goods or backing politicians or supporting ideas in the name of love. Not for nothing has this psychological operation to install the authority of Christianity in our consciousness been dubbed "The Greatest Story Ever Sold".

A few centuries later, Iraneus's four gospels were combined with the *Acts of the Apostles*, a score of epistles and then rounded off with the *Revelation of St John Divine* to provide the scriptural authority of a command and control mechanism for a new world order based in Rome.

The table in **Figure 26** shows how the 12 tribes of the Children of Israel could be paired with each of the 12 disciples and to their astrological signs. It is not the final word – just an educated interpretation that is open to further suggestions. [25]

Figure 26 The zodiac of the Bible

Zodiac sign	Tribe of Israel	Disciple of Jesus
Aries	Gad	Simon the Zealot
Taurus	Ephraim	James the Lesser
Gemini	Manasseh	Thomas (the twin)
Cancer	Issachar	Judas Iscariot
Leo	Judah	Thaddaeus Lebbaeus Judas Juda Jude
Virgo	Naphtali	Andrew
Libra	Asher	Philip
Scorpio	Dan	Simon Peter
Sagittarius	Benjamin	Matthew Levi
Capricorn	Zebulun	Bartholomew Nathanial
Aquarius	Reuben	John the Baptist
Pisces	Simeon & Levi	James the Greater and John the Apostle

The meaning of the cross

The Passover, in which a lamb is sacrificed, is another common theme that is found in both the Old and New Testaments, and it is also a zodiacal allegory. What actually "passes over" is the Sun of God, when it crosses the Spring Equinox line. This is the same Platonic Cross of the Universe that Justin Martyr refers to in his *First Apology*, which is created by the line between the two equinoxes of Spring and Autumn crossing the one that runs between the solstices of Summer and Winter.

If you refer back to **Figure 24**, you'll see the equinox line of the zodiac. It represents a horizontal plane that is extended in all directions which the Sun crosses twice a year: once on 21st March and secondly on 21st September, when both these days are of equal length.

The horizontal equinox line is crossed by a perpendicular line that marks the time of solstice, a word that comes from sol-sistere, which is Latin for "Sun stops". The Sun appears to stop its journeying, either north or south, for three days before returning again. This occurs on June 21st, leading to the longest day of the year, and December 21st, or Winter Solstice, leading to the shortest day.

Another cross associated with Christianity is called the saltire cross; it is X-shaped, like the one upon which St Andrew was crucified in Patras, Greece,[26] and that cross is currently the emblem of the Scots, as shown on their blue-and-white flag.

However, this cross pre-dates Christianity by thousands of years, when the equinox line stretched between Taurus and Scorpio, and the solstice line ran between Leo and Aquarius. It also represents where the line of the celestial equator crosses the starry river of the Milky Way, the birth canal that the gods travel down to reach this dimension and human incarnation.

The celestial equator is a huge circle of the celestial sphere – an abstract orb which is concentric to the Earth. It is on the same plane as the equator of the globe which is currently tilted at 23.44 degrees with respect to the ecliptic, the plane of the Earth's orbit. So, the line of the celestial equator currently enters the zodiac at Pisces, and then crosses directly through to Virgo. St Andrew is the disciple associated with Virgo.

According to the Hermetic system, the Milky Way river rises between Gemini and Taurus and the gods are born into human bodies when it reaches a point between Scorpio and Sagittarius.

As you saw earlier, the two crosses are superimposed upon each other, just as they are on Leonardo da Vinci's *Vitruvian Man*. The first Tau cross stretches between the equinoxes and solstices and the other X-shaped cross of St Andrew is created by the trajectory of the Milky Way traversing the line of the celestial equator.

At the time that he compiled the *New Testament*, Iraneus attributed the four gospels to four fictional apostles called Matthew, Mark, Luke and John. As the gospels grew in popularity, the zodiacs in the artwork and architecture of churches were changed. Originally, they had been based on the *Old Testament* Ezekiel's vision of the four elemental cardinal points of the Man (Aquarius, air), the Bull (Taurus, earth), the Lion (Leo, fire) and the Eagle (Scorpio, water).

The church masons of Constantine's new world order soon got to work in replacing the Bull, Lion, Eagle and Man with the four apostles.

Thus, the airy Man of Aquarius became Matthew, the earthy Bull of Taurus became Luke, the fiery Lion of Leo became Mark and the watery Eagle of Scorpio became John.

In artworks that feature them all together, these four are known as the tetramorph, as shown in the **Figure 27**.

Jesus the Sun of God

We are told that Jesus taught in parables; in other words, he told stories containing metaphors which carried hidden meanings. And despite the attempts of Iraneus to make a dog's breakfast of a myriad of ancient Mesopotamian myths, the gospels are still chock-full of hidden metaphors for astrological and alchemical processes, if you know how to identify them.

However, in order to understand the metaphorical meaning of the parables, it is first of all necessary to realise that they are not in classical order. On the contrary, it is as if Iraneus took a sledgehammer to a temple floor mosaic illustrating the story of the pilgrimage of the zodiac hero and then mixed up all the tiles and put them back together again to create an entirely new journey.

In other words, the events making up the chronology of Jesus's 33 years do not follow the traditional pattern of the mythological hero, who begins his adventures around the astrological Wheel at the Spring Equinox.

The pick-and-mix fashion in which the stories of the gospels have been edited, revised and collated effectively disguise the circular evolutionary development of the great warrior hero as he passes, like the Sun, through the different signs of the zodiac in order to meet his trials at Beltane, the Summer Solstice and the Autumn Equinox. He is then bitten by the Scorpion and falls down into the Underworld to face further challenges which, if he passes, allows him to be reborn on the Winter Solstice.

Festival	Sun sign	Older symbol	Christian symbol
Imbolc	Aquarius	Man	Matthew
Beltane	Taurus	Bull	Luke
Lughnasadh	Leo	Lion	Mark
Samhain	Scorpio	Eagle	John

Figure 27 *The Hermetic year*

Many pre-Christian temples had the pilgrimage of the zodiac hero mapped out in a mosaic on their floors or painted on their ceilings, like the one at Dendera in Egypt.

The following chart, in **Figure 28**, is a result of my attempts, over the years, to sweep up those mosaic tiles, dust them off and then reconstruct the original zodiac story of the mythological hero from which, I believe, Iraneus selected and compiled his four gospels. Once again, I should stipulate that it is a work in progress and I am open to further suggestions.

Figure 28 *The astrology of the Jesus mysteries*

Sun Sign	Event
Sun of God moves into ARIES *Spring Equinox* **Matthew 27. 32-36** **Mark 15.21-25** **Luke 23.26-34** **John 19.16-24**	Aries the Ram is synonymous with the Spring Equinox and the Passover, which is when the Sun passes over the equinoctial line on its journey north. Passover is traditionally celebrated, by the Jews, with the sacrifice of a lamb. This might by why the sign of Aries is symbolised by a male sheep or ram. In the stories of the pre-Christian heroes, the Spring Equinox was traditionally when our champion set off on his adventures around the rim of the zodiac wheel. This also coincides with the season for calcination, when alchemists would begin to fire up the first stage of the seven-stepped process of the Marriage of the Sun and the Moon. However, in the *New Testament*, which replaced the old one, Jesus himself becomes the sacrificial lamb. In other words, the death of the hero has been put at the

beginning of his journey instead of the end.

In much older myths, the death and subsequent rebirth of the mythological hero takes place in the Underworld signs of Scorpio, Sagittarius and Capricorn, in which he becomes the scapegoat.

To make a person a scapegoat is to punish them for the misdeeds of all the people. In this way, it is said that Jesus took on the sins of the world. The sign of Capricorn is symbolised in the Alexandrian system by the goatfish. It is the sign of the resurrection, with the rebirth of the hero on the Winter Solstice, December 21st.

The Nativity therefore should have been about rebirth, not just the birth, of the hero. Instead, it seems that Iraneus mixed up the two stories and then divided them between Easter and Christmas.

Sun of God moves into TAURUS

The ancient Mesopotamians used the image of the bull to symbolise Taurus because it was when the

Beltane

**Matthew
13:18-23**

**Mark
4:14-20**

**Luke
8:11-15**

**Matthew
2:1-12**

constellation of the Plough was prominent in the night skies. This starry omen signalled the season for their bulls to start pulling their ploughs across the land in preparation for the sowing of new crops. Jesus's parable about the sower of the seeds comes to mind.

The end of the Age of Taurus could be signified in *the Old Testament* by the story of Moses forbidding the Children of Israel from worshipping the Golden Calf.

Archaeologists can find evidence or rites of passage initiations involving the riding and taming of bulls throughout the whole of the cradle of civilisation, going back to the Minoans. The Druids would sacrifice a bull at rites involving the mistletoe, which they considered symbolised death and rebirth. (**Note 27**).

To the Hindus, the bull is Nandi and he protects the Kritika Sisters from Orion the Hunter, who is pursuing them across the skies. These seven stars begin to set at the time of Beltane and we know them as the Pleiades.

We also find Taurus in the story of the three wise mages who followed a star in the east to find the newborn King of Jews. That star is thought to have been the Orion of the Greeks (**Note 28)**, but the Hebrews of the *Old Testament* called it Ephraim.

The Orion constellation appears to be striding across like a giant who is wearing a belt of three stars. Due to precession, it would have signified the birthplace of the avatar in Taurus, 4,000 years before the supposed time of Jesus, when the Spring Equinox fell in May.

Sun of God moves into GEMINI	Gemini is symbolised by the twins and the name of Jesus' disciple Thomas also meant "twin".
Numbers 14:34	In the *Old Testament*, the Children of Israel wandered in the wilderness for 40 years facing trials sent by God, while Jesus in
Matthew	the *New Testament* was sent by

4:1-11 Mark 1:12-13 Luke 4:1-13	Spirit into the wilderness, where he fasted for 40 days and 40 nights and faced trials sent by the Devil. The latter is the gospels' version of the traditional mythological wrestling match between the twins, such as the Egyptian Set and Horus, and the Babylonian Gilgamesh and Enkidu. (**Note 29**). It represented the time of "increase" or "doubling", when the Sun reaches its greatest potency.
Sun of God moves into CANCER *Summer Solstice*	In the *New Testament*, Jesus triumphantly rides into Jerusalem on Palm Sunday on an ass with its foal. These two asses are found in a Greek myth about the constellation of Cancer. (**Note 30**).
Matthew 21.1-11 **Mark 11:1-11** **Luke** **19.28-44** **John** **12.12-19**	Judas's 30 pieces of silver represent the 30-day month, or lunation, the "pieces of silver" symbolising the different phases of the Moon. Judas Iscariot was associated with the Moon's sign of Cancer, as were the Issachar tribe of the Children of Israel. Today, the sign of Cancer is signified by the Crab. But in older

John
13.21-30

Matthew
26.36-46

Mark
14.32-42

Luke
22.39-46

John
18.1

Sumerian myths, the symbol for Cancer was the Carpenter, which was the profession of Jesus and his father, Joseph.

In much older Mesopotamian myths, going back to the Epic of Gilgamesh, the Summer Solstice is associated with a water initiation in which the hero may feel as if he drowning in a sea of overwhelming emotions, just as a sorrowful, angst-ridden Jesus is portrayed in the Garden of Gethsemane before the crucifixion.

Sun of God
 moves into LEO

Lughnasadh

Matthew
14.1-13

Mark 6.14-29

Luke 9.7-8

Regulus, the star of rulership, moved into Leo around 2,150 years ago, and it is now on its way out again, heading for Virgo. Regulus is governed by Mars and Jupiter, and in Leo has been associated with violent rule and oppression – such as that wielded by the tyrannical King Herod, who waged the massacre of the innocents in order to murder the newly born "King of the Jews".

Leo also plays a role in Herod's

beheading of John the Baptist in an astronomical process that is explained in **Note 31.**

Sun of God moves into VIRGO

Matthew 1.18-25

Luke 1.26-38

Luke 8.1-2

The Virgin Mary and Mary Magdalene would have been ciphers for different aspects of Virgo, which I explain further later on. There is a third Mary, Mary of Cleophas, and all three keep vigil together at the foot of the cross during the crucifixion. They are the three faces of the Triple-Faced Goddess of antiquity known as Maiden, Mother and Crone.

Matthew 27.55-56

Mark 15.40-41

John 19.25-27

The dogmatists of Roman Catholic Church have spent much time arguing over whether Mary Magdalene was a prostitute. Speaking mythologically, she probably was. I believe her character comes from a much older and honoured tradition of sacred prostitution, where the divine whore or *hierodule* was the lunar prerequisite for producing the avatar of the age through her marriage to the Sun god.

In the ancient Mesopotamian

world, the word "virgin" in myths did not mean a person who had not yet had sex. It meant a woman who only has intercourse with a god or holy Spirit.

The impregnating god, in the case of Virgo Mary, was the winged messenger Gabriel, the equivalent of the Roman Mercury or the wing-footed Hermes.

Mercury is the governing planet of Virgo. He was known to the Celts as Gwythyr and Gwyddion, to the Saxons as Woden and to the Vikings as Odin.

When the fruit of the union, Jesus, becomes an adult, he meets the sacred prostitute Mary of Magdala and is sexually initiated by her into the Mysteries, which is the final fire initiation.

Sun of God moves into LIBRA

Autumn Equinox

This sign did not exist before the time of the Romans, who took the claws of the Scorpion to make the scales of justice that nowadays symbolise Libra. But the trial of the judgment was a perennial

Mark
15:1-5

Matthew
27.1-14

Luke
23:1-6

John
18.29-37

feature in the ancient story of the mythological hero. None could avoid being judged, whether it was in the Egyptian Hall of Ma'at, where the soul is weighed against a feather, or in the Underworld where they are hung on a hook, which was the trial faced by the Babylonian goddess Ishtar.

The Greeks named Ishtar Venus. Mary was also a version of Venus. Venus is the planet that rules Libra along with Taurus.

The Autumn Equinox is at the beginning of Libra. It is directly opposite Aries and could perhaps be described as the eastern transept to the western transept of the cross of the equinoxes.

So, Jesus finds no exemption to the rule of this law when he is delivered by the Elders and the scribes to stand before the Roman governor, Pontius Pilate, prior to being hung on a cross.

Sun of God moves into

Jesus tells Simon Peter that his closest disciple will deny him

SCORPIO

Samhain

Matthew
26.58-75

Mark
14.54-72

Luke
22.55-62

John
18.15-27

three times before the cock crows at dawn. Thus, it may seem confusing that same apostle goes on to become so trusted that he is appointed the gatekeeper of heaven, complete with keys.

However, it makes more sense when we understand that this imagery goes back to ancient myths about the gatekeeper of the Underworld being a cock, and it will not let the Deceased pass until it crows three times, at dawn.

The zodiac hero is always bitten by the scorpion or serpent in Scorpio, which represents the gateway to the Hell, or the Underworld.

The cock was, even back then, a symbol for the penis. This is quite apt because the sign of Scorpio is associated with sex and death – in other words, the sort of sacred sex that we learned about in Virgo, which leads to resurrection, and there will more about that later on.

Sun of God moves into SAGITTARIUS

John 19.34-37

I Peter 3:19

Sagittarius is represented in the gospels by the Roman centurion who pierces Jesus' side while his body is still alive, on the cross. The centurion is a word play on "centaur", the half-man, half-horse symbol of Sagittarius, who holds a bow with an arrow ready to fly.

In ancient myths, it is the vindictive archer who stabs and side-wounds the failing Sun as it falls down into the Underworld. In the Taurean Age, it was the half-bull, half-man Minotaur at the centre of the labyrinth.

When the centurion pierces the side of Jesus, both red blood and white water is emitted. This represents not the blood and semen of the vials of Jesus's tin merchant uncle, Joseph of Arimathea, but the red and white of the alchemical operation of the Marriage of the Sun and the Moon. Sagittarius is ruled by Jupiter, the planet that governs the metal tin.

So, like all mythological heroes, Jesus is also required to go through the Underworld and, before being reborn on the Winter Solstice or Christmas Day, has to face trials which, if successful, will release the tormented souls.

The allusion is found in the following: "In the spirit, he went and preached to the imprisoned spirits." (**Note 32**) It is actually about redeeming the DNA or Rivers of Blood, which shamans do for their tribe or family line.

Sun of God moves into CAPRICORN

Winter Solstice

John 18.12-14

"Now Caiaphas was he, which gave counsel to the Jews, that it was expedient that one man should die for the people."

This verse in John, from the trial of Jesus before the Jewish Sanhedrin, clearly represents the sacrifice of the scapegoat king and, as we learned in the section on Aries, the Babylonians associated the symbol of the goatfish with the sign of Capricorn.(**Note 33**)

Capricorn is the sign of death and rebirth, just as the Sun "dies" on the Winter Solstice and is "reborn" again three days later.

The year of Jesus's nativity is given as 1 AD (Latin: *anno domini*, "the year of our Lord"). This date was invented by a scribe in the employ of the Roman story machine during the sixth century, named Dionysius Exiguus. Dionysius may or may not have been aware that his mythological namesake had also experienced a Christmas birth in a nativity story that could go back as far as the Minoans.

Dionysius decided to back-engineer the mishmashed story of Jesus's life that Iraneus had concocted hundreds of years before him, in order to come up with the year in which Christ was born in a little town called Bethlehem.

Bethlehem means "house of wheat", which is the astrological house of the wheat sheaf-carrying Virgo.

Sun of God moves into

Jesus's baptism takes place at the River Jordan, where we meet

AQUARIUS *Imbolc*	John the Baptist, who is associated with the Sun sign of Aquarius. (**Note 34**)
Matthew **3.13-17** **Mark** **1.9-11** **Luke** **3.21-22** **John** **1.32-34**	Aquarius is symbolised by the Man of the tetramorph carrying water. This is a water initiation in which John the Baptist tells the assembled crowd that one follows him who will baptise by fire and light – in other words, it is allegory for the baptism of the Lesser Mysteries that lead to the Greater Mysteries.
Sun of God moves into **PISCES** **Matthew** **15.:37** **Mark** **6:43**	Jesus famously fed the multitudes at his sermons on the mound with fishes and loaves. Pisces is symbolised by two fishes and Virgo, which is directly opposite Pisces, is represented by a grain of wheat. When the Sun is in a certain sign, the full Moon always falls in the opposite sign. So, when the Sun is in Pisces, the full Moon falls in Virgo. Therefore, this story about fishes and loaves is really about the Marriage of the Sun and the Moon.

We can find further hidden

meanings by combining both of the accounts found in Mark and Matthew, because they are slightly different.

Matthew 15:37. The feeding of the four thousand: "And he took the seven loaves and the fishes, and gave thanks, and brake them, and gave to his disciples, and the disciples to the multitude… "

Four thousand relates to the four cardinal points of the zodiac – the Man, the Bull, the Lion and the Eagle of the tetramorph. We have already learned about the number four symbolising power and dominion in the magical rite surrounding the murder of Abbot Whiting by Henry VIII.

Regarding the seven loaves:

Mark 6:43. "… and the disciples picked up twelve basketfuls of broken pieces of bread and fish."

In other words, this sounds like an old creation myth:

> Jesus the Sun god distributes the seven loaves or planetary rulers – Mars, Mercury, Jupiter, Venus, Saturn, the Sun and the Moon - to the 12 baskets or signs of the zodiac.
>
> The pre-Christian "Mistress of the Earth and Sea, multiplier of loaves and fishes" was Demeter, the daughter of Chronos or Old Father Time. And so, the loaves might also refer to the grain that is harvested by the Grim Reaper.

The Massacre of the Innocents

You will be familiar with the story of King Herod's massacre of all the babies in Judea in the hope that one of them will be the "King of the Jews", who the three kings have prophesied will replace him on the throne. Again, this is not a historical event but a metaphor for a scientific process.

Scientists who study how fossils evolve have found that while change occurs after a slow, steady, plodding evolution, the ultimate transformation at the end comes as a revolution, which is swift and sudden. This revolution "eats its own children", which means that it burns up all that has gone before it in order to provide a fire to fuel its path into existence, like the phoenix that rises from the ashes. It is also the occult meaning of the *ouroboros*, the snake that can only survive by eating its own tail.

So the "massacre of the innocents" is another of those themes that runs through the primordial carpet of myths worldwide, to demonstrate that cosmological law in metaphor.

For instance, the Greeks told tales about the god Chronos, who is terrified of eventually being replaced as the supreme god by one of his children. Chronos is determined that he should be never be toppled, so whenever his wife, Rhea, gives birth to a child, he devours it whole. Chronos dispatches six of his children in this fashion, until the seventh, Zeus, is born. This time, Rhea gives Chronos a stone to swallow, fooling him that it is the newly born child. He swallows it, then Rhea sends Zeus to be hidden with friends on the island of Crete.

Once Zeus has grown into his manhood he returns, imprisons his father and forces him to regurgitate his six brothers and sisters. His siblings then go on to fight by his side in the 10-year war of the Titanmachy, after which Zeus releases his father and crowns him king of the Elysian Fields.

The myth about Chronos and Zeus is the whole story of the mythological hero in a nutshell. Just like the baby Krishna, who is taken into hiding to escape the massacre of the innocents of King Kamsa, and the baby Arthur who is taken into hiding to escape the wrath of King Uther, the newly born avatar is always first sent into a sort of captivity in another land until his teenage years. Then he is called to meet his challenges in order to be able to grow into manhood, before he can return as the chosen one to save humanity and redeem his father.

Viewed through this more zoomed-out lens, I hope you can see that the story of King Herod's massacre of the innocents is well-founded in myths.

The Mysteries of the Holy Grail

And so, the sun-bleached bones of the dreams of the Desert Fathers were transplanted into this green and pleasant land of wetlands, of rushes and reeds, lush green rolling hills and joyfully bubbling silver streams.

And just as thousands used to walk many miles to reach the Lesser Mysteries of Eleusis, so the Christians of Britain were encouraged, during the early centuries, to make a pilgrimage across the Channel to Burgundy.

There, a winding path would take them through the hilltop town of Avallon and on to the Benedictine Basilica of Sainte-Marie-Madeleine in Vezalay, which housed the purported bones of Mary Magdalene and where the sculptures engraving its capitals and portals celebrated the Acts of the Apostles.

Many a Christian soldier of the Crusades set off from Vezelay Abbey and today it is a starting point for another famous camino – one that follows the Milky Way to Santiago de Compostela in Spain.

However, after the Norman Conquest, the authorities decided to bring these lengthy pilgrimages closer to home. The landowners were no longer willing to spare their peasants for weeks at a time when they were needed to tend the fields.

There was a huge scriptorium at Glastonbury Abbey at that time, which seems to have had the sole aim of churning out a stream of narratives designed to underpin various and changing political imperatives. And so, there was a confluence of convenient events that, it seems to me, had as their aim the persuasion of hearts and minds to a much shorter pilgrimage route that ran between St David's in Pembrokeshire and the new Avalon of Glastonbury Abbey.

William of Malmesbury wrote, in the 12th century, that he had found documents in the library recording that St David was one of the first bishops of Glastonbury. He claimed that David had arrived at the abbey on his way back from Jerusalem, and that he was carrying a travelling altar that was embossed with a large blue sapphire.

Modern historians are as sceptical about the existence of St David as they are about St Patrick – and we will be untangling that web later on. However, many local folks are convinced that there was a sapphire; that it was stolen by Henry VIII and that it eventually made its way, via the Stuarts, to the Imperial State Crown of Queen Victoria.

What we do know is that a similar-sounding stone, whatever its origins, was eventually moved to the back of the crown of the current queen, Elizabeth II, to make way for the Second Star of Africa.

But to my mind, it is at the very least convenient that stories about a St David, and a sapphire given to him by the Patriarch of Jerusalem, were spun into existence at a time when the abbey was trying to give itself power and influence by claiming to be on the site of the first Christian church.

Then, by grafting the tale of the tin merchant Joseph of Arimathea, Jesus's uncle, on to that narrative, it gave Glastonbury Abbey, with its extensive land holdings all over Somerset, a potent autonomy over a wide region that lasted for hundreds of years.

Around the same time, a school of Norman scribes, like Geoffrey of Monmouth, began composing a whole raft of French Arthurian literature, such as the *High History of the Holy Grail*, which bedded down the cognitive seed in the consensual reality about Joseph of Arimathea's Holy Grail in the new Avalon.

Set in the arid wasteland of the wounded Fisher King, in which the well maidens of the waters that normally fertilised the marshy lands had fled their posts, the barrenness of this alien grafting may have been what inspired the Irish poet W. B. Yeats, half a millennium later, to rhyme-up the lines: "twenty centuries of stony sleep, vexed to nightmare by a rocking cradle" and of a strange beast "with a rough gaze, pitiless as the sun" slouching towards Bethlehem to be born.[35]

The *High History of the Holy Grail* was a dramatic production that came straight out of a Norman mytho-industrial complex that had been tasked with supplying a pseudo-historical back-story designed to win back the hearts and minds of those who had lapsed back into a more Celtic-Druidic way of thinking since the Romans had left.

One of its playwrights, John of Glastonbury, set about composing a script that would exchange King Arthur's Celtic grael or cauldron for another - the Holy Grail of Joseph of Arimathea, who used it to found the first church here.

These days, it would be impossible to make a serious case for an openly Christian community being allowed to live free from interference on the island known then as Ynis Witrin any more than the members of the People's Front of Judea - or was it the Judean People's Front? - were left in peace in the Roman-dominated Jerusalem of *The Life of Brian*.

As the researcher and illustrator Yuri Leitch wrote in his book *Gwyn: Ancient god of Glastonbury and key to the Glastonbury Zodiac*:

> *There is far more evidence to show that Ynis Witrin functioned as a sacred pagan site well up to the 4th century (and possibly beyond) than there is to prove Joseph of Arimathea ever came here at all. In fact ... there is plenty of evidence to show that Christianity could not have survived here until the late 3rd century at best, as it was actively persecuted by the Roman Empire ...*
>
> *The Celtic Church attempted to claim Ynys Witrin some time during the middle of the 5th century. This ties in with the accepted date of the dawn of the Celtic Church and the Christian evidence appearing in archaeological digs in the surrounding area.*

Nevertheless, in the 13th century, there were no archaeologists around to debunk John of Glastonbury's story about Joseph of Arimathea's boat arriving at what was then a port of an inland sea, below Wirrall Hill. He was the first to write that he was carrying a sort of cruet of two vials containing the red and white fluids from Jesus's crucified body.

John didn't actually use the word "grail" in reference to these vials. But he would have got the idea from the Norman author Robert de Boron, whose near-contemporary work Joseph d'Arimathie was used to shore up part of this new narrative.

De Boron's literary poem recounts how Joseph of Arimathea used a chalice from the table of the Last Supper to collect his nephew's blood after he'd been taken down from the cross. He apparently separated those fluids into the red and white liquids of blood and semen, and put them into a cruet. On his way to Britain, de Boron tells us, Jesus's uncle was thrown into prison and apparently, while there, he received a vision of his dead nephew, who explained to him the mysteries of the Holy Grail.

In the word "mysteries", we have stumbled upon a clue. The cruet of red and white fluids is crucial to the Mystery teachings and makes perfect sense as an alchemical metaphor, representing the Sun and the Moon, the yang and yin, of the Divine Marriage that leads to the birth of the Philosopher's Stone.

Robert de Boron describes Joseph's eventual release from prison whereupon, he says, he gathered his in-laws and other followers to travel to Britain, where he established a dynasty of Grail Keepers.

In this context, the "keepers of the grail" could only mean those Norman scribes and Templars, and those who followed in their footsteps over the centuries to hide the Mystery Teachings in multi-layered, allegorical artworks, architecture, plays, poems, songs and dances that are only visible to those with the eyes to see – which, by the end of this chapter, you will be well on the way to developing yourself.

Grail Secrets in the Churches

Now that you have gained some of the keys for unlocking the secrets of the Holy Grail, it will bring alive your visits to the many churches of these Summerlands, which are like treasure troves or Arks of the Covenant, in which successive generations Grail Keepers have hidden the Mystery teachings.

For instance, you really should check out St Peter's Church at Hornblotton, West Bradley, just off the Roman road of the Fosse Way. The Victorian church is not particularly prepossessing from the outside but go inside and you'll be amazed to find some quite stunning Royal Arch masonry artwork.

The high walls are covered with extraordinary murals in the pink *sgraffito*-style, which is achieved by applying layers of plaster. Two of the illustrations depict the fire and water initiations from the Mysteries of the Desert Fathers. In one, water gushes forth from a rock after Moses has struck it; in the other, he is holding up a bronze serpent on a rod.

You will also find a cosmological design of Plato's on the Cosmati pavement in front of the altar. It is a much smaller version of the one that was on display at the high altar in Westminster Abbey, which was revealed to the world after hundreds of years when they pulled back the carpet in 2012 for Prince William to marry Catherine Middleton, now the Duke and Duchess of Cambridge.

On this design, the four elements rotate, changing from one to another as they impress their forms on the impressionable but unchanging *prima materia* or First Matter of the alchemists. Plato's concept of an animate universe was also crucial to the concept of the land as a living organism whose wellbeing depended upon the health of its king, in which the Sovereignty sex rites are crucial.

At the centre of this intricate pattern of circular motifs there is a disc of onyx marble and gold; this is considered, by natural philosophers, to be the most highly evolved of material substances upon which kings were crowned and it symbolised their vital role in the divine enactment of the celestial order or the hierarchy.

The Cosmati pavement was a great source of inspiration to medieval alchemists such as Roger Bacon, who wrote the alchemical treaty the *Secreta Secretorum*, based on the teachings that Aristotle gave to Alexander the Great on nature, astrology, physiognomy and the Philosopher's Stone.

Another fascinating place to visit is St Andrew's Church at Compton Dundon, which is just a few miles along the road between Street and Somerton.

Its churchyard is also the location of a great, sprawling 1,700-year-old yew tree. As an aside, it's always a good idea to head for the yew tree when visiting any church when you want to connect with the *genius loci*, or the power of place. This is because the yew is often a descendant, if it's not the original, of the yew which marked the most sacred point before the Normans arrived to set up their own buildings nearby. As the tree that governs the processes of death and rebirth, I can tell you that praying or in any way communing with this particular ancient yew packs a highly potent punch.

At Compton Dundon, during certain times of the year, you can find yourself standing directly under the Milky Way, the river of the gods that makes up the saltire cross or the cross of St Andrew – hence the name of the church.

The window at the front of the 13th century nave is segmented into a saltire cross. Inside, on the back wall, you'll see a painting of three disciples, one of whom is St Andrew holding the two pieces of his wooden cross in the shape of an X.

[1] *Astrology of the Old Testament* by Karl Anderson.
[2] There is a more detailed breakdown of the passage of the zodiac hero in my book *Stories in the Stars*.
[3] Old Testament, *Genesis 28:10-17.*
[4] *Old Testament,* Exodus 1 and 2:23.
[5] The newly-born hero of a zodiac age is usually kept in captivity or hidden away and often amid a massacre of the innocents by an evil king. We find this same meme in the nativities of Krishna, Jesus, Moses and Arthur, to name but a few.
[6] *Old Testament,* Exodus 3:1-10.
[7] *New Testament,* Acts 2:3-4
[8] *Old Testament,* Exodus 12:1-51; 13:17-22, 14:1-15.27.
[9] *New Testament,* John 1:32-34
[10] *Old Testament,* Numbers 14:34
[11] *New Testament,* Luke 4:1-13
[12] *Old Testament,* Leviticus 9:23-24
[13] *New Testament,* Acts 9: 3-9.
[14] *Old Testament,* Exodus 15:22-25; 16:1-3, 11-15; 17:1-6
[15] *New Testament,* John 6:14-21
[16] *Old Testament,* Numbers 21: 7-9
[17] *New Testament,* John 3:5-15
[18] *Old Testament,* Exodus 13:21
[19] *New Testament,* John 19:16-24
[20] *Old Testament,* Exodus 17: 1-7
[21] *New Testament,* John 2:1-11
[22] *First Apology*, Chapter 60, entitled Plato's Doctrine of the Cross.
[23] Plato's *Timaeus* 34.
[24] *Old Testament,* Numbers 27:18
[25] The zodiac comparisons for the tribes of Israel is from a chart published by Albert Pike, Sovereign Grand Commander of the Scottish Rite, in his *Morals and Dogma* (1871); discussion of the 25th Scottish Rite degree of "Knight

of the Brazen Serpent". Also from Samuel Liddel MacGregor Mathers' essay, *Twelve Signs and Twelve Tribes*, reprinted in R. A. Gilbert's *The Sorcerer and His Apprentice* (Aquarian Press, 1983). The matching of the tribes with the disciples of Jesus is my own interpretation, and is in no way meant to be the final word on the subject.

[26] The apocryphal *Gospel of St Andrew*.

[27] According to the Roman historian, Pliny.

[28] The three stars of Orion's Belt. According to American author Barbara Walker in *The Women's Dictionary of Symbols and Sacred Objects*: "Ancient Hebrews called [Orion] ... Ephraim." This is cognate with the Ephraim tribe that corresponds with Taurus the Bull. Early 20th century Egyptologist Gerald Massey wrote: "The three kings or three solar representatives are as ancient as the male triad that was first typified when the three regions were established as heaven, Earth and the Nether-world, from which the triad bring their gifts ... When the birthplace was in the sign of the Bull (approx: 6,500 – 4,400 Before Present) the Star in the East that arose to announce the birth of the babe was Orion."

[29] Early 20th century occultist Albert Churchward wrote in *The Origin and Evolution of Religion*: "The equinox was figured at the top of the mound on the ecliptic and the scene of strife was finally configurated as a fixture in the constellation of Gemini, the sign of the twin brothers, who for ever fought and wrestled "up and down the garden", first one and then the other being uppermost during the two halves of the year."

[30] There is much more about the asses and the manger in Chapter Nine: The Quest for Avalon.

[31] "The greatest denoument awaits the investigator who makes use of the Julian calendar in the Roman Catholic calendar of Saints with the large zodiac. He will find that the death of John the Baptist is fixed for August 29th. On that day, an especially bright star, representing the head of the

constellation Aquarius, rises whilst the rest of his body is below the horizon, at exactly the same time as the sun sets in Leo (the kingly sign representing Herod). Thus the latter beheads John because John is associated with Aquarius, and the horizon cuts off the head of Aquarius." Godfrey Higgins, *Anacalypsis*.

[32] 1 Peter 3:19. The reference is thought to have come from the 5th-6th century apocryphal text: DESCENSUS AD LNFEROS (the Descent of Jesus to Hades or Hell), which is in the second half of the Gospel of Nicodemus.

[33] This Mystery ritual was common in the early centuries around the Mediterranean. French writer Edouard Dujardin wrote: "The god is anointed king and high priest. He is conducted in a procession, clothed in a mantle of purple, wearing a crown, and with a sceptre in his hand. He is adored, and then stripped of his insignia, next of his garments, and scourged ... He is killed and the blood sprinkled on the heads of the faithful. Then he is affixed to the cross. The women lament the death of their god ..."

[34] *John answered them all, "I baptise you with water. But one who is more powerful than I will come, the straps of whose sandals I am not worthy to untie. He will baptise you with the Holy Spirit and fire." Luke 3:16*.

[35] *The Second Coming* by W. B Yeats, first printed in *The Dial* in November 1920.

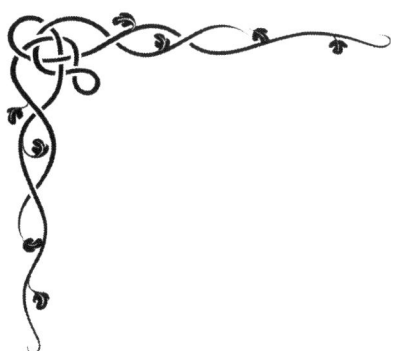

Chapter Seven: Guiding Spirits of the Summerlands

The Earth is alive: living, breathing, pulsing. It lives, but sleeps, stirring at times: and the people of the cities try to ignore it, hoping it will stay asleep.

It breathes: and the wind batters the grimy arrogance of the townsman, who dreams of "Man's increasing control over the blind forces of Nature."
It pulses, its seasons and cycles turning in all their subtleties: and those pulses are accepted and realised in the lives of everyone and everything in the countryside.

"Needles of Stone" by Tom Graves.

You may not realise it because we've been so busy chatting - but we have made considerable progress along our camino.

Back along, we came through the dense fog of the

Mirkwoods, where the mists of Avalon are at their most dense, and so we can now see clearly through the woven overlays of the authors of various authorities of old. We have even dug under the sand dunes of Time in an arid desert to discover the Elysian Fields below – or John Bunyan's lush garden of Beulah. So, we are now ready to meet the guiding spirits who inspire the dreams of all those who walk these Green Roads of the soul.

As you will have realised from some of the places we have visited thus far, we are presently emerging from a philosophical Dark Ages that has lasted for more than 2,000 years. During this time, our innate, natural wisdom has been dulled and blunted by receiving either no information or mis-information but all based on our ancestors' wisdom stories that have been twisted almost out of all recognition. So, despite the so-called Enlightenment of a few centuries ago, we know far less today about the world we find ourselves in than the ancients who painted on the walls of the caves or those who built the pyramids.

However, to the shaman, the land itself is buzzing and alive in its efforts to communicate with us through a two-way, interactive narrative that would be familiar to the storytellers of old, who used the night skies as a silver-screened film theatre upon which to stage their heroic sagas, containing cosmological metaphors and wisdom teachings. They "pulled down" those stories from the stars into the land by building earthworks of the stellar giants who "trod the boards" above. It was a genius-inspired way to interact with the *genius locii* and one that it is possible to use today, if you know what, where and how to stage your great works.

Faeryland and the Hollow Hills

Perceiving the multi-level and multi-dimensional story that the land of the Druids is trying to express and then passing it on to others "around the campfire" of various modern-day media, is the role of the shamanically-minded Dreamer or *awenwyddion* who is expert at "walking across the worlds". They are skilled at transmitting the wisdom teachers of those parallel dimensions, an Elder race that our ancestors knew well. And even though we have been taught to forget the existence of these beings, they have never forgotten ours.

All these "worlds" are found arranged across many a World Tree or Tree of Life on the primordial carpet that forms the backbone of these narratives. In Celtic faery lore, these extra-dimensional worlds are known the Hollow Hills.

So where are the Hollow Hills, you might be asking?

We all visit the Hollow Hills regularly in our dreams at night and our subsequent daytime thoughts, words and deeds are influenced by what we learn there, whether we realise it consciously or not. Any inspired work of art, great musical masterpiece or magnificently designed building or groundbreaking idea has its genesis as a sound or pictorial metaphor in this nation of images, known to us as the Imagi Nation.

Many of our greatest scientists and philosophers gained their "Eureka!" breakthroughs from entering into this same Nation of Images. The masterworks of the best painters and composers sprouted from seeds that grow in the Hollow Hills.

Once through the tunnels of the kaleidoscopic Looking Glass, we are taken by guides to be shown various phenomena — extraordinary landscapes, paintings, tableaux and moving pictures which speak a thousand words, all in unimaginably vivid colours and all containing metaphorical messages that slowly unfurl themselves, upon our return, like the petals of a rose.

Sometimes, the spirits speak directly to us in the words of our own language. We may hear it as a voice in our ear, often couched in an archaic form of expression that uses songs, poems and riddling rhymes shot through with kennings and puns. After you've been so lucky to hear a spirit recite a poem, you're only ever attracted to listening to human poets whose works spring from the Hollow Hills, and you know these works when you hear them because they ring like bells. At other times, we can receive an instantaneous direct download; the message will appear in writing in front of our eyes in a billboard poster, or with lines scrolling upwards, like the credits after a film.

In my experience, the *genius locii* are made up of two kinds of spirits: the faeries and the ancestral spirits who are also sometimes known as Threshold Guardians. The roles of the Elder race within the multi-tiered biome is to act as conduits between the humans and the ancestors who live in the Realms of the Dead in the Underworld. It is a vital requirement for the human to secure the protection and guidance of the ancestors when he comes to face the challenge of redeeming his family line. He reaches them by sailing down the red and white serpent-entwined Rivers of Blood, a Celtic kenning term for the double-helixed DNA.

There are almost as many names for faeries as there are tales about them, courtesy of the exiled Irish, Scots and the Welsh whose *Under Milk Wood* dreams still hover at night like silvery holographic films flickering under the Moon in the morphogenic fields of a land that stretches down to the "sloeblack, slow, black, crowblack, fishingboatbobbing sea".[1]

The Irish faeries are known as the Tuatha da Danaan or the Sidhe (pronounced *shay*) and they are the guides to the ancestors in the Underworld. They are also the pilots who guide the shaman in trance along the Rivers of Blood to help them in redeeming their family line.

The Scottish fae are very much like the Irish fae, which is hardly surprising since they come from the same mythological root stock. The beings who inhabit the parallel dimensions of the Highlands and Lowlands are called the Sith but it is also pronounced *shay*, like their cousins on the Emerald Isle. There are too many races of Sith to name here but they include the Black Angus or Cu Sith – named after a faery dog, the Fachan – who are all as ugly as their tempers and to be avoided at all costs, and the Selkies who are seals in the lochs but who, from time to time, shapeshift into human form.

In Wales, we find the Tylwyth Teg (pronounced *till-with-teeg*) who are famous for their skills in alchemy and you might catch a glimpse of them as we go along, riding through the skies on their yarrow stalks. They are divided into five races: the Ellyllon (elves), the Coblynau (dwarf miners), the Bwbachod (guardians of the hearth), the Gwragedd Annwn (well maidens) and the Gwyllion (crones or hags of the mountains).

Those who know them are respectful about using their names, because just naming them can call them. So, they are often referred to more obliquely as the Gentry, the Little People and the Dod, while to the Scots they are the People of Peace, the Prowlies, the Silent Moving Folk, the Wee Folk and the Pixies.

So yes, we really do have faeries living at the bottom of our gardens, although they rarely look like the tiny gossamer-winged Tinkerbell of Victorian fantasies, or the Moth and Peaseblossom of Shakespeare's *A Midsummer Night's Dream*. On the contrary, some of them are huge hags and giants, or have just one eye, one arm and one leg, while others are covered in fur. But more often than not, they look very much like you and me and if you passed one on the street on your way to the supermarket, you may not even notice them.

The Fae tend to live in prominent hollowed-out mounds, which is where the Hollow Hills come into the story. Glastonbury Tor, for instance, is the home of the King of the Faeries, Gwyn ap Nudd, the guide of the souls of the dead into the Otherworlds, who he gathers up during his Wild Hunt. These mounds are also known as sidhes and, in Scotland, burghs from which music can often be heard at night, especially during their fiddling, riddling and jigging *cèilidhean* on the cross-quarter festivals of Imbolc, Beltane, Lughnasadh and Samhain.

There are all sorts of stories about people who are out late on such nights and who stumble unwittingly upon these mounds. Some are never seen on Earth again or they may return a century later to find that all their friends and relatives are long dead and buried. However, those tales are usually just bastardisations of archetypal myths about the hero falling into the Underworld to redeem his ancestors, and then salted-and-peppered to become a cautionary tale of Christian clerics.

The Fae are the spirits of the land and so should not to be confused with goddesses or angels who are from another part of the World Tree, called the Upper World.

The Fae are often referred to as the Elders, because they "fell from the stars" at a much earlier Time than we did. In old folk tales that still survive in parts of the British Isles relatively untouched by modernism, it is said that the Fae came into incarnation on Earth at the First Utterance or primordial vibration. It is also told that the animals descended on the Second Utterance and we humans arrived on the Third.

Bridie and the Sleeping Beauty

The Fae, apparently, "fell" at the same time as the Bright One and they are her protective guardians. The Bright One is the Celtic equivalent of the Dreamer in Land, the *genius locii* who is known variously as Brigit, Brigid, Bridie and Breed and, in Roman times, as Brigantia and Britannia.

In the oldest faery lore, Bridie is the sleeping beauty who is dreaming under the green mantle of the Hollow Hills. She is protected by thick, tangled briar rose thorn thickets that only the most ardent suitor would be able to cut his way through. She will only awaken when the Three Utterances — man, animal and faery — come together in a Venus "kiss" on this Earth to sound the Fourth Utterance.

I love the use of the word "utterance". It brings to mind the Word of the gospel of St John or Aum, the primordial vibration of the Vedas. It is the "god particle" of the physicists, in other words, the sound resonating at the heart of every atom born from the Vesica Piscis. When you understand this concept, you realise that to insist upon a division between material nature and spirituality is to create a false dichotomy. That our ancient forefathers knew this is clear from the fact they put so much into effort into creating such extraordinary sacred sites. To my way of thinking, the three Utterances can be brought together by the guidance received from those who bring it back from their journeys into the Three Worlds.

The Indo-European root word *brig* means "high", "elevated" and "noble", just as the Indian rishis were signified as "nobles" in the Vedas. In Sanskrit, *bhrati* or *brihati* means "exalted one", which was one of the qualities attributed to the Persian storyteller Scheherezade. The word "high", in this case, is not derived from the power of a ruling hierarchy on Earth, although Brigit-types are often depicted in faery tales as beautiful princesses.

When the young princess of Sleeping Beauty pricks her finger on the spinning wheel, it is a metaphor for menstruation or coming of age in a rite-of-passage story, which in modern versions focusses almost exclusively on the female's role. But the hero prince, who awakens her with a kiss, will have had to face many dragon slaying adventures before reaching the challenge of the dark and tangled rose briar forest – and you will be learning all about that further on.

The first Bridie-type most of us hear about is in the faerytale *Sleeping Beauty*, although we are mainly familiar with the Walt Disney version, which harks back to the ancient Greeks in naming her Aurora, after their goddess of the dawn.

However, there are elements of *Sleeping Beauty* that come from the sagas of the Old Norse *Edda*. The three good faeries who first appear at the christening are very much like the three Norns of the spinning wheel of destiny.

The three Norns were known to the Greeks as the three Fates or Furies. They are also probably the three witches of Macbeth, although that trio were badly bent out of their original shapes. In the Old Norse tradition, these three Norns were said to govern the three wells of Wyrd, which were the Scandinavian equivalent of the Celts' Three Cauldrons of Poesy.[2]

Wyrd is our reality, which here is characterised as a kind of matrix or web of destiny that is spun and woven by the Norns but which is under the ultimate control of Orlog, the same omnipotent, omnipresent and eternal law of the universe that Hermeticists call the hierarchy.

Wyrd is made up of a sweet, nectarous liquid that flows down through the three wells situated on a Tree of Life called Yggdrasil, which is an ash tree, and on which are found the Three Worlds of the shaman.

The well at the top of the tree is in the Upper World of Asgard. It is overseen by an old crone Norn who is named Urd, and she governs the past. Wyrd flows down from Urd's well until it reaches the well of the mother Norn called Verdandi. Verdandi rules the present day in the Middle World of Midgard, of which Earth is a part. So, if our cup in the present is tasting bitter, the storytellers would tell us that it is because the streams of Wyrd that are reaching us from Urd's well in Asgard are polluted by past actions that need unravelling and reprocessing. This is rarely about the individual, though, and much more often about the actions committed by others further back up our family line. So, it is part of the shaman's work of redeeming the ancestors.

For instance, most doctors recognise that alcholism or addiction is a disease that runs in families. Many of us face that challenge in this lifetime. And yet it makes all the difference when we realise that we are supported by ancestral guidance that shows us how to clear and purify the streams of Wyrd for future generations.

After leaving Verdandi in the Middle World, the river of Wyrd continues down the trunk of the ash until it reaches Skuld's well in the Underworld or Nifleheim. Skuld is the Norn who rules the future and that part of Wyrd will only taste clean and delicious once we have completed the work in the present with Verdandi and cleaned up the pollution of the past that came down from the well in the Upper World ruled by Urd.

The Ancestors live in the Underworld where Skuld's well is situated and they know that her role is to send fresh, clean Wyrd up to Urd in the Upper World if the family line is to continue and thrive. This can only be the case if the streams Skuld receives from

Verdandi's present-day well in the Middle World are unpolluted and clear.

We can see this Old Norse philosophy is the inspiration for the three faeries in Sleeping Beauty.

When the teenage princess pricks her finger on the spindle of the spinning wheel there is a deliberate poetic resonance between the words "spindle" and "spinster". She is then sent to sleep and can only to be awakened by her true love, the Prince, who has to thrust and carve his way, with his magical sword, through a thick and tangled forest of briar rose thorn bushes. Once through, he finds a royal court of servants and courtiers that has been asleep for a hundred years. This is a metaphor for the human being who is born into a state of ignorance and unawareness of the reason for their human life, making them "children" on the path of the initiate until they awaken.

The three faeries, or Norns, are also an allegory for the three stages of the alchemical process – nigredo, albedo and rubedo – which all of Nature goes through to re-create itself. The kiss of the Prince symbolises the final stage of the Marriage of the Sun and the Moon, in which we are "kissed awake" to the realisation of our true selves and that only happens when we recognise that our consciousness ranges across an inner landscape of the Three Utterances or Three Worlds. Enlightenment involves bringing them back together to make the individual whole.

So that is the deeper meaning of the story that Kroy-Khasis so loved about the Dreamer in the Land who, in our tradition, is Bridie the Bright-browed.

Many of believe the British Isles and Brittany in

France were named after Bridie or Brigit. Current academic thinking would disagree but then few of them realise about the Druidic-inspired magical and mythological underpinnings of the whole layout of Britain, which comes from these stories.

Recent research is bringing scholars increasingly to the view that the whole of Europe was surveyed and mapped out with roads long before the time of the Romans.[3] The Druids constructed long, straight tracks between towns, often in alignment with stellar cycles according to calculations based on the summer and winter solstices. The sort of maths needed for this kind of intercontinental surveying is found in the Welsh myth about Lludd and Llevelys, the battling Red and White Dragons of Dinas Emrys, and in Celtic and Pictish art, and we will be examining all that much later on.

The story of the naming of Britain after Brigit can perhaps be found in a tale of treachery that begins in what is now Yorkshire. It was occupied during the Iron Age by a tribe called the Brigantes, which was the largest and one of the most influential at that time. They named their territory Brigantia and they honoured Brigit as the High One and the Bright One.

The queen was named Cartimandau. However, she was not faithful to her land and her people. The Roman historian Tacitus describes Cartimandau as being loyal to Rome and he records that she "defended by our arms". She had agreed to an arms deal with the enemy in which her part of the bargain was to hand over to them, in chains, Caratacus, the leader of the British resistance.

The Emperor Claudius rewarded Cartimandau with great wealth – and possibly flattered her too by naming the whole country after her tribe, as Britannia.

However, it wasn't long after that before the Romans launched their attack on Britannia. They began with the Brigantes and eventually Cartimandau and her whole treasonous court was forced into exile.

According to the Greek geographer Claudius Ptolemy, at around the same time there was an influential tribe across the Irish Sea also called the Brigantes[4]. They were situated around Wexford, Waterford and Kilkenny and are thought to have become, in medieval times, the Uí Brigte clan.

However, all the indigenous mainland British tribes were eventually pushed to the west and south of the country by various successive invasions of Romans, Saxons and Jutes.

It wasn't an overnight exodus. It took many hundreds of years. The Welsh were then referred to as foreigners, which is the meaning of the word "Welsh". And so, Brigid's peoples thus became foreigners in their own nation of Britannia, which they still, to this day, longingly refer to as "the lost lands" or *Loegres*.

According to the Anglo-Saxon Chronicles[5], the seventh century king of Wessex, Centwine, was responsible for pushing the real followers of Brigit out of Somerset. But we can still hear their voices in the places they named after her – such as Bristol, which was originally Brigstow or Brig's Town and the centre of which is still called Bridewell today.

One of Bridie's totem animals is the swan, which is found in the name of Swansea on the north-east edge of the Bristol Channel. There have been actual white swans in the moat of the Bishop's Place next to Wells Cathedral for longer than anyone can recall. She is certainly not forgotten in Glastonbury, where we find Bridie's Mound. And she is also remembered across the whole of the country in the towns of Bridgnorth, Bridgwater, Bridlington, Bridport, Brigg, Brighouse, Brixham and Brighton.

Druids and bards who channelled the *awen* were often referred to as "Bright-browed", which gives us a clue to who they believed was responsible for their enlightenment.

The earliest mythological source for Brigid is the 11th century Irish *Lebor Gabála Érenn* (The Book of the Taking of Ireland), which portrays her as the daughter of the primary deity, the Dagda.

The Irish Brigid had two sisters, who are both also called Brigid: one was Brigid of the healers and the other was Brigid of the smiths. In other words, she was a classic Celtic triple-faced goddess – and also perhaps an Irish version of the Three Norns of the Norse myths?

Her pre-Christian festival on February 1st is called Imbolc, which means "womb", because it marks the time when the seeds that had remained dormant when the Earth stood cold and hard as iron are now germinating and preparing for their births in the Spring.

As you would expect, the mytho-industrial narratives of the Christian centuries made an effort to historicise Brigit. From those religion-inspired sources, it seems there were up to up about 11 women named Brigit, Bride or Breed, at different times, who held high ecumenical offices. These Brigits were abbesses who came from the convent at Kildare in Ireland, where a candle dedicated to Brigit was always kept alight.

The medieval art historian Pamela Berger believes that the Christian monks "took the ancient figure of the mother goddess and grafted her name and functions on to her Christian counterpart"[1], thus turning Brigit into a human saint. The late professor of Irish folklore, Dáithí Ó hÓgáin, believed that Brigid had been chief druid at the temple of the goddess Brigid in Kildare and was responsible for converting it into a Christian monastery [2].

I think both ideas are likely to be true, in that a succession of highly placed female spiritual leaders within Celtic Christianity could very well have named themselves after their guiding, eternal spirit guide, who they canonised. In this way, Brigit would have been a title rather than a name.

So now that we understand Brigit or Bridie represents fertility and birth, we might be wondering who provided the yang to Brigit's yin in the Summerlands of the Celts. Who was the dragon-slaying hero who fought through the tangled rose briar forest to awaken her with a kiss?

The Faery King to her Faery Queen changes, according to the seasons. In winter, this role is played by her brother, Gwyn ap Nudd. The brother and sister are like bookends of the whole process of hatching, matching and dispatching. Gwyn is a psychopomp who

---

[1] From *The Goddess Obscured: Transformation of the Grain Protectress from Goddess to Saint by Pamela Berger.*
[2] From *Myth, Legend & Romance: An Encyclopaedia of the Irish Folk Tradition by* Dáithí Ó hÓgáin.

carries souls of the deceased to the realms of the dead, the lands of the ancestors in the Underworld. [6]

Gwyn ap Nudd

I have been where the warriors of Britain were slain,

From the east to the north:

I am the escort of the grave.

I have been where the warriors of Britain were slain,

From the east to the south:

I am the escort of the dead![7]

While the faery midwife Brigit the Bright One's time is Imbolc in February, when the snowdrops and crocuses are just beginning to be born into the light, the season of the saturnine Gwyn ap Nudd is at the start of the Plutonic dark of winter, over which he wins rulership in a duel with the Lord of Summer at another cross-quarter festival, Samhain.

The two faery lords govern the whole Wheel of the Year and so Gwyn has to fight this contest again at Beltane in May – and this time he is the loser, so that his challenger can reign over the Summerlands, otherwise we would be in permanent winter.

The lower-half months of the zodiac represent the Underworld in the Hermetic system, which makes the Celtic Gwyn the psychopomp whose role it is to guide the initiate down into the lower deeps for the

Judgement, much as the Egyptian god Anubis escorts the Deceased into the Hall of Judgement of Osiris.

The Sumerian psychopomp Nabu ferries Gilgamesh along a river into the Realms of the Dead, while the Arthurian scribes of the Norman Conquest personified that character as Morgan of the Fae, who takes the wounded Arthur in her boat through the mists of Avalon and into the Otherworlds.

In alchemy, the mythological psychopomp is symbolised by Mercury, who was known to the ancient Greeks as Hermes, the so-called "trickster god" who conducts souls into the afterlife. This is why the term Hermetic Arts is often used for the practice of alchemy. The metal quicksilver, which is governed by Mercury-Hermes, can be quite tricky and slippery to work with!

Trickster gods, such as Puck in Shakespeare's *A Midsummer Night's Dream*, are representatives of Mercury, who is the catalyst of the Marriage of the Sun and the Moon. Mercury is vital to the success of the work. No matter the prodigious amount of painstaking effort put in, without his divine intervention the Child of Philosopher will be stillborn.

So viewed through that lens, you may be now realising that the psychopomp guide is not just there for the dead but for the living shamans who journey through the veil into the Underworld. Gwyn attends to the quick and the dead. Add to that our earliest ancestors' propensity for dreaming themselves into shamanic trance in the pitch-black recesses of caves and we can also understand why no skeletons have yet been discovered buried within the Egyptian pyramids.

Gwyn ap Nudd has several epithets, such as

Lord of the Wildwoods, King of the Faeries and Leader of the Wild Hunt - the latter shared with Arthur Pendragon.

The researcher who has done the most to uncover Gwyn's ancient legacy in this land is local artist Yuri Leitch. He dedicated decades to historical and mythological research and contemplation into this Otherworldly phenomenon that many who live here encounter shamanically. The results can be found in his book, *Gwyn: Ancient God of Glastonbury*, which, to my knowledge, is the best and most comprehensive work on our spirit of place or *genius loci* ever written.

Yuri examined many local myths and also stories within the medieval Welsh literature to find the roots of our ancestors' knowledge and experience with this powerful spirit. From all this, one gathers that Gwyn was honoured by the indigenous Britons right up until they were forced from the land, giving him cause to lament:

> *I have been where Llacheu was slain,*
>
> *The son of Arthur, extolled in songs,*
>
> *When the ravens screamed over blood.*
>
> *I have been where Meurig was killed,*
>
> *The son of Goheleth, the accomplished,*
>
> *The resister of Lloegyr, the son of Lleynawg.* [8]

As Yuri writes:

The poem of Gwyn in the Black Book of Camarthen is quite clearly the British Hunter God lamenting the death of British heroes and mourning a lost land.

But Gwyn's dominating presence in the morphogenic fields of memory has never been erased, despite being "left behind" by the exodus of the Irish and the Welsh fleeing the Romans and the Saxons.

The scribes of the new religion tried to demonise Gwyn out of existence.

The seventh-century monk St Collen claimed he had exorcised the King of the Faeries from Glastonbury Tor and re-presented him as the demon king of a Celtic Hades to an audience no longer taught that Hades was not a hell of fire and brimstone, and that horns on an ancient god denote a great wisdom teacher.

But Gwyn has just taken all those slings and arrows, and he has so far refused to budge.

When we examine his name more closely, we realise that just like Brigit, he is remembered across all of Britain.

Ap means "offspring of" in Welsh and thus in their myths, Gwyn is the son of Nudd. However, double-d in old Welsh is pronounced "th" and the "u" usually sounded more like "ee". And so the word *Nudd* was pronounced "Neath" and sometimes "Nedd".

So, Gwyn is not forgotten in the Vale of Neath of the Brecon Beacon mountains of Wales, otherwise known as the last abode of the Welsh faeries, the Tylwyth Teg. He is also the spirit of place at the source of the River Neath that runs through the Vale in a mountain called Fan Nedd.

Druidic bards would often compose their magical poems and songs in the darkness of dream incubation sanctuaries. There is one at Lydney, which is in the Forest of Dean in Gloucestershire. The Romans turned it into a temple for their god Nodens. But the rectangular shape gives us a clue to who built it. It's in the Celtic style, similar to the chapel of St Dunstan's in Glastonbury Abbey. Roman temples tended to be round, so their Nodens was probably originally Gwyn's father, Nudd.

Venturing into the south-west, we come to the pretty village of Tintagel, in Cornwall, where they would have tourists believe Arthur Pendragon was born, in the ruined castle on the edge of a cliff. But we find more evidence for the Nudd family than we do for the Once and Future King in the tumbling silvery waterfalls of a nearby area of outstanding beauty called St Nectan's Glen.

Local folklore tells of a St Nectan who came to Tintagel from the Welsh Vale of Neath. "Nectan" is the Cornish rendering of the Latin name Nathanus, which is cognate with the Welsh "Neath" or "Nudd". Thus, it seems probable that both the Welsh Vale of Neath and the Cornish St Nectan's Glen were named after Gwyn or his father, Nudd.

We celebrate Gwyn here in Glastonbury every Beltane (May Day) and Samhain (Halloween) in a drama that goes as far back as anyone can remember and which is based on a story in the stars that is thousands of years old.

Gwyn plays the part of Orion the Hunter, who

appears in the night skies with his hound in the form of the Dog Star of Sirius, within Canis Major.

The two duels are over the hand of the beautiful maiden who was once depicted in the night skies as the Vesica mandorla-shape, which was all that remained of the Southern Cross as it began to gradually fall into the southern hemisphere.

Gwyn always loses the battle of Beltane, to give way to the Summer King, Gwythyr, until he returns again at Samhain and, this time, he conquers Gwythyr to become the holly-crowned Winter King.

Gwyn ap Nudd appears in the family tree of gods and goddesses found in the tales of the Welsh Mabinogion[9] as the grandson of the great matriarch Don. The realm of Don is found at Compton Dundon, five miles to the south of Glastonbury. "Dun" meant "hill" and thus "Dundon" was "the hill of Don".

Gwythyr ap Greidawl

Gwythyr is a pivotal character in the stories of the Summerlands and yet he is only now being rescued from the deep, buried caverns of times forgot.

There is just one brief line about him in the Mabinogion's *How Culhwch Won Olwen*, a story we will examine in more detail later on. The Welsh Triads also name him as the father of Arthur's second wife, Gwenhwyfar. There's not much else… However, once you know how to read the stories in the stars, you can soon figure out where all the bodies are buried.

The Winter King is represented by Orion and the Summer King by Ophiuchus, which the ancient Greeks depicted as a strong-muscled man grappling with a huge boa constrictor snake wrapping itself around his waist. The snake is the Serpens constellation and, underfoot, the hero is trampling Scorpius.

History tells us that those whose sagas starred this serpent-slaying hero went first to Cornwall. From there, some carried on to Brittany, while others eventually fanned out into Wales and Ireland. So, we can look for correspondences in the tales about the Irish mythological hero Fionn mac Cumhaill. In these, we find that Fionn, Gwyn and Gwythyr are closely related. Fionn is descended from Nuadu of the Silver Arm, who is also known as Necht and Nudd to the Welsh, while the Romans called him Nodens.

There is also an Irish folktale about Fionn that might enlighten us further to Gwythyr's identity. It was passed on to the mythologist W.Y. Evans-Wentz[10] more than a hundred years ago and it is set at a pilgrimage site of great renown, the lake of Lough Derg in Shannon, Ireland:

> *In his flight from County Armagh, Finn mac Coul took his mother on his shoulder, holding her by the legs, but so rapidly did he travel that on reaching the shores of the lake nothing remained of his mother save the two legs, and these he threw down there.*
>
> *Some time later, the Fenians, while searching for Finn, passed the same spot on the lake-shore, and Cinen Moul, who was of their number, upon seeing the shin-bones of Finn's mother and a worm in one, said: "If that worm could get water enough it would come to something great." "I'll give it water enough," said another of the followers, and at that he flung it into the lake ... Immediately the worm turned into an*

enormous water-monster. This water-monster it was that St. Patrick had to fight and kill; and, as the struggle went on, the lake ran red with the blood of the water-monster, and so the lake came to be called Loch Derg (Red Lake)

Today, Lough Derg is the site of St Patrick's Purgatory or Chapel - a popular pilgrimage destination for those who wish to visit the lake where St Patrick fought and conquered the terrifying worm or wyrm – in other words, the water serpent.

However, mythological water serpent-slaying heroes go as far back Hercules vanquishing Hydra, Indra conquering Vrita and Thor subduing the Midgard Serpent. So it seems more likely that it was Cinen Moul (or Mac Coul or Mac Cumhaill) who was the original Irish protagonist of that mythic deed and whose character had "fallen" from Ophiuchus, who is the only giant in the skies portrayed in a contretemps with a serpent.

Add to that the knowledge that the monastery at Lough Derg was the last hold-out of the retreating Druids who were also known as wise serpent teachers and a clearer picture starts to emerge through the haze of glosses that make up the legend of St Patrick slaying all the serpents in Ireland.

And I can't help feeling that introducing a St Patrick into the Miss Havisham-style wedding cake of layered misinformation that makes up the pseudohistory of Glastonbury Abbey would have been the perfect device for replacing the existing indigenous heroic *wyrm*-slayer, Gwythyr ap Greidawl, with the archangel St Michael.

I will leave you to do your own further research on the historicity of Patrick, as there are only so many hamburgers made from sacred cows that one can eat in a day. However, I will share just a couple of *hors d'oevres*, to whet your appetite.

The belief that Patrick was the first abbot of Glastonbury is based on the 12th century writings of William of Malmesbury, which are no longer available to us. The story was embellished by John of Glastonbury about 100 years later as he constructed the Joseph of Arimathea narrative.

In addition, accounts of Patrick's entry into Ireland on a Spring Equinox more or less exactly map on to the ingress of the Irish mystical poet Amergin 1,500 years before, but on Beltane. However, both of their trajectories cross the River Boyne, the name of which is derived from the Milky Way or *Bealach na Bó Finne* (Way of the White Cow).

Rolling back the clock to the times of Amergin, archaeo-astronomers have found that, because of precession, the Hunter Orion was falling down from the skies into the Hill of Slane during Beltane, just as the serpent-slaying Ophiuchus was rising.

It is interesting that these two giant "men" of the sky, Orion and Ophiuchus, the "warrior" and the "healer", are not only in opposition to each other but they both appear to guard the great "starlit ford of night", where the Milky Way is crossed by the sun and moon. [11]

At Beltane, Orion would have been "falling" out of the Milky Way while Ophiuchus was rising in victory over the slain hunter. The Hill of Slane is where Patrick is said to have lit the Paschal fire of Easter more than a millennium later.

As we local authors, poets, artists and musicians begin to resurrect Gwyn and Gwythyr in our various works[12], these heroes seem to be coming alive again like Tinkerbell, in Peter Pan, who can only be saved from death when humans really believe in her. And this is why, every Beltane and Samhain, we drum Yuri's carved, red and white dragons through the town and then up to the Fairfields of the Tor, where we reconstruct, in ceremony, the duel of Avalon.

We also need to take into account an older system of primogeniture to understand why Gwyn, as the Lord of the Underworld, is so protective of his sister. It was not like ours today, in which the son of the king is automatically installed as ruler upon the death of his father. It was the offspring of the sister of the monarch who inherited the throne and so this duel may also have been trial of strength to test Gwythyr's fitness to be Bride's groom and produce a worthy heir to rule the Underworld.

Merlin

The Round Table was constructed, not without great significance, upon the advice of Merlin. By its name the Round Table is meant to signify the round world and round canopy of the planets and the elements in the firmament, where can be seen the stars and many other things.[13]

The above lines are extracted from *La Queste del Saint Graal*, otherwise known as the *Lancelot-Grail*, the

Vulgate Cycle and later the *Pseudo-Map Cycle*. It was composed by the Norman mytho-industrial complex that was in the process of updating various 12th century works, including Geoffrey of Monmouth's *Vitae Merlin* which contains the first mention of Merlin. It later inspired *Le Morte d'Arthur* by Thomas Mallory, who was probably a Knight Templar, and much of the Arthurian media material that we are familiar with today comes out of that mishmash of politically expedient overlays.

The word Merlin meant "sea dragon". The Normans called the sea *la mer*. The Anglo-Saxon word for dragon was *lin* or *lind*.

Geoffrey of Monmouth had reinvented his character of Merlin from an already existing dramatis personæ of a native shaman called Myrddin Wylt. Myrddin was an *awenywddion*, a Dreamer in his own self-enforced captivity in the vast, wild forests of Caledonia. Welsh myths[14] portray Myrddin's primary role as that of upholding the Sovereignty of the Blessed Isles, which, for that reason, were known as Myrddin's Precinct [15].

Myrddin's surname of Wylt meant "wild". It comes from Welsh stories in which he is portrayed as a hermit living in the darkest depths of the wildwoods. The old man is riven with grief over the loss of so many lives during a furious military engagement, which, according to the *Annales Cambriea*, was the Battle of Arfderydd of the year 573.

In the original Celtic stories that the Normans drew upon, there is no connection between Myrddin and Arthur.

Myrddin's main task was to bury The Thirteen

Treasures of the Island of Britain[16] in order to protect the Sovereignty of the land. The number and nature of these talismanic objects varies according to the whims of various storytellers, bards and troubadours but they usually include magical chalices, weapons, chariots, cloaks of invisibility, stones, precious rings, chessboards and cups or cauldrons.

However, for reasons best known to themselves, the Norman propagandists decided to site those protective symbols of guardianship away from mainland Britain. They had their Merlin bury the Thirteen Treasures in Bardsey Island, which is just off the county of Gwynedd in Wales. This could have been to provide a distraction away from a much more sacred burial ground fit for those precious protective talismans of Sovereignty. It is a 10-mile wide circle of 13 giant earthworks currently known as the Glastonbury Temple of the Stars, and we will be coming to it soon, once we have crossed a few more meadows and stiles.

In Welsh myths, we hear that Myrddin stores the treasures in a Glass House. In the old sagas based on Hermetic lore, the word "house" often signifies an astrological house or sun sign.

The oldest name for Glastonbury is Ynis Witrin, which meant Isle of Glass, and that may have been the inspiration for the Norman author of *Lancelot*, Chretien de Troyes' story about the kidnapping of Arthur's queen, Guinevere.

Queen Guinevere is abducted by an Otherworld god called Meleagant and taken to the kingdom of Voirre, or glass, which is reached by crossing over water. In another version of this story[17], where her abductor is named Melwas, the place Guinevere is taken to is named Glastonbury. These associations strongly suggest that Glastonbury acquired the name of Ynis Witrin or the 'island of glass' as a version of the Welsh Caer Wydr, or glass castle.[18]

I have restored what I believe to be this earlier Celtic narrative in my book *The Grail Mysteries*, in which you can follow Myrddin Wylt and his whole crew of Manawydan, Taliesin, Gywddion and Arianrhod, as they go around the Isle of Glass burying each of the 13 treasures to protect the Sovereignty of the Blessed Isles.

Nature Spirits and 'Shrooms

We first become familiar with nature spirits at an early age through illustrations in our nursery books of rhymes of tiny fairies, elves and pixies sitting on toadstools and mushrooms. Once again, there is a hidden message in these works of art which, once understood, transforms the child into an adult. It is a metaphor for those who are our true Elders, the Underlords and the Overlords of the green mantle of this Earth, who are known to biologists merely as fungi.

It is amazing how so many take the existence of fungi for granted, given its absolute dominion over the land. Every single animal and insect on the planet, including mankind, comes originally from fungi, from which we began to separate about 650 million years ago.

Mushrooms are our true Common Ancestor, which might be why we have far more in common with 'shrooms than with apes. Human cells and fungal cells are remarkably similar, so we're able to obtain physical healing from mushrooms, in the form of penicillin, and also spiritual healing from the pixie-capped psilocybin and red-and-white flyagaric.

Our relationship with these Elders might be the reason why our brain synapses have doubled in size over hundreds of thousands of years. We can certainly trace the use of hallucinogenic mushrooms back that far, anyway, from votive offerings and burial goods archaeologists have found all over Europe, Eurasia and America.

Even modern bio-science recognises the intrinsic intelligence of these eukaryotic organisms, in that they organise the flows of groundwater to the roots of trees. It's like an enormous brain under the soil - a humungous, luminous network of branching, threadlike mycelium *hyphae* that act like telegraph wires, sending along the instructions to bring in more water to a tree when its roots are deemed too dry, or moving ground water tables when they are needed elsewhere.

This knowledge opens up a whole new meaning to the Arthurian-era myths about the well maidens who deserted their posts, turning the whole country into a Wasteland.

And of course, we must not forget the three Norns of the Edda who water the roots of the World Tree, Yggdrasil, to create a sort of shimmering, foaming loam that sounds a lot like fungi.

So, it can be no coincidence that rock art paintings of mushrooms have been found in the caves that used to be inhabited by the rain shamans of the Nevada desert. This is because one cannot bring the rains by merely consulting with the thunder god above; one also has to communicate with the organisers of the water in the land below.

There are millions of different "races" of fungi, just as diverse types of yeast are used to bake Mediterranean flatbreads, Irish bannocks, Polish bagels, Indian naans, Danish pastries and so on. It wouldn't do if we all ate the same kind of bread.

In other words, just as our own stories have been customised to flow better in our own Rivers of Blood, so do our own mushrooms "talk to us" in language we have been cultured to understand.

Wise women herbalists know that there are no such things as "weeds"; that when a plant erupts through the soil unexpectedly in our garden, it is unwise to treat it as an unwelcome guest. It may have only turned up because we need its specific healing qualities. Charity begins at home.

Of course, there will always be those who are lured to try more exotic experiences in the jungles of the Amazon with ayahuasca, datura and San Pedro. I have no doubt that the visions derived from the intelligences of those psychotropic plants are invaluable to the shamans who are indigenous to the land where they grow.

But it has become almost a brain tic of our times – the idea that the grass is always greener on the other side.

Yet when flying back from abroad, it is always evident, to me anyway, that as the plane swoops down for its long, slow descent over the patchwork pastures of the Home Counties, that there is no greener and more pleasant land than our own.

The Land of Milk and Honey is surely the true epithet for the Blessed Isles which were renown, in ancient times, for their bee-keeper shamans?

Speaking of bees, you will be aware of the current decline in these vital pollinators. It is due to many factors, including pollution and over-chemicalisation.

But another important cause is the modern tendency to want to stock our gardens with exotic plants from foreign climes. Bees fail to recognise colours and patterns on flowers from other countries that they have not been genetically programmed, over millions of years, to see – so they pass them by.

That is why I prefer to follow the ways of the bee shamans of the Blessed Isles when contacting the innate intelligence of this land. I find it's best to pick the tiny pixie-caps of psilocybin in the silver dawn dew of autumn meadows and take them home to make tea.

I avoid the red-and-white spotted flyagaric mushrooms because, unless you are an expert in these matters, which I'm not, there is a danger of toxic overdose[19].

The Grail Keepers

The Grail Keepers of Avalon are part of a worldwide shamanic oral tradition who appear in myths as types of "threshold guardians", "gatekeepers" or "keepers of the hearth". So, while the elementals and spirits of place may often be conflated in our minds with these localised custodians of the magical lore, they are not identical in nature or purpose, although to beginners the difference can appear to be moot.

To my understanding, the spirits of place are disembodied entities who inhabit the morphogenic waves of memory which are then woven by the threshold guardians into stories, plays, artworks and magical rituals that become impregnated in our nightly dreamscapes.

Some spirits of place, I've learned, were once in human bodies and have held up their own liberation in order to stay and teach the initiates. Others have never been incarnate on Earth, or anywhere else. Conversely, threshold guardians, such as the Grail Keepers, are ex-humans who have now moved on from their incarnation on Earth. They have left their resonant mark in the fields of memory, both in our inner landscapes and dreams, and in the soil and structures of the outer world too.

Those who are aware can sense their holographic presence in the rolling hills and vales to which they gave their hearts. The intricate silken weaves of the messages from the Grail Keepers are subtle overlays that are hidden in plain sight but which can sometimes glance your cheek like a butterfly's wing. In that way, their presence is experienced or felt at a deep, cognitive level, sometimes for many generations.

Often, the challenge is to find words for the concepts they are expressing that have fallen out of consensual reality, and thus our language, even before Chaucer put pen to paper. But it is necessary if we are to recover what we have lost and then use these resurrected cognitive tools to help enrich our lives today. In this way, we ourselves become the Grail Keepers for future generations.

So let's begin with the Druidic scribes and bards, who were among the earliest keepers of the hearth, who kept the primordial carpet around the fire clean and alive by retelling its stories, dances and songs, many of which have come down to us in the form of faery stories and nursery rhymes.

The Druids were banished from the Blessed Isles in the early centuries by the Romans. The most well-known and bloodiest massacre is the one led by Suetonius Paulinus in 60 CE. He routed them at their innermost sanctuary, to which they had retreated: the passage tomb mound of *Bryn Celli Ddu* at Mona Insulus, now Anglesey.

Even so, they left their mark. The architecture of this passage tomb alone gives us a clue to their cosmological wisdom, because a beam from the Sun hits the back of the central passage on the Summer Solstice.

In addition, recent excavations there have uncovered stones decorated with weaving serpentine patterns, similar to those found at the prehistoric mounds at Newgrange and Knowth in Ireland. These indicate a mindset that was familiar with the concepts of the Web of Wyrd: one that did not divide matter into particles of matter and waves of energy, knowing full well that the two flow into and out of each other all the time.

There was a brief hiatus after the collapse of the Roman Empire in the fourth century, which meant that the imperial invaders had to return to Italy. In their absence, there was a revival of Druidic stories and bardic songs that carried, in their underlayers, the star lore of the Hermetic system. The three main religious centres were the islands of Iona, Lindisfarne and Glastonbury, which formed a scalene that mirrored the Summer Triangle of the three "birds" or stars – Deneb,

Vega and Altair[20] - as shown in **Figure 29**.

Figure 29 The Summer Triangle aligned with three holy islands

It was during this heyday of Celtic Christianity that the sixth-century bard Taliesin composed a poem in which he stated that he was born in the "land of the summer stars".

Reading about the lives of St Colombo of Iona and St Cuthbert of Lindisfarne, they can seem more like awenwyddions in that they retreated to caves, had healing powers and close relationships with animals.

In those days, monkish scribes would make endless copies of the books of the New Testament, and they kept the "grail" by faithfully preserving the star parables. They penned them in Latin on to vellum and papyrus, and then decorated them with beautifully illuminated illustrations.

These early iterations of the Christian scriptures are known as codices – which is sufficient hint, I think. If it hadn't been for those monastic codists, most of our ancestors' wisdom would be completely lost to us today.

However, the revival lasted only a couple of centuries.

In 664 CE, a meeting or synod was convened at Whitby – on the land that used to be the territory of the Brigantes. The outcome was that all the religious institutions of Britain were brought back under the aegis of Rome. And from then onwards, all the Hermetic Arts were ostensibly banned – apart from for those in the royal courts, which carried on the practices secretly.

It may come as a surprise to know that until only fairly recently, a practising alchemist would either have to be in the employ of the ruler of the land or locked up in prison. There were no freelancers. So, some would hide their expertise under the more socially acceptable profession of "blacksmith".

Both the smith and the alchemist were skilled in the transmutation of metals, which is at the heart of the science first developed by the sages and mages in the cradle of civilisation. Thus, in this way, the blacksmiths became the new Grail Keepers, although there was nothing new about their practices.

As you know, even before the glaciers melted and drove our ancestors south, the tales around Tabiti's campside fire featured an all-powerful goddess called Satana who has to appeal to a blacksmith, Tlepshw, for help in birthing her child. Tlepshw's role in this Circassian myth highlights the more sacred and respectful approach to the mining of the Earth's resources, which is still practised today by some aboriginal tribes.

In this understanding, the ore is a child that is birthed from the womb of Mother Earth, as much as the Child of the Philosopher is born through the congress of the Sun and the Moon. Mines were only opened in elaborate ceremonies by the smiths, the midwives of metallurgy, when the ore was considered to be "ripe". These ancient prospectors feature in the myths of antiquity in the characters of the dwarves who quarry gold from the caves of mountains.

The Seven Dwarves, in the story of *Snow White*, are a metaphor for the seven planetary gods and their associated metals. Each metal is required to be present at one of the seven different stages of the operation of the Marriage of the Sun and the Moon, and their qualities and at what stage of the process they are introduced is shown in the table of **Figure 30**.

Planetary god	Metal	Quality	Stage
Saturn	Lead	Dark	Calcination
Jupiter	Tin	Exuberant	Dissolution
Mars	Iron	Masculine	Separation
Venus	Copper	Feminine	Conjunction
Mercury	Quicksilver	Transformative	Fermentation
Moon	Silver	Soulful	Distillation
Sun	Gold	Spiritual	Coagulation

Figure 30 Planets, metals, qualities and alchemical stage

The underlying meanings of the names of the seven dwarves Grumpy, Happy, Sleepy, Bashful, Sneezy, Dopey and Doc is not clear in Walt Disney's 1931 animated film *Snow White and the Seven Dwarfs*.

But another version was broadcast in 1995 on the American HBO service, in the animated series *Happily Ever After: Fairy Tales for Every Child in America*. This programme gave these miniscule miners epithets that hinted at their metallic associations: Bright Silver, Sharp Flint, Fools Gold, Smelly Sulfur, Heavy Metal, Rough Copper and Hard Jade.

The power of the smith should perhaps come as no surprise to those who have been journeying through their own Rivers of Blood to meet with their ancestors and have found themselves being advised by the spirit of a smith rather than a shaman.

We find evidence in folklore worldwide for the smiths eventually replacing the shamans as spiritual leaders[21] during the Bronze and Iron Ages.

There is a Siberian proverb: "A shaman's wife is respectable, while a smith's wife is venerable."

According to the Dolgans, a shaman could not

"swallow" the soul of a smith because smiths keep their souls in the fire. On the other hand, the same source tells us that a smith could catch a shaman's soul and burn it.

The Buryat of Mongolia had a creation story about the nine sons of Boshintoi, the celestial smith, who came down to Earth to teach men metallurgy. Like the ancient Celts, the Buryat smiths practised the horse sacrifice known as the *asvamedha* in the Indian Vedic culture. It is a theatrical sacred ritual that is designed to establish Sovereignty and so it has the Marriage of the Sun and the Moon as its understory.

The Indian horse sacrifice is also the original, and far more ancient, source of the character of the ass named Bottom in Shakespeare's *A Midsummer Night's Dream* [22].

The horse represented the Sun in these *asvamedha* rituals. According to the lore of the Buryats, the redeemed soul of the sacrificial horse returned to the celestial smith, Boshintoi.

Boshintoi's sons married the daughters of the Earth and thus they became the ancestors of all the smiths. It wasn't so long ago when no-one could claim the family name of Smith unless they were in the bloodline of the Boshintoi. And just as the stonemasons formed themselves into secret societies in order to preserve their knowledge and share it with only a chosen few, so the smiths organised themselves into arcane guilds, some of which still exist today.

And so now, with all that previously occulted grail lore packed into our rucksacks, we are ready to meet the most illustrious blacksmith, bard and Grail

Keeper of not just Glastonbury but the whole of the Blessed Isles.

Dunstan

There is a lot told about Dunstan's role in helping to rebuild Glastonbury Abbey after the fire of the ninth century and we are told he was bard and a blacksmith. But not much is ever discussed about what I want us to concentrate on now if we are to proceed along this path – and that was his role as an alchemist.

To my understanding, the forge of the 10th century abbot of Glastonbury Abbey would have been one of the earliest magical hearths of Avalon.

Through knowledge that I've acquired, tiny though it is by comparison, I believe that Dunstan had a relationship with the Otherworldly experts in alchemy known as the Sidhe or the Fae. This association would have made him so knowledgeable in the esoteric arts that it was natural he would go on to become a close adviser of kings, one of whom he crowned in Bath Abbey, to assume the mantle of the Archbishoprics of London and Canterbury and to be canonised after his death.

In getting closer to this extraordinary man, in the next chapter, we will be going to small village of Baltonsborough, which is just a few miles from Glastonbury and which was his birthplace in 909 CE. We will be visiting a 15th century church there named after Dunstan. On display, over the altar, there is a beautiful stained-glass window which was bequeathed by a Grail Keeper of the 19th century [23]. The design depicts, in glorious iridescent hues, the processes needed to create the Philosopher's Stone. We will, I promise, be examining this great masterpiece in more detail soon. But just to say, at this stage, it can be no coincidence that this unique alchemical window is found in Dunstan's own church, in his own birthplace.

On the wall near the altar, there is a famous illustration of Dunstan, in which he is holding the Devil by the nose with his blacksmiths' tongs. Now, it goes without saying that there is no Devil in alchemy; this demonisation of the fiery Hades was a way of smearing horned gods and blacksmiths in one foul swoop. You could almost say, if you wanted to be annoying, that if the Christians hadn't invented the Devil, there would be no-one to blame for our "sins". However, what small documentary evidence is left to us about Dunstan's life indicates to me that holding the Devil by his nose with tongs was a metaphor for the conquest over forces required to create the Philosopher's Stone or Child of the Philosopher at the stage of the Child Tension Victory.

I'm bolstered in this view by the fact that Dunstan did not appear to have followed the Christian doctrine of Heaven and Hell – at least in artwork attributed to him, as shown in the drawing in **Figure 31**. It is a black-and-white sketch of the cover design of what has been termed *St Dunstan's Classbook*, which is stored in Oxford's Bodleian Library, and it is subtitled *Four manuscripts written in 9th-11th century in Brittany, Wales and England*.

The cover sketch is considered to be a self-portrait of St Dunstan as a monk lying at the foot of the cross during the crucifixion. The scribbled words underneath the prostrate figure are thought to read

"Remember, I beg you, merciful Christ, do protect me, Dunstan, and do not permit the Taenerian storms to swallow me up," and it is signed "D".

Taeneria was a Greek peninsula of that name, although today it is called Cape Matapan. There was a cave at Taeneria that local legend decreed was the entry to the Underworld and which was guarded by the multi-headed dog Cerberus, who the zodiac hero Hercules slew on his down through there at Sagittarius.

So, I find it interesting that Dunstan did not ask Christ to save him from the fires of the Roman Christian abyss of fire and brimstone, "Hell", but from the "storms" that the older mythological hero meets as he proceeds towards the Judgement of the Underworld. This is more in line understanding of the Druids about the Three Worlds, the Old Norse three wells of the Tree of Life or Wyrd, and the astrological-alchemical pilgrimage of life around the rim of the Wheel.

It looks to me as if the four-armed cross within the halo of Christ is symbolising the cross formed by the equinoxes and solstices. The halo is slightly tilted, just as our the globe of our Earth is.

Note that Dunstan has placed himself in the far bottom-right corner, which, on the zodiac, is where the initiate or hero falls down into the Underworld at Sagittarius, after being bitten at Scorpio.

There is no explanation for the diagonal line going across the body of Christ. But it is in the same place as the river of the Milky Way found on the zodiacs of the Hermetic system, which runs downwards from between Gemini and Taurus to Scorpio and Sagittarius.

There is some sort of sash that appears to be

flying out from the Christ figure with the end marked by a black dot at exactly where Pisces would be located, which is the Age that was ushered in by Jesus and the one that we are currently leaving, after 2,000 years, to move into Aquarius.

Figure 31 The cover of St Dunstan's Classbook

You will find a lot more about Dunstan in the public sphere which is more historical and political in nature, and you might want to look that up at a later date.

At this stage of our journey, I just wanted to highlight some clues that indicate he was probably an initiate of the Mysteries and his self-portrait could have been his way of leaving a message for future generations to eventually unravel, just as any self-respecting Grail Keeper would do.

The Avalonians and the Astral Planes

The Avalonians is the title of a book by Patrick Bentham about a colourful group of real people who were drawn to Avalon in the early half of the 20th century, perhaps sensing the magic of the land and thus seeking to employ its forces in order to influence – to their minds, for the better - the destiny of a nation.

The Avalonians were well-meaning in that they wanted to break the knowledge about Hermeticism out of the private, locked vaults and curtained salons of secret seances, and disseminate the keys among the people. But they were hampered by a combination of factors.

One was that, like Frederick Bligh Bond, they were trying to broadcast an idea whose time had not yet to come. The churchgoing folk of Glastonbury were just not ready for it. In addition, these Avalonians were saddled with a musty potpourri of assorted systems that was derived from the early, and thus incomplete, study of archaeology in Egypt and Assyria. Then they were forced to politely cover it all with a lace doily of revived Jacobean politics. So the few seeds that they managed to plant in the wastelands have been slow to develop and some were so twisted out of shape that they have given rise to alien, anachronistic creatures, reminiscent of W.B Yeats's "strange beast slouching towards Bethlehem", which refuse, even today, to remain in their graves.

Most of the Avalonians were not able to contact the spirits of the Three Worlds. The secret societies from which they hailed – such as the Rosicrucians and the Golden Dawn - although rich in access to hidden vaults of research material had long lost the ability to receive the Otherworldly guidance necessary to correctly interpret the contents found there.

In short, they were stuck in what Dion Fortune called the Astral Planes.

The Astral Planes are etheric fields constructed, in the morphogenetic waves, by earlier Hermeticists whose role was to protect their employer, the incumbent power of the land. They built a sort of etheric, cognitive platform in Time from which, even today, their shadows can confuse and baffle as much as educate and enlighten. They mean well; they are just doing their jobs. But unless your consciousness is rooted in a deeper, more primordial understanding, you can find yourself going down long, winding rabbit holes that eventually turn into brick walls.

Bligh Bond benefitted, initially, from the messages of the astral monks because their purpose was – and still is - to protect, in memory, the Benedictine abbey. But even that advantage was short-lived. He was eventually banished from the town because his findings, although real and tangible, went against the preferred narrative of the day.

Glastonians were strict churchgoing types in the first half of the 20th century. The aristocratic elite tended to be High Anglican, while the ordinary people were mostly Congregational chapel goers and Methodists. And, in the shadows, pulling the strings behind it all, were the "Lost Tribes of the Children of Israel".

British Israelism, as a movement, was born in the late 19th century and by the time of the Avalonians it had grown so much in size and influence that it had secret cabals in all English-speaking countries throughout the world.

It had won adherents through reviving an older back-story that had its roots in the post Ice-Age migrations of the peoples of the Caucasian Steppes. However, they claimed to have followed a different migratory route and taken a detour through Palestine. From there, they claimed that their ancestors followed alongside the exodus of the Children of Israel out of Egypt and then to Spain, from where they had finally sailed to Ireland. Thus, they contended that they were the original Druids, who were Jewish.

These days we know that there is no evidence for any of this – either archaeological, ethnological, genetic or linguistic. In addition, such a narrative can only survive as a succubus that feeds on a bed of ignorance about the real underlying meaning of the stories found in the Bible.

However, the British Israelites were not spinning this story out of thin air; it was based on the same tall tale that the Jacobeans had used, in the 16th century, to give the reign of the Stuarts some legitimacy. Once it had achieved its aim, it died a natural death in the public consciousness and there it would have been allowed to rest in peace had not the British Israelites decided to resuscitate it.

The influence of the British Israelites on the Freemasons at the turn of the 20th century explains why the nexus of masonic ritual work is, even today, focused around the imagery and geometry of the Temple of Solomon. Many of these faux Hebrews were hoping to build a Second Temple of Solomon here in Britain, and they considered the site of Glastonbury Abbey – if only they could eject the Church of England incumbents – to be ideal for their purposes.

As their justification, they needed to be able to prove that Joseph of Arimathea had established the first church on that land and to that end, they were quite content for Bligh Bond to dig there, in order to uncover the "original wattle-and-daub" building. However, Bligh Bond and the Company of Avalon not only failed to uncover this mythical structure but what they revealed instead was that the original builders, the Benedictines, were brilliant and wise Hermeticists who understood the alchemical process that led to real magical power.

As we discussed backalong, the story of the exodus of the Hebrew slaves was part of an allegorical Gnostic template and not a historical event. The Twelve Tribes of Israel constitute an astrological-alchemical metaphor for the zodiac path to enlightenment, which is symbolised by the Vesica Piscis.

And so, for uncovering this inconvenient truth, Frederick Bligh Bond was sent into exile himself.

The influence of the British Israelites eventually faded after they failed in their bid to buy the ruined Abbey when it came up for auction. The bishop of the Diocese of Bath and Wells stepped in and bought it up, and the Church of England has remained its owner ever since.

However, in continuing to overlay a dry, sandy kilim rug of more desert climes on to the sacred primordial carpet that underlies this green and fertile land, our ancestral Rivers of Blood slowly came to reject it - just as the cells of an immune system will always spurn and eject a foreign body. Thus, the fertile, healing waters of wisdom turned back, leaving a barren and arid wasteland in the spiritual hearts of the people.

To my mind, Frederick Bligh Bond and Dion Fortune – plus Katharine Maltwood, another contemporary whose work we will examine in more detail later on - were the most gifted and inspired among these Avalonians and they have left the strongest mark in the morphogenetic fields. But given the stifling political climate, even they were only able to hint at a deeper lore of geometrical knotwork buried under the Arthurian overlay established after the Norman Conquest. So, you have to read between the lines of their writings and artworks to find evidence that they understood that the magic of this land is essentially Celtic or Druidic in nature.

Fortune set her novel *The Sea Priestess* on her imaginary Bell Down and Bell Knoll, but it is no secret that she was inspired by the local Brean Down and Brean Knoll – in other words, they are named after Breed or Bridie. It is thought that Fortune changed their names to "Bell" to denote Belinus, the Celtic sun god, to hint towards a solstice alignment[24] that runs through there.

There were several other prominent Avalonians, such as John Goodchild and William Sharp (who wrote under the pseudonym of Fiona McLeod), who did much to bring Bridie's Mound and the Salmon of Wisdom to public attention.

Alice Buckton and Wellesley Tudor Pole, to whom we are most grateful for the creation of the Chalice Well Gardens, did not seem much concerned, in the end, with connecting with the native lore of this land. They became adherents of the Baha'i faith, which was co-opted by the United Nations for its globalism agenda along with other more Theosophic systems such as Alice Bailey's *Lucifer Trust*, later renamed to the more palatable sounding *Lucis Trust*.

I'll leave it up to you if you want to find out more about the Avalonians. Right now, we need to keep moving in our quest to unearth the native antecedents of our own Mystery teachings – and there is still a way to go. It is only in recent times that the understanding about the power of place is being revived again among a much larger *cognoscenti* and, with it, the knowledge is germinating that to ground a philosophy successfully in the soil of the collective consciousness of a land, it must first find resonance in the ground.

The Company of Avalon and the Watchers

No section on Grail Keepers would be complete without the inclusion of the Company of Avalon, the Otherworldly guides of the architect Bligh Bond, who told him where to dig in order to uncover the buried ruins of early medieval Glastonbury Abbey.

Bligh Bond has recorded the conversations with these monks in Project Gutenberg's *The Gate of Rememberance* and it is there that I found they had signed themselves as The Watchers.

In the Preface, the author describes them thus:

Still small Voices from a distant Time! — thrilling through the void and stirring faint resonances within the deeps of our own being — the great Telepathy, the true Communion of Mind, the gate of the Knowledge, the Gnosis of the apostle, whose key is Mental Sympathy, the key that the lawyers took away, neither entering themselves, nor suffering others to enter.

No discord can mar this communion, since love and understanding are its law. Death cannot touch it: rather is he Keeper of the Gate. Time, as we know it, here, counts for naught, for to the deeper dream-consciousness, a day may be as a thousand years, and a period of trance or sleeping as one tick of the clock.

Bligh Bond's words completely chime in with my own experience of the Watchers, of a timeless realm of which Chronos or Saturn is the gatekeeper.

In receiving their messages, I sense my state transforming on a deep cellular level as they transport me, sonically, to a slower, gentler existence. These voices, which remain in our landscapes - both inner and outer - make the Watchers truly the Threshold Guardians, the *genius loci* and the power of the place of Glastonbury Abbey.

Those who revealed themselves to Bligh's spirit

mediums had names like Johannes, Reginaldus and Ambrosius, and there was also John Camel, a treasurer of England that died in 1487.

I've met one of them, David, a gentle, self-effacing soul, who taught me how to interpret the Massacre of the Infants. There was also a tall, slim, aristocratic-sounding Benedictine who didn't give his name but just instructed me to "Sit back and watch the show". Then he waved his arms and somehow banished some sort of entity or "fetch" that had been spying on my house. It tore off, and I heard it screeching in agony, all the way down Glastonbury High Street.

However, I won't say any more about the Watchers because I don't want your experience to be coloured by mine. Instead, I will enjoy watching you receive from them your own customised experience of pilgrimage - one perfectly in line with the destiny written in the stars at your birth - as we progress through the hills and vales of Avalon.

1 From *Under Milk Wood* by Dylan Thomas
2 There is much more about the philosophical system of The Three Cauldrons of the Celts in my book, *Stories in the Stars*.
3 *The Ancient Paths* by Graham Robb.
4 Ptolemy's 2nd century *Geographica*.
5 Created in the 9th century during the reign of King Alfred.
6 In other Celtic myths, Arawn is the Lord of the Underworld and his sister is named Creiddylad.
7 From poem XXXIII in the *Black Book of Camarthan* that dates to the 13th century. It is the oldest surviving manuscript written entirely in the Welsh language and thought to include the works of bards who composed between the 9th–12th centuries.
8 The words of Gwyn, from poem XXXIII in the *Black Book of Camarthen*.
9 The *Mabinogion* is a compilation of Welsh folk stories that are thought to date from the 12th-13th centuries, but reach back to a much earlier oral tradition.
10 *The Fairy-Faith in Celtic Countries*, by W.Y. Evans-Wentz.
11 This is from Anthony Murphy, who has done an extraordinary job in dissecting the astrononomical metaphors found in Irish myths, and you can find much more on his blog *Mythical Ireland*.
12 Gwyn is the main protagonist in two of my novels: *The Bright World of the Gods* and *The Grail Mysteries*.
13 *La Queste del Saint Graal* (13th century).
14 *The Black Book of Carmarthen* and *Red Book of Hergest*.
15 The Welsh Triads (*Trioedd Ynys Prydein*, Triads of the Island of Britain)
16 The Welsh Triads (*Trioedd Ynys Prydein*, Triads of the Island of Britain)
17 *The Life of Gildas* by 12th century cleric Caradoc of Llancarfan.
18 *The Star Temple of Avalon* by Nicholas R. Mann and Philippa

Glasson.

[19] Disclaimer: Please do consult your doctor or take professional advice before taking any fungi.

[20] The alignment of the "birds" with the holy islands was discovered by Holly Hazeltree.

[21] *The Forge and the Crucible: The origins and structures of alchemy* by Mircea Eliade.

[22] I explain the alchemical and astrological underlays of Shakespeare's *A Midsummer Night's Dream* and show how the Marriage of the Sun and the Moon compares to the *Asvamedha* horse sacrifice in my book, the *Sacred Sex Rites of Ishtar*.

[23] *The Squire of Butleigh*, Ralph Neville-Grenville.

[24] *The Terrestrial Alignments of Katharine Maltwood and Dion Fortune* by Yuri Leitch.

Chapter Eight: Hill Lucre and the Philosopher's Stone

Now they were come up with the Hill Lucre, where the silver mine was which took Demas off from his pilgrimage, and into which, as some think, By-Ends fell and perished; wherefore they considered that. But when they were come to the old monument that stood over against the Hill Lucre, to wit, the pillar of salt that stood also within view of Sodom and its stinking lake, they marvelled, as did Christian before, that men of knowledge and ripeness of wit, as they were, should be so blind as to turn aside here.

The Pilgrim's Progress by John Bunyan.

We know the saying that "all that glitters is not gold". However, before the Alexandrian Greeks rescued the practice of alchemy from the Late Period Egyptians, it was – or at least it had been for a thousand years.

The aftermath of the Santorini earthquake had destroyed much of the knowledge of the civilised world, including the understanding about the transmutation of metals and their interaction holographically on the microcosm within the macrocosm.

What followed after the island of Thera exploded in the second millennium BCE was a millennia-long Dark Ages in which pharaohs happily accepted gold bars that were in fact merely metals that had only acquired their glittering hues after being dipped into solutions and gilded with different alloys. It is where the word "guilds" comes from.

However, after the fourth century BCE, a system came to the fore that was strongly influenced by the natural philosophers of the cradle of civilisation of Alexandria and Antioch.

Following in the traditions of the shamans of the steppes before the ice caps melted, these alchemists re-envisioned the material world as alive and the life force was contained in the form of a spark of light that was indwelling deep inside the darkness of matter – a spirit, if you like. The purpose of their alchemy was to purify and release this spirit, which they named variously as the Magisterium, the Grand Elixir, the Child of the Philosopher or the Philosopher's Stone.

So, there was a relatively brief heyday in the West that was based on the natural philosophy of Parmenides, Plato and Aristotle, until the curtain was brought down for the next Dark Age, courtesy of Roman Christianity.

However, the Arabs managed to keep a lot of it alive and so those who wanted to study the Great Art spent time in the desert with them - such as the Knights Templars in the years of the Crusades – and then they brought back the knowledge to the royal courts of Europe. And, as I'm sure you can imagine, just as with any great spiritual teaching, its surface story was misappropriated by those who wanted to manipulate others by claiming that they had found the way to produce gold from base metal.

The alchemists who propagated this means of easy wealth were known, derogatively, as "puffers", for the continual blowing of their bellows in order to increase the heat under their operations. When the gold failed to materialise, they would often resort to trickery and guile, such as painting a real piece of gold and then dipping it into an acid solution to dissolve the paint so that, "hey presto!", the gold appeared.

It often worked on gullible princes and kings – but not all of them. Others, though, like Frederick of Wurzburg, had special gilded gallows built for those guilty of such crimes.

However, metal coins gilded in this fashion did eventually infiltrate our currency. In the 15th century, the weak and ineffectual King Henry VI, who was in need of a war chest for holding royal lands in France, issued licences to guilds of alchemists, and they were eventually put in charge of the nation's Mint. These puffers would probably still be there today, using their secret methods of gilding metals, if it hadn't been for the introduction of promissory notes made of paper.

And so, this is how the practice of alchemy became divided into two camps: puffers and Hermeticists. The former just blithely carried on with their guilds and gilding of metals on behalf of the ruling classes. But the Hermeticists understood that the word "laboratory" came from the Latin *ora* and *labor*, meaning "prayer" and "work". In other words, inner contemplation, meditation and journeying were vital to a spiritual process in which the transmutation of metals was a metaphor for the transformation of the soul.

Those who carried the *gnosis* were not ignorant that enlightenment, when the spark of the life-force is born or reborn as the Child of the Philosopher or Philosopher's Stone, was the outcome of what the Celts called the Four Joys and Four Sorrows that are the challenges encountered along the pilgrimage of any alchemical process, including that of the human lifespan.

The true adepts were a select fraternity of initiated alchemists to whom the laboratory work was part of a comprehensive philosophical and spiritual system based on the teachings of Thoth and Hermes. The experiments of the true adepts to transmute metals were carried out as a demonstration of Hermetic principles and not just as a way of accumulating wealth[1].

Perhaps another way of dividing these two camps is into Templars and tempters.

It seems that the tempters will always be with us on this path, such as the aforementioned Demas in The Pilgrim's Progress, and like By-Ends, we are being continually seduced off the narrow pathway into the certain death – spiritually, anyway – and ending up like Lot's wife, who was turned to a pillar of salt beside the silver mine of Hill Lucre.

We can compare these lurers to our doom to the Devil who offers up dominion over the whole world in his temptation of Christ in the wilderness. But in fact, every mythological hero, from time immemorial, has had to face and overcome the siren song of the irresistible allure of gold, such as Bilbo and Frodo in J.R.R. Tolkien's *Lord of the Rings*.

So, this temptation must be one of the intrinsic challenges along the path of the Called.

In other words, these trickster tempters are metaphors for the adversarial processes and catalysts that aid in the evolution of our self-realisation, and who variously attempt to turn us back, challenge us to a duel, lock us up into captivity or try to steal our powers.

You're probably already recognising these landmarks along the path of the Fool in Major Arcana of the Tarot deck but it is also the quest that most of us are on as we step into Avalon, whether our conscious minds realise it or not.

You may have had moments in your life where you reached a crossroads and had to make a difficult decision which tested your integrity and how you decided dictated your life's journey for the next x-number of years. These potently energetic crossroads are called "nodes", where the male and female aspects of "leylines" cross – and the god who governs all crossroads and nodes is Hermes, aka Mercury.

There is a famous zodiac hero who fell foul of tempters who you may not have previously recognised as such. His name is Pinocchio and he was not merely a naughty little puppet who got up to pranks and misadventures involving magical animals and faeries, which so many of us enjoyed in our childhoods, courtesy of Walt Disney's animation.

If we go into the Way Back Machine, beyond Hollywood's superficial, truncated treatment of the story, there is a much longer 19th century tale, by Carlos Collodi, which is far more authentic to the original. The story is divided into 36 chapters or adventures – one for each decan of a zodiac sign – so we can more clearly see the bones of the archetypal, alchemical champion poking through it.

Therefore, in Collodi's *The Adventures of Pinocchio*, we are presented with a much more comprehensive teaching on what causes us, as a fractal, microcosmic part of the macrocosm, to go round on the Wheel of our own lives, like a rotating cog within other rotating cogs that make up the much larger grandfather clock of Old Father Time.

In **Figure 32**, you will see how these adventures follow the order of the sun signs of the classical zodiac. It also shows how the Hollywood cartoon jumps from Cancer to Scorpio.

Thus, in ignorance of the older story, we are not cognisant of a large and formative part of this little hero's journey. Instead, Disney fast-forwards us into the final step of the Redemption of the Ancestors, in which he has to demonstrate great intelligence, integrity and courage to rescue his father from the belly of the whale. And it is only cognitive dissonance that stops us from realising that the wooden puppet has not yet had enough time, or faced sufficient challenges, to develop such heroic qualities. He goes from zero to hero in a matter of minutes.

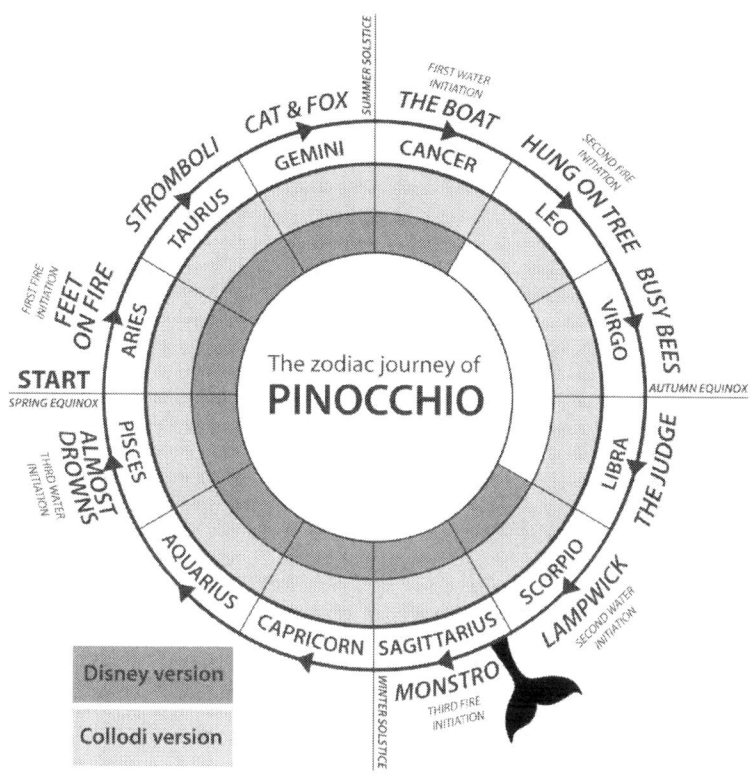

Figure 32 The astrological journey of Pinocchio

So, let's unpack this older Tuscan tale of Pinocchio's a little further, in order to familiarise ourselves with the structure of the story of the zodiac hero that is found on the primordial carpet worldwide [2].

His father, Guiseppe, is a clockmaker and thus he represents Chronos or Saturn, the Father of Time.

In Collodi's version, the temptation of Pinocchio begins almost immediately after he leaves home at the same place as heroes always do, at the Spring Equinox in Aries.

He is supposed to be going to school. But on the way, he is lured into becoming an actor at the theatre that he reaches at Taurus. There, he is trapped in a cage by Stromboli, a terrifying, bullish impressario. Even his conscience, Jiminy Cricket, cannot find a way to pick the lock.

Eventually, he is released by the magic wand of the Blue Fairy of Venus, who governs Taurus.

The Blue Fairy then bestows upon him the boon of five gold coins and he sets off again, quite jauntily, with his treasure jingling in his pocket.

But when he reaches a crossroads, at Mercury-ruled Gemini, he is waylaid by the villainous trickster-twins of Fox and Cat. In this scene, we are reminded of the expression "meeting the Devil at the crossroads". It isn't that Mercury is the Devil. But in his trickster form, in which he challenges our integrity, he is quite happy to play the role of the Devil's advocate.

The pair instantly set about persuading him that if he plants his money in the Field of Wonder, it will grow a thousandfold overnight.

They take Pinocchio to the field, and show him an ideal place to bury them. He follows their direction and plants his five coins and then as night falls, he leaves to go to bed. Naturally, when he returns the next morning, his treasure has disappeared.

This mistake, in trusting the more cynical, worldly-wise Fox and Cat, is the mercurial catalyst for a whole series of dangerous and life-threatening escapades he cannot avoid. But he learns many valuable lessons as he goes through Cancer, Leo and Virgo, until he reaches Libra, where has to come before the court, whereupon the judge throws him in jail for the crime of having his five gold coins stolen.

And so, by now you are probably wondering what all this has do with Avalon. Well, do bear with me, because we are almost at our destination of Baltonsborough, which is just a few miles from Glastonbury.

Next, though, in order for you to be able to gather the learning from that visit, we are going to examine a series of events in the life of the Elizabethan alchemist, John Dee.

The temptation of John Dee

John Dee was one of the most learned men of his time. Perhaps this was largely due to him only sleeping four hours a night during his student years at Trinity College, to make time for his voracious consumption of books on alchemy.

Upon graduating, he turned his attention to the stars and went to study astronomy among some of the best scholars of Europe, not least the renown geographer Gerard Mercator. He also spent a few years in Paris, where he held lectures for the elite few on sacred geometry.

However, not long after his return to Britain in 1553, Dee was falsely accused, in his own words, of being "...a companion of the hellhounds, a caller and a conjuror of wicked and damned spirits" who had used his magical powers to try to take the life of Queen Mary, for which he was thrown into jail at Hampton Court.

Five years later, when Queen Elizabeth came to the throne, she played the role of the Blue Fairy and released him, and saw to it that Dee's fortunes changed for the better. She bequeathed him a quiet but sizeable grace-and-favour property on the banks of the River Thames in Surrey.

So finally, Dee was free to practice his occult arts to his heart's content and his inner life grew as he meditated inwardly and received ecstatic visions of angels carrying important messages.

His Mortlake house soon became famous all over Europe as the repository of the most comprehensive esoteric library of the times and it was there that he produced a number of books[3] on what he called Enochian magic – which went on to inform budding alchemists for centuries afterwards, right up to the present day.

However, at that time, Dee had yet to learn the lesson that knowledge without its attendant delivery system of wisdom can lead you on a merry dance. The quote at the top of this chapter reminds me of this highly esteemed man of letters.

> ... they marvelled, as did Christian before, that men of knowledge and ripeness of wit, as they were, should be so blind as to turn aside here.

And so, the Elizabethan equivalent of John Bunyan's tempter Demas was sent to appear at a staging post along the pilgrimage of Dee's life, in the form of one Edward Kelley.

If Dee's sixth sense had been working properly, he would have realised that Kelley was a bit of a scoundrel, to say the least. He invariably wore a strange-looking black skull cap with long flaps on each side to hide the fact that his ears had been cut off in punishment for counterfeiting coins. But our "hero" was apparently unable to recognise that Kelley was the sort of disreputable type who longed to be wealthy but who never had any intention of doing even one honest day's work to achieve such a desired state.

Kelley had managed to gain entry into Dee's house by producing a vial of mysterious-looking red powder and with which, he insisted, it was possible to create the Philosopher's Stone that would turn base metal into gold.

There is no documentary evidence for what transpired next so what follows is my own educated guess.

Dee would no doubt have excitedly invited Kelley into his laboratory. Once inside, Kelley would have produced another vial from the inside pocket of his coat, this one containing a sort of whitish powder. He would have mixed the red and white powders together in a clay cup called a cupel. The cupel would have been put into the brick oven - also known as the Philosophical Furnace – which was capable of reaching very high temperatures. Then the two would have watched the mixture carefully until it ignited and – abracadabra! – before their very eyes, what materialised was gold.

Sadly, for all his great learning, Dee had not studied metallurgy so he may not have realised that if you combine red iron oxide with white sulphur – as these puffers often did - you get pyrite, or what is known as Fool's Gold, and it can look almost like the real thing under sunlight.

The rest of this Fool's journey is well-documented, so we can leave my imagined reconstruction. His "discovery of the Philosopher's Stone" meant instant world stardom for the pair. It was of no small interest to Queen Elizabeth and her explorer "privateers", who were often little more than pirates By Appointment, that Dee had actually found the secret to turning base metal into gold. So, the Mortlake house suddenly became very busy with the comings and goings of all sorts of well-heeled and illustrious visitors, from dukes and earls to princes and princesses, some from as far afield as Europe.

Kelley was in his element! It turned out that he was also a necromantic master of illusion and a practised ventriloquist. So he became a great hit with his mediumistic channellings from the "realms of the angels" with names such as Gabriel, Jubanladace, Uriel and Nalvage, and who had copious advice on how to make the Philosopher's Stone. [4]

Eventually, such was their popularity that there was nothing else for it but to undertake a Grand Tour of all the courts of Europe, demonstrating their magic trick. Thus, they spent more than three years being feted by various minor princes of Europe, just as it was beginning to bubble up into the Thirty Years War.

There was no Germany or France then. The continent was a patchwork quilt of tiny principalities that were starting to stretch their limbs from being under the iron grip of the Holy Roman Empire after Martin Luther pinned his notice to the church door in Wittenberg, calling out the corruption of the indulgence-taking popes and priests.

So, this was the volatile setting to Dee and Kelley's travelling fairground show, which they took, along with their wives, from one royal court to another, pretending to produce gold from base metal.

Their first port of call was the court of Prince Lasco in Poland, after Kelley had received "a message from the spirits" that Lasco and his descendants were "destined to rule all of Europe into all eternity" and that, therefore, he would need gold to raise an army.

When the gold failed to materialise, their host quickly tired of them and sent them packing with enough funds and an introductory letter to carry them as far as the court of Prince Stephen in Krakow, who, coincidentally, Kelley had just heard from his spirits, was "destined to rule all of Europe ... etc, etc.

Three months later, the rogues were sent packing again by a disappointed host and they headed for the court in Prague of Emperor Rudolph who, coincidentally, was "destined to rule ..." etc, etc.

Kelley received a similar channelled message about Count Rosenberg in Bohemia a year later, when they had to leave Prague.

His spirits even told him, apparently, that they should swap wives! Dee fell for it and, nine months later, poor Mrs Dee gave birth to a tiny Kelley.

But whenever their royal hosts had asked Dee how he had uncovered the alchemical process to create gold, he would tell them he had found the mysteries of the Philosopher's Stone in Dunstan's grave at Glastonbury Abbey.

Now, whether or not he actually visited Glastonbury, there is no record of it. But if he had meant

"Mysteries" with a capital M, he could have been telling the truth.

As we have discussed in previous chapters, the sacred geometry of the Vesica Piscis that produces the Philosopher's Stone must have been crystal clear to anyone trained in the Hermetic arts, as Dee surely was. It is writ large in the medieval architecture of the Old Church in Glastonbury Abbey, although Dee would have visited it centuries before Bligh Bond made the same discovery and forged its image on the lid of the Chalice Well.

But as you have probably guessed, I wouldn't be recounting the adventures of John Dee if I didn't have some fresh intelligence on the matter. There is another place in Avalon where, if John Dee had possessed a Time Machine, he could have found the Mysteries of the real Philosopher's Stone.

It is in the village of Baltonsborough and we will reach that destination once we've crossed a few more cognitive ditches and fences.

Soul Alchemy

Let's halt for a short while to discuss the processes of inner alchemy a little more deeply. Because what we will discover in Baltonsborough suggests that the coders of the codices were not selfishly hiding this alchemical process for just the privileged few to hoard the secret of making gold from lead. Well, not necessarily, anyway.

Of course, we could put it down to the Law of Unintended Consequences, which acts through a sort of blinkered short-termism that is blind to the Fibonacci spiral shell of reality. But to my way of thinking, some of these encoders were Grail Keepers acting as way-showers along the hidden path out of the labyrinthine matrix of Saturn's stygian, leaden realm into the golden sunlight of inner transformation and spiritual enlightenment.

I've heard it said that the great initiates of old were just using their masterworks to talk to each other, to signal to their peers that they were one of the *cognoscenti* who had the gnosis. I beg to differ – because it's a no-brainer to me that once you know the language of creation, your heart would be so full that you would want to use it to send a Valentine's Card to the creatrix itself. And wouldn't it be the greatest gift ever if your love letter to Mother Nature contained coded instructions for future generations to help them discover who "she" really is?

Well, I'll just park that thought with you for now because we need to get on to understanding the true nature of the Philosopher's Stone.

One of my favourite writers on soul alchemy is Catherine MacCoun, and here is her view[5] on the real meaning of the Philosopher's Stone.

> *The Philosopher's Stone is not a metal or a mineral. It's not a material object at all. So, what is it? Here's a hint from Mahatma Gandhi. Be the change you wish to see in the world.*
>
> *Maybe right now you read that as just a bumper sticker slogan. But one day you may be astonished that you've heard it for free, that it isn't buried deep in some Himalayan cave, guarded by high priests, dragons, vestal virgins and blood-guzzling Tibetan*

deities.

For Gandhi has let the cat entirely out of the bag, and given away the most mysterious and potent alchemical secret of them all. This is in the power to overthrow an empire. Take that literally.

So, let's break down the processes of the Great Work to see how the Philosopher's Stone could be used to overthrow an empire!

The metal lead was chosen by alchemists to represent the raw state of the unenlightened human because at its heart, it contains a tiny spark of gold which acts as the seed of its own resurrection. Some of them even referred to lead as "unripened gold", but that didn't mean it would turn to gold over time; it is a metaphor for the Saturnic captivity that humans are born into. We are the lead, the First Matter, the raw material that is to be taken through seven processes in order to release the gold spark. In the tale about Pinocchio, wood is used to represent the same unevolved state of the First Matter. The wooden puppet, through its adventures, was the subject of the Great Work of which the Philosopher's Stone is the fruit.

Changing lead into gold was only a metaphor for a larger process that involved the rejuvenation of the body; the integration of the personality, and the perfection of the human soul. Though they spoke of retorts, furnaces, acids and chemicals, the alchemists were really talking about changes taking place in their own bodies, minds, and spirits.

One of the central ideas of alchemy is that no transformation is complete and lasting unless it occurs simultaneously on all levels of reality – the physical, the mental and the spiritual. The distinction is what makes alchemy a unique discipline that combines the methods of science, psychology and religion.

"On the spiritual level, alchemy seeks to unite the opposing essences of soul and spirit in an operation known as the Sacred Marriage. The product of this union is the Philosopher's Stone, which in spiritual alchemy is the embodiment of a permanent state of perfected consciousness. [6]

This means that alchemical and astrological symbols in churches are like Trojan horses that carry the seeds of our own salvation. Clues have been left to us, in cipher form, by the wise church scribes, artists, sculptors, architects and builders, which represent the seeds of true Christianity. In other words, it is the real spiritual teaching in its purest state, before it was corrupted and bastardised into a literal history by Iraneus and subsequent Roman emperors.

The Hermeticists were also known as "natural philosophers" because they had discovered in Nature universal patterns that led to its ultimate transformation. It is a process in which a gold spark is held Captive in the metal lead, which can only be released by the Calling – otherwise known to the mythologist Joseph Campbell as the Call to Adventure – through the seven steps of the process of the Great Work that each represent the challenges needed to turn the lead into the Chosen, the gold.

Natural philosophers found that this organic blueprint could be applied as much as to the material creation of new worlds as to the transubstiation of the human soul. And so, their myths, paintings, stained-glass windows and sculptures all tell a tale that depicts the original pilgrim's progress through his Captivity in the dark Vale of Despair, which King David lamented in his *Psalms*, into becoming the Chosen and finally being reborn into the golden sunlight of day.

This seven-stepped process is also known as the Ladder of the Wise and the timings for each step of the process carried out in their crucibles or cruxes were crucial, which is why alchemists were also experts in astrology. **Figure 33** shows each step of the operation with its matching governing planets, Sun sign and astrological timings. It is a ladder, so you will need to read it from bottom to top. Begin with the first process, calcination, on the lowest rung.

The Ladder of the Wise is the alchemical blueprint for the passage of our lives. We slowly climb its rungs as we face the challenges that mould us and lead us towards metamorphosis. Each of us is born at differing stages of the pilgrimage of the Great Work. But we all benefit from progress that is accrued over previous lifetimes and the work of our ancestors in their relationships with the Fae.

In other words, this is the real meaning of the eternal life sought by the champions of many a heroic tale, from Gilgamesh to Arthur.

According to this philosophy, the day, time and place of our births were all carefully planned, right down to the second when we took our first screaming lungful of air. The stars that greet us as we emerge from the birth passage are organised in a customised arrangement in the skies. Thus is set in motion the spinning Wheel to provide the major landmarks, milestones, crossroads and way stations of the long and winding road of our lives, and all of which create the needed challenges for our eventual transformation at the last stage of coagulation. The final step, which is the result of the Child Tension Victory, is considered to be something of a miracle, an act of Grace if you like, and it is also referred to as the "quickening".

You may have noticed at certain times that there seems to be something of a quickening that is taking place in your own spiritual or psychological evolution.

Pilgrims who visit Avalon often get a sense of the quickening as soon as they arrive. We think that the cause is a sort of landscape geometry which creates terrestrial alchemy and you'll learn all about this in subsequent chapters. But in one person's opinion "the Glastonbury Experience" was like living in a deck of Tarot cards. Yuri Leitch says Avalon is "a very powerful synchronicity accelerator", which would certainly explain why you always seem to bump into just the right person on Glastonbury High Street – or even just the wrong person if you're trying to avoid your fate. It can be fun; it can be blissful; but it is by no means always a path of perfumed roses.

Figure 33 Timings for seven stages of alchemical operation

Rung	Process	Planet	Best times
7	Coagulation	Sun	Gemini (Fixation) Aquarius (Multiplication) Pisces (Projection)
6	Distillation	Moon	Virgo, (Distillation) Libra (Sublimation)
5	Fermentation	Mercury	Capricorn, (Fermentation) Leo (Digestion)
4	Conjunction	Venus	Taurus (Beltane)
3	Separation	Mars	Scorpio
2	Dissolution	Jupiter	Cancer (solution)
1	Calcination	Saturn	Aries (calcination) Sagittarius (incineration)

Many of us feel Avalon has been a very special place for a long time and that the medieval monks would have likely had the role in helping the pilgrims through their own personal quickenings. They have certainly left enough evidence that they knew of this inner path. And so, once we learn how to decode the great masterpieces that are preserved in the churches, abbeys and cathedrals, they reveal themselves as way-showers for the process of the transformation of metals in which we ourselves are subjects of the Great Work.

Quicksilver Messenger Service

Each metal is assigned a god or goddess to encapsulate its qualities and we can see these characteristics writ large in the classical Greek dramas about the gods and goddesses of Mount Olympus.

For instance, Ares (the Roman Mars) is always portrayed as passionate and warlike, while Chronos (the Roman Jupiter) is jubilant, outgoing and adventurous. And so, if they are combined and processed, in the right way at the right time, with the quicksilver messenger, Hermes (the Roman Mercury), they manage to charm and trick the strict schoolmaster Chronos (the Roman Saturn) into dissolving some of his stiffly held boundaries. When the walls of the old world fall, it creates chaos in the short term. But then Aphrodite (the Roman Venus), the personification of harmonious beauty, sweeps in with her blessings of order and proportion for the new world.

Each of these deities rules one or more astrological signs and thus the timings of the seven stages of the Great Work. The first stage of calcination is always begun under the fiery Aries, which is ruled by Mars, at the Spring Equinox. Then the second stage of dissolution is performed during the time of watery Cancer, which is under the rulership of the Moon, and so on.

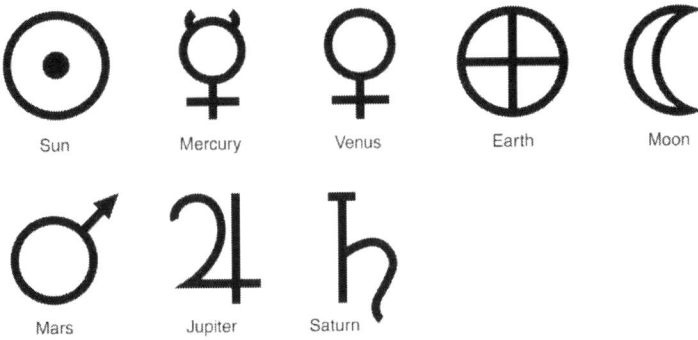

Figure 34 The ciphers for the gods and goddesses of the zodiac

Figure 35 below shows Yuri Leitch's illustration of the order in which the Roman gods and goddess are arranged around the zodiac. He based it on a carving of the birth of the god Mithras found on Hadrian's Wall, which was built in the second century to delineate the northern limits of the Roman empire.

Yuri's drawing illustrates the doubling or mirroring functions of the rulers of each Sun sign. For instance, Mars rules Aries and Scorpio, Jupiter rules Sagittarius and Pisces, Venus rules Taurus and Libra, Mercury rules Gemini and Virgo, and Saturn rules Capricorn and Aquarius.

The zodiac hero always meets his judgment in Jupiter-ruled Sagittarius and his death in Saturn-ruled Capricorn. He is then reborn as the Radiant Child and his earliest years are spent going through Aquarius, which is also ruled by Saturn. So, because Saturn rules both the beginning and end of life, he is known as the Alpha and Omega, the First and the Last.

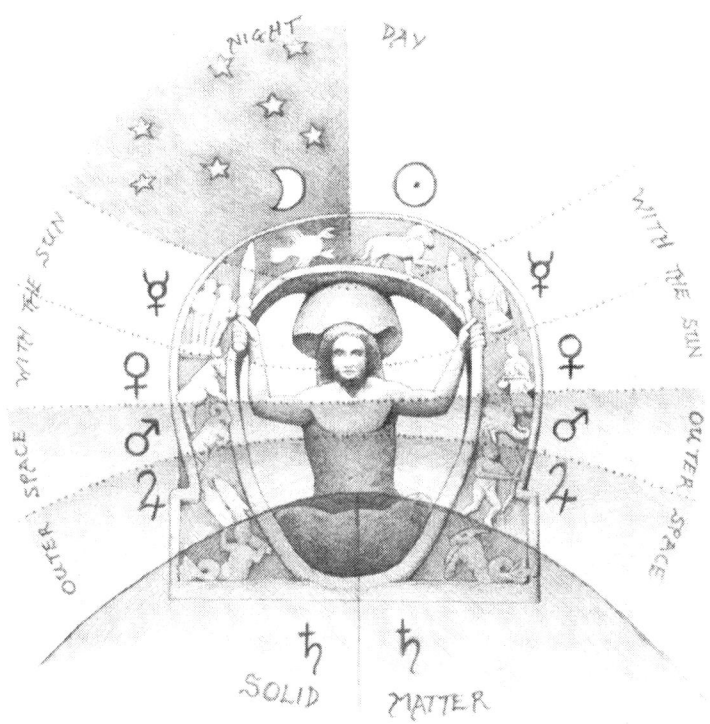

Figure 35 The Mithraic Rock Birth by Yuri Leitch

Now let's look at some religious stories and paintings from medieval and Renaissance times, to identify symbols within them for the transmutation of metals that are in themselves metaphors for the spiritual transformation of the human being.

In much of Renaissance art, the Madonna is depicted in a blue cloak with a red lining, or a blue cloak covering a red dress underneath. It is an alchemical cipher for Venus and her associated metal of copper, which burns with a blue-green flame that flashes sporadically with red sparks.

She is often found with the Child of the Philosopher, or Philosopher's Stone, on her lap or at her breast. It is meant to imply the nature of copper as the mother of the Great Work, because it has the ability to balance and raise the energies of other metals in the same way that harmony and order is expressed through the feminine nature of the mother of the family.

The Philosopher's Stone is the same stone out of which the mythological babes Sosruquo and Zeus are born. If you remember, Satana needed a smith – a transmuter of metals - to break open the stone and reveal within the Radiant Child, which symbolises the success of the Great Work.

Next we will talk about Jupiter, which is appropriate as we are currently coming on to that part of Avalon that is ruled by the jovial, expansive one, and I'll explain how that all works in the next chapter.

There is a local legend about Jesus's uncle of whom it is said: "Joseph was a tin man." As already discussed, it is unlikely that Joseph of Arimathea was a tin trader or even that he existed in history. It is more probable that the J in his name stood for Jupiter, which governs the metal of tin. It would certainly be quite fitting for the "uncle" of the Child of the Philosopher because Jupiterian-ruled tin releases the divine spark from its dark Saturnic captivity in the metal lead, much as Jesus was released from his gloomy, tenebrous tomb.

And now we come on to Mercury, whose role is vital. No alchemical operation can succeed without the intervention of the quicksilver messenger. Mercury's metal is called quicksilver and that might be because it is the only one that remains liquid at room temperature and thus flows more quickly and easily than any others.

Alchemists regard the god Mercury as the messenger who carried the catalytic life principle and so mercury-ruled materials are used as the animator or life-giving force of their operations. The symbol for this life principle is found in the twisting serpents that crawl up the caduceus and also in the double-helix of DNA. In Celtic lore, this vital messenger force is known as the Rivers of Blood; in the gospel stories of the New Testament, it is the "message" that is delivered to the womb of Mary (Venus) by the angel Gabriel, which leads to the birth of the Radiant Child.

The poetic children of the quicksilver god Mercury are the words "message", "memory", "measure", "meaning", "marine", "metal", "mettle" and "memes".

And so, in understanding the metaphors for the processes of the alchemical Great Work, we benefit from the messages carried by the once and always and forevermore mercurial force, which those who came before us intoned sonically into our Rivers of Blood.

Those messages come to us in our dreams as memes that invoke memories which reach out to us, over the submarinal oceans of Time, like messages in a glass bottle blown from the sands of Saturn's hourglass: the trickling sands by which our human span is measured. And while the costumes of the characters or the scenery may change over the ages, the meaning of the messages are always the same: we are being ground in these dark Saturnic mills in order to test our mettle.

Fools and Heroes

And so, here we find ourselves, the star, the hero of the drama, playing the lead-ing role of the Fool, the unevolved, leaden human, who takes birth with a series of pre-arranged missions designed to evolve his soul but who, once here, drinks a draught of forgetfulness and falls asleep to who he truly is and the purpose of his life.

Thankfully, the symbols and metaphors used in these multi-level, textured works appeal to a part of the brain that is beyond logic and reason. Thus, they reawaken the dormant Self of the Fool through the shamanic dreams and visions sparked by the subconscious mind, and then steered into conscious awareness by the gods and goddesses in the forms of our spirit guides.

We sometimes call these Otherworldly "voices" our instincts, which are continually making us feel that we came here on Earth to do something… but what it actually is escapes us. However, this feeling drives us like an incurable itch and it turns us into sleuths and truth seekers in the hope that some day we will become a truth finder. Then as we proceed, we begin to realise that what we once thought was "the truth" about history is turning out to be a mirage. As Count Tolstoy once opined: "History would be a wonderful thing if only it were true."

As we proceed, we begin to realise that our "history" has been written by the victors and any story that doesn't fit the new narrative, at such times, is just used as fuel for the book burnings.

However, it takes a huge leap of faith – in a

world that has been lying to us ever since we took birth – to head for the *omphalos* rock upon which to build our new cognitive "house" now that the Clockmaker's sands are shifting under the old one.

The real truth about the meaning of human life has been hidden deep in multi-layered stories that have been intoned by the ancients into our Rivers of Blood within our subconscious minds, memories of which are triggered in our dreams and visions by alchemical and zodiacal symbols found in medieval architecture and Renaissance art.

Like the iceberg that sunk the Titanic, seven-eighths of who we really are is invisible to us, under the sea of consciousness. Yet it is the captain that steers the Captive's ship. In other words, the subconscious mind knows why we have incarnated into human life and it is ready to help us sail towards that destiny.

But, as Carl Jung discovered, until we can learn how to make our subconscious conscious, through the practice of the Mystery Teachings, we will be for ever at the mercy of terrifying sea serpents, beguiling sirens and wicked brigands and pirates.

Like Luke Skywalker in the Star Wars films, the pilgrim is challenged by the old Empire's Stormtroopers or the trickster Jabba the Hutt – all prototypes of antagonists that are vital to the process of transmutation.

Luke Skywalker follows the archetypal hero in that he learns a little more from each encounter with the "enemy", and thus becomes more and more adept at working with the Force until the final showdown of the death-rebirth experience in which he has to face and defeat his father, Darth Vader, who has "fallen" down into the Underworld of the Dark Side.

Harry Potter is another character whose journey follows an alchemical trajectory. J. K. Rowling's books about the schoolboy magician evolve over three parts, which correlates with the three alchemical stages of nigredo (black), albedo (white) and rubedo (red).

Harry's initial long, black nigredo phase culminates in Harry Potter and the Order of the Phoenix. All that he tries to achieve fails and goes badly wrong, and this reaches a chilling climax in the death of his adored godfather, Sirius Black.

In Harry Potter and the Half Blood Prince, the narrative centres on the death of Albus Dumbledore – Albus is Latin for "white" and hence it symbolises the white albedo stage of the operation.

Then Harry has to face the Deathly Hallows. Harry's friend Rubeus Hagrid is forced to take part in a death march, symbolising the fall into the Underworld, to commemorate the "killing" of Harry. Thus, this last section of the series represents the final processes of the Great Work, the red rubedo stage.

The Grailkeeper of Baltonsborough

So, we have now reached the final stage of a winding path that has led us to the small village of Baltonsborough.

There we can see a stunning artefact that seems to be a recipe for the Great Work writ large in glorious vivid colours on a stained glass window that was bequeathed to St Dunstan's Church in 1850 by the then Squire of Butleigh's wife, Julia Neville-Grenville (see **Figure 36**). The design on the west window is a classic example of how one story can hide and yet also reveal another, perhaps reminiscent of the saying "the bee pollinates the flower that it robs". The occluded message is woven through a surface Christian story with a golden thread only visible to those trained in how to read it.

I only discovered this window recently and the first signal that alerted me to look more closely, to see if it was an alchemical cipher, was when I noticed that the four evangelists - Matthew, Mark, Luke and John – although represented as the winged beasts of the tetramorph are in a different order.

It is the same order that Iraneus used in compiling the canon of the four gospels and that caused me to me wonder whether that ordering was to give a clue to astrological timings for the Great Work.

If all this sounding way too complicated, let me break it down further.

Bible scholars are still arguing today about when the canon of the four gospels was ordered as Matthew, Mark, Luke and John. But the general consensus is that it was somewhere between 200 and 400 CE. However, my point is, coincidence or not, they are ordered to show the timings of the processes to create the Philosopher's Stone, as they are also on the window in St Dunstan's Church, Baltonsborough.

If you remember, the original saltire cross is governed by the beasts of the tetramorph, a shown in **Figure 37**. It shows a much older way of dividing the festivals of the year, known as the cross-quarter days of Imbolc, Beltane, Lughnasadh and Samhain. The four creatures are the Man (Matthew) at Aquarius, the Bull

(Luke) at Taurus, the Lion (Mark) at Leo, and the Eagle (John) at Scorpio. These are the same four creatures found in the Book of Revelation[7] and can be seen as a progression of the pilgrim Man who begins his progress at Aquarius after the birth or rebirth at Capricorn.

Each of the four panels on the stained glass window at Baltonsborough is governed by a member of the tetramorph, the governors of the four quarters, and they are shown as winged beasts on the lower panes. However, they are not in the "right" order for the older saltire cross-quarter festivals.

They are, however, in line with the canon, indicating to my mind that the sequence of the four gospels could have been intended to show the timings of the processes of the alchemical Great Work.

Figure 36 Symbols on west window of St Dunstan's Church

Figure 37 *The tetramorph symbols and cross-quarter days*

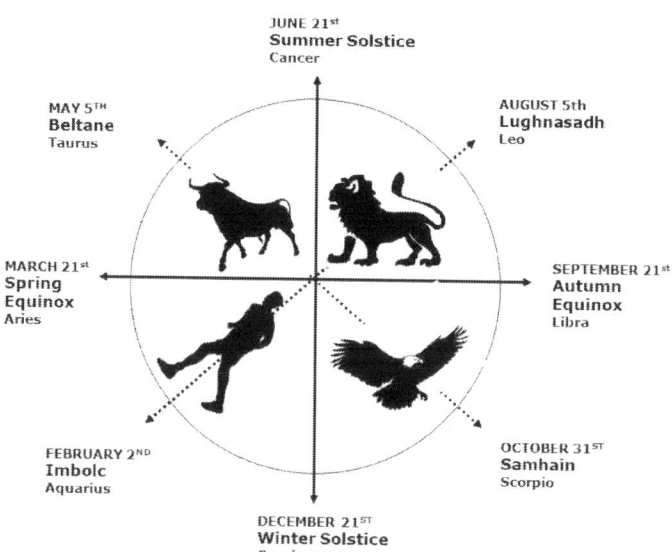

Decoding the window

What follows is a chart, in **Figure 38**, containing my interpretation of the illustrations on the stained-glass window above the altar in St Dunstan's Church, Baltonsborough: [8]

Figure 38 Alchemical interpretation of stained glass window

PANEL ONE – IVY

Metal: Lead
Element: Fire
Governing planets: Saturn and Mars
Astrological timing: Imbolc/ Spring Equinox
Alchemical stage: Calcination

The design of the backdrop is of Ivy, a plant ruled by Saturn.

The symbol at the top of this panel is the Alpha and Omega, which was the "first and last". Some Christians call Jesus the "first and last". However, under the Hermeticists, the Alpha and Omega is the god who rules the first and last signs of the Saturnic mill of the revolving zodiac at Capricorn and Aquarius. It is Saturn, the Father of Time and the Grim Reaper.

The middle frame shows a lamb or ram, which is the sign for Aries, at the Spring Equinox, ruled by Mars. Medieval alchemists would begin their operation of the Great Work on the day of the Spring Equinox in Aries, when fiery Mars was dominant, in order to fuel their fires. This first stage is known as calcination.

The lower frame represents Aquarius with the sign of Man. In other words, the Man is presenting himself as the base material to be purified and transformed by the Great Work. He represents the unrefined lead that has taken incarnation for his soul, the spark of gold, to be released from captivity. The alchemical process of the Four Joys and Four Sorrows releases the spark of divinity held captive within the leaden spirit, to transform the man into the gold of the winged man seen here.

The winged Aquarian Man of Imbolc is represented on the Christian tetramorph by the apostle Matthew.

----000----

PANEL TWO – OAK

Metal: Tin
Element: Water
Governing planets: Jupiter and the Moon
Astrological timing: Lughnasadh/Summer Solstice
Alchemical stage: Dissolution

The design of the backdrop is of Oak, which is a tree ruled by Jupiter.

The symbol at the top is of Jupiter with its moons. Jupiter is also found in the mythic character of the tin merchant Joseph of Arimathea; the metal of Jupiter is tin. The Romans considered tin to be a perfected form of lead, naming it *plumbrum album*, or "white lead".

Jupiter is always portrayed as a jovial, expansive and adventurous god. Here, he represents the light and energy that is needed to break the soul out of the prison of its heavy, Saturnic darkness. But it must also be carefully controlled. It represents the stage of dissolution, which is best carried out during the time of Cancer, ruled by the Moon.

While the chalice of the middle pane symbolises the Eucharist to Christians, it represents, alchemically, the vessel containing the liquid of dissolution which is made up of the red and white serpentine drops, which we will come on to in more detail later.

The winged Lion in the lowest pane is the Red Lion of alchemy. It symbolises the control that must be achieved at this stage, which, if successful, results in the production of the sublimated salt that will be used to make the Philosopher's Stone.

The winged Leo Lion of Lughnasadh is represented on the Christian tetramorph as the apostle Mark.

PANEL THREE - LILY

Metal: Quicksilver/Mercury
Element: Air
Governing planets: Mercury
Astrological timing: Beltane
Alchemical stage: Conjunction, Separation and Fermentation

The design of the backdrop is of Lily which is ruled by Mercury.

In mystic Christianity, the lily represents the regeneration of life through sacrifice, just as the lily's bulb ferments and decays in the ground to be "reborn" again.

However, the lily is also ruled by Mercury, which is symbolised by the Dove at the top – or the Holy Spirit. This holy spirit is the catalyst which brings the magic to the operation.

The middle pane shows an image of three nails in the crown of thorns. In Christian symbolism, this is the Passion of Jesus's sacrifice. But it also represents, alchemically, the Three Magisteriums.

These are the three different stages of purification that initiates pass through to reach the Marriage of the Sun and the Moon. The same metaphor is found in the Nativity story about the three *magi* or kings who follow the star to find the baby Jesus in the manger in Bethelehem.

It is about three different types of functions of the metal mercury which leads to what 17th century alchemists called "wise man's sulphur".

The winged bull of the lowest pane represents Taurus, or Beltane, which is the best time to begin the Conjunction phase of the operation.

The Taurean Bull of Beltane in the Christian tetramorph is the apostle Luke.

PANEL FOUR – VINE

Metal: Copper
Element: Earth
Governing planet: Venus
Astrological timing: Winter Solstice
Alchemical stage: Distillation leading to Coagulation

The design of the backdrop is of the grapevine, which is ruled by Venus.

The symbol at the top is IHS - the Greek letters *iota*, *eta* and *sigma*. When capitalised, it spells out ΙΗΣΟΥΣ or Jesus who, in his own words, is the True Vine.

The Marriage at Cana (**Note 9**) – in which Jesus turns water into wine – is thought to be a Hermetic metaphor for a different kind of wedding, one in which the transformation of a base substance into its true divine inner nature leads to the alchemical Marriage of the Sun and the Moon. Venus is also the Christian Mary Magdalene, the *cuen* of Jesus Christ.

The middle panel shows a classical alchemical symbol – a pelican that is feeding its young with the blood it pecks from its own breast. The bird represents the long-necked, two-armed vessel which is used for the Distillation phase.

The Marriage of the Sun and the Moon in Avalon takes place on May Day, or Beltane, when the Sun is in Taurus at Beltane, and the moon is in Scorpio, which is represented, in the lower pane, by the winged Eagle at Samhain.

The Scorpio Eagle of Samhain in the Christian tetramorph is the apostle John. The resulting birth of the Philosopher's Child – the goal of the whole operation - takes place nine months after the conception, on the Winter Solstice.

----000----

You will soon be learning much more about how the story of the Marriage of the Sun and the Moon has been carved into the land of Avalon.

Now that we have a few basic principles packed into our rucksacks, we have ample provisions for our journey into the next level where we will meet the Call to Adventure.

[1] *The Complete Idiot's Guide to Alchemy* by Dennis W. Hauck.
[2] There's a whole chapter in *Stories in Stars* that dissects, in much greater detail, the astrological and alchemical understory in *The Adventures of Pinocchio* by Carlos Collodi.
[3] *Monas Hieroglyphica* (1564), *De Trigono* (1565), *Testamentum Johannis Dee Philosophi Summi ad Johannem Guryun Transmissum* (1568) and *An Account of the Manner in which a Certayn Copper-smith in the Land of Moores, and a Certayn Moore Transmuted Copper to Gold* (1576).
[4] *A True and Faithful Relation of What Passed between Dr. Dee and Some Spirits; Tending, Had it Succeeded, to a General Alteration of Most States and Kingdoms in the World* by Meric Casaubon.
[5] *On Becoming An Alchemist: A guide for the modern magician* by Catherine MacCoun.
[6] *The Complete Idiot's Guide to Alchemy* by Dennis W. Hauck.
[7] Just to make matters even more complicated, *Revelation 4:6-7* gives a different order: "And before the throne there was a sea of glass like unto crystal: and in the midst of the throne, and round about the throne, were four beasts full of eyes before and behind. And the first beast was like a lion, and the second beast like a calf, and the third beast had a face as a man, and the fourth beast was like a flying eagle."
[8] After studying and practising alchemy for about 10 years, I still regard myself as a complete beginner. So I offer this interpretation in the spirit of the proverb: "In the land of the blind, the one-eyed man is king." However, if there are any two-eyed emperors out there, who can offer a more informed view, please do get in touch.
[9] John 2:1-11, John 2: 3-5 and John 2:6-10

PART TWO: The Called

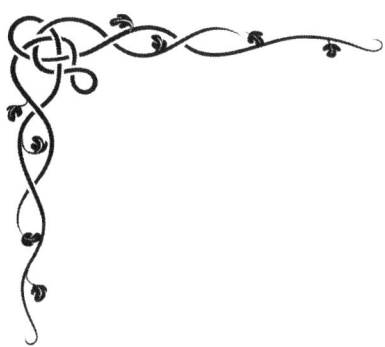

Chapter Nine: The Quest of Avalon

Just as the medieval Glastonbury monks sifted and sorted the wheat from the chaff in the inner cognitive landscapes of their flocks, in order to replant and cultivate the seeds of a new narrative into consensual reality, so they also altered the outer landscape. They drained the salt marshes of the low-lying alluvial levels and re-routed the rivers so that the green and fertile valleys and hills could be used for the growing of barley and the grazing of sheep and cows.

However, in emptying a miles-wide, cauldron-shaped bowl rimmed by the limestone caves of the Mendips and the chalky hills of the Poldens, they unwittingly revealed the outlines of actors of a drama much older and far richer than even the black peat which was lain down after the glaciers of the last Ice Age melted, and saltier than the seas that had submerged them.

As you proceed into this Call to Adventure, you

will be learning about a few of those tales. Like those that Tabiti recited in her sing-song voice around the campfire, they have a haunting and visionary quality, and contain seeds that flower and fruit over time. So, don't be surprised if they come tiptoeing softly into your dreamscapes to wake up your Rivers of Blood to the wisdom of an Age that Time forgot, when a man's dreams were valued more than gold and a real song could birth new worlds from old.

To the modern way of thinking, it seems scarcely credible that our earlier ancestors would have gone to such enormous efforts to geo-engineer the land into a nocturnal theatre. We would be hard pressed today to even find the words to justify any kind of rationale for such an enormous task. However, by entering into the timeless realms ourselves, we shamans meet the ancient sages and *mages* who transmit to us the same wisdom teachings, through stories, song and dance.

So now some of us are beginning to get more tuned to the thinking of those who had a more holographic or shamanic understanding about their place in the Universe. And in bringing our own way of seeing into line with theirs, their rhyme and reason reveals itself to be *sine qua non*. After all, we too have had our cognitive processes carved into shape by the sagas we've been told.

As Shelley once said: "Poets are the secret legislators of the world."

Stories are what makes the world go around. We all live according to the weave of the narrative that we've received from birth, so much so that we'd find it difficult to leave our beds in the mornings unless there was an Ariadne-like red thread or winding yarn to show us the way through the labyrinth of our day.

We become attached to our own stories because they are all we have to guide us, and that's why we get quite upset when someone tells us another that doesn't chime with "our own". I put "our own" in inverted commas, because unless it's one that can be traced back to the mythological seedbed on our part of the primordial carpet, it is rarely actually "our own". But Nature abhors a vacuum. So, in the absence of the sagas, songs and rhymes from our old folk to guide our life's path, we tend, like a sleepwalker stumbling along a landing, to grab hold of the rope railings of any tall tale we're given.

I'm finding that the further back in time we go, the more wisdom the old myths contain. That's why I dig and dig and dig, looking for the indigenous teachings of those ancient ones whose Rivers of Blood run through our veins in the Bright World Above, and through the dark caverns of the Land Below in which those who came before us are buried – often in the very spot where they fell fighting to defend this sacred soil for future generations.

The Blessed Isles of Britain have been our homeland for at least six thousand years, due to the efforts of innumerable generations who worked with the spirits of the land in protecting the Sovereignty and holding the sacred space. They were not altruistic. They were acting in their own enlightened self-interest, because they understood the importance of claiming the Sovereignty of their territory for their children and grandchildren to be able to survive and thrive into the future.

It seems to me that the more a civilisation comes away from the stories of the wise Elders who came before us, the more it can be persuaded, to the point of bullying, to act in the interests of pathological altruism rather than in its own enlightened self-interest. It is how our enemies weaken us from within, making us much more susceptible to falling to those who have no compunction about acting in their own good, and Nature will favour the, because they are more intelligent than us in the matter of survival. After all, why would She bother to keep around beings so blasé about the extraordinary gift of human life as to throw away their own inheritance and that of future generations?

We can see this throughout history, even in the past few centuries. How many indigenous tribes have been removed from their traditional lands? How could that happen if these native tribes were led by people wiser than us? Or was it because they lost touch with their roots, with their ancestral spirits in their own soil, and thus were more easily persuaded to adopt foreign stories that their enemies gave them?

This is why we owe a huge debt of gratitude to the Grail Keepers like Taliesin, Dunstan and the Company of Avalon, for weaving the golden threads of allegorical codes into their illuminated codices. They have also allowed us to discover the raison d'etre for our human pilgrimage of life by preserving these Mystery Plays in the "aspic" of unchanging mathematical, astrological and alchemical formulae that contain great wisdom about the genesis and meaning of life. Their hope was that one day, millennia hence, their descendants would rediscover their place within the vast cosmological processes and mark their joyous gratitude for such an opportunity, to take part within this cosmic Dance of the Hours, with ceremonies held at the right Space and Time around the face of Saturn's grandfather clock.

The birthing of new worlds from old was a constant preoccupation of our earliest ancestors. They fully understood themselves to be in a holographic relationship with the realms Above and Below, through which Nature continually resurrects Herself with sequences of numbers, frequencies and vibrations that continually spin to create spiralling symphonies of energies which dance to the beat of the Sun and the rhythm of the Moon.

So, they told their young people stories about a divine coupling and intercourse between the Sun and the Moon that produced the Radiant Child.

It was both a science teaching and a spiritual one. And as it was Above, so Below in that it was as much about the marriage of the Sun and Moon within our own inner landscapes, the one that governs our own spiralling spiritual evolution. Thus, the fruit of this union, the Child, was called Radiant because he or she represented the inner light of pure illumination that shines through the brow of one such enlightened.

So, for the next few chapters, I'm going to show this story has been built into the very fabric of the Earth of Avalon. As usual, it will be a stepped learning process, so your mind won't get boggled with too much information all at once. Instead, I will give you just enough to help build your foundation first and then gradually add each new concept block, one upon the other, until you have the whole construct.

Earth Mysteries and Astro-Archaeology

It is well known that our earliest ancestors, before the Agricultural Revolution, were hunter-gatherers who led a nomadic lifestyle. What is not so well-known is that they didn't just wander randomly, following their noses. They followed circular paths delineated by huge earthworks that matched where the constellations fell to Earth, and they formed the foundations for the earliest zodiacs.

The surprising number of these peripatetic courses across the globe are currently only known to a handful of visionary researchers in the field of Earth Mysteries. One of them is Anthony Thorley, a retired psychiatrist who is currently doing a PhD on the conceptual basis of landscape zodiacs as sacred space. He told me recently that he has found more than 80 possible examples of such astrologically aligned earthworks worldwide and that there could be more than 40 in the British Isles alone – which begs the question "Why?".

As Anthony Thorley said, in a speech to the 2010 *Megolithomania Conference* in Glastonbury:

> *A landscape zodiac is a representation of the signs and symbolism found in the texture and morphology of rural and urban landscapes which broadly mirrors the zodiac in the constellations of the ecliptic.*
>
> *It is created by something called informational coherence: an accumulating aggregation in a*

landscape, across and through time, of a matrix of closely related information leading to a recognition, or a moment of recognition, of the nature of the whole. A tissue of synchrony with the whole being greater than the sum of the parts.

It is a phenomenon too complex to be solely and simply coordinated and created by men and women.

In other words, Thorley intuits that there is another agency at work, besides that of humans. It may be the same force that causes so many who visit or live in Avalon to believe that they have been called here, although they can often spend years and years in trying to discover just why they have been so summoned. Eventually, some stumble across what has been termed, by author and medieval scholar Hank Harrison, "astro-archaeology". This is the study of how the stories that our ancestors carved out in the stars and mirrored on the land have been used since time immemorial to help initiates along the path of self-realisation.

The Glastonbury Temple of the Stars

So here we are now in the most sacred part of the land of Avalon - a 10-mile-wide circle of giant earthwork effigies that are delineated by water courses, contour lines, tracks, lanes and field boundaries, which are mirror images of the constellations above. It is as if the starry giants have had a great battle in the heavens and fallen to the land. Some call it the Glastonbury Zodiac. But it is much more than a just a flat circle divided into Sun signs and, probably for that reason, the Grail Keeper who discovered it in the early 20th century named it the Glastonbury Temple of the Stars.

This huge, sprawling earthwork ring of "sleeping giants" first came in a visionary way to the freemason and sculptor Katharine Maltwood as she sat at her desk by her study window, which overlooked the Somerset Levels. Already an artist and sculptress of some renown, she was designing a cover for a new edition of The High History of the Holy Grail[1].

Her travels worldwide had given her an abiding interest in Buddhism, Egyptology and Theosophy, and so she was able to view these earthwork characters through the lens of myth and magic. She was married to a millionaire whose company invented the Oxo cube, so she was able to commission the Royal Navy Air Service, as the Royal Air Force was called then, to take aerial photographs of the area, to see if her hunch was correct.

Once she began to study these photos in more detail, she soon realised that there were 13 gigantic humans and creatures marked out in a huge circle on the landscape. Over time, she gradually came to realise that not only were these "giants" laid out in a way that reflected the constellations above but they seemed to be characters from the Arthurian sagas recounted in the book for which she was creating the new jacket.

In 1934, Maltwood published her first book on the subject, *Glastonbury's Temple of the Stars*[2]. In it, she showed the outlines of these giant earthwork effigies with their "thirteen heads all designedly pointing towards the sunset", all arranged in a circle and each one mirroring where their matching constellation "fell to the Earth."

She brought out a further book on the subject,

Enchantments of Britain, published toward the end of the Second World War and in which she wrote:

> *King Arthur's Round Table was not just a piece of furniture as might be supposed but something vastly more worthy upon which to found a Knightly Order; it was the Round Table of the Stars. This design was found laid out on the ground near Glastonbury and it is 30 miles in circumference, the earthworks which form it were constructed by the Early Bronze Age inhabitants; it constitutes a sculptural relief of unequalled magnitude.*

Figure 39 is based upon Maltwood's vision of the Temple of the Stars. Now I can quite understand if you're wondering whether this is some kind of practical joke or a Rorschach ink blot test. It confused me too, at first sight. However, once I began to investigate this map more carefully, by which I mean journeying into to it, shamanically, to gain guidance from the spirits, I soon began to learn more about it.

Firstly, I discovered that the effigies were characters from ancient, orally-transmitted myths that are freeze-frozen in motion, like cartoon characters in an old-fashioned, flickering flip book – which was all we had for animation until Walt Disney came along.

Secondly, you get a much better sense of the narrative of this revolving theatre of the gods when the map is flipped the other way around, as if you are viewing the action from the vantage point of above Glastonbury Tor, as shown in **Figure 40**.

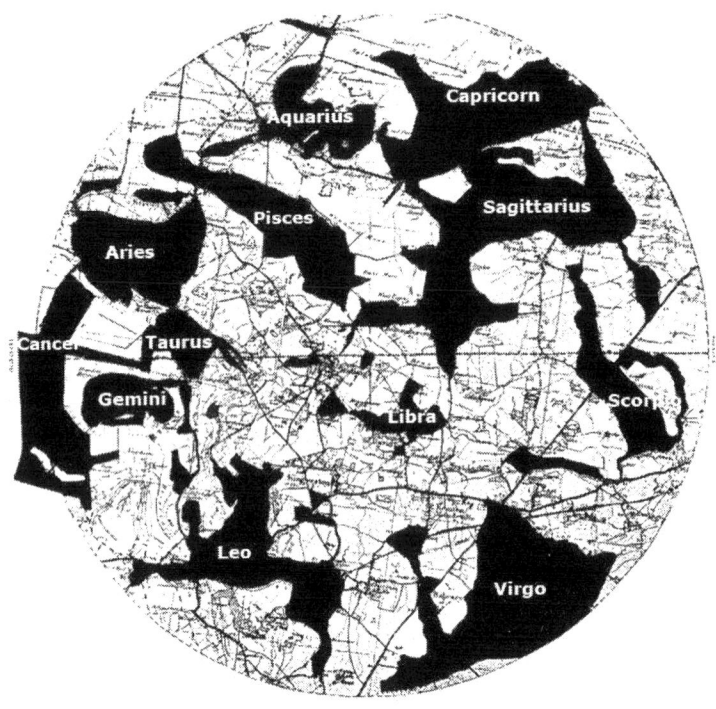

Figure 39 The constellations on the Temple of the Stars

An added benefit of this vantage point is that it allows the astrological symbols to follow the perceived passage of the Sun from its zenith at the Summer Solstice and its nadir at the Winter Solstice. This puts it in line with older zodiacs.

The new viewing point southwards puts Cancer and Leo closer to the top to reflect the Sun rising to its highest, most northerly point, which peaks on the long, bright days of the Summer Solstice. Equally, Sagittarius and Capricorn are at its base, which is when the Sun "sinks into the Underworld" at its most southerly extreme, on the Winter Solstice.

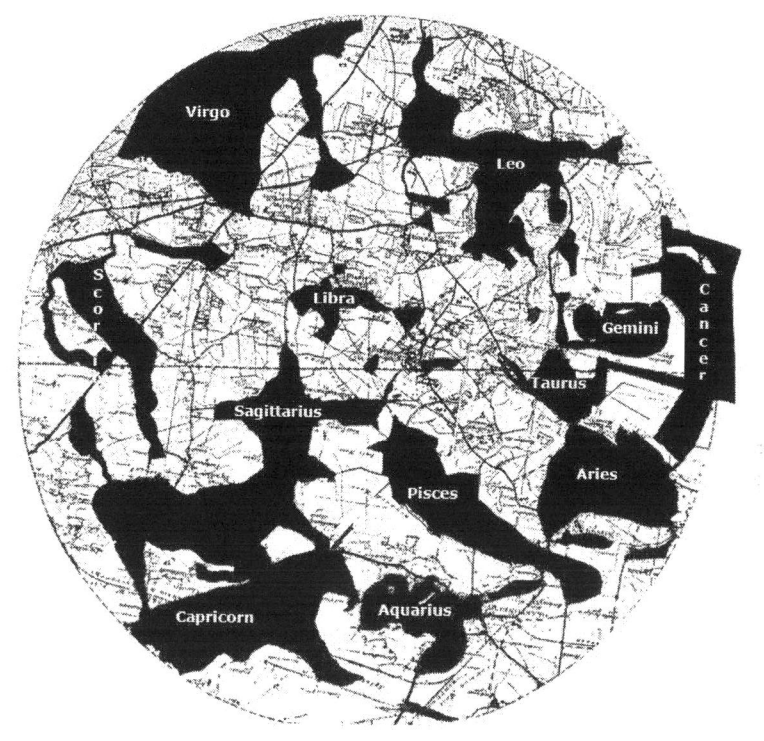

Figure 40 Glastonbury Temple of the Stars looking south

Glastonbury Tor resembles a long-necked bird in flight. Both Maltwood and Fortune saw, in this shape, a firebird or phoenix, which would have fitted with the politically fashionable views of the Theosophists that the tin-merchant Phoenicians were here in Britain.

However, if you dig under that gloss, it could be a long-necked swan in flight. Irish lore is full of these graceful birds so beloved of monarchs, from the Children of Lir who were turned into swans by their jealous stepmother to Aengus, who wandered all over the world looking for his beloved, Ibormeith, only to find she had shapeshifted into a swan.

There is a carving of a swan at the prehistoric Avebury stone circle. Another was found more recently, at the equally old Irish passage mound of Knowth, which is aligned with the Winter Solstice. It depicts a swan gazing at a sunburst. This is a familiar motif found in megalithic artworks worldwide and it is considered to be a sort of timestamp view of the heavens showing the position of Cygnus the Swan at the Winter Solstice.

Richard Wagner would have been inspired by these tales for his opera about the Grail Knight Lohengrin, who travels in a boat drawn by swans. The most popular part of the opera is the *Bridal Chorus*, better known as "Here Comes the Bride". I wonder if Wagner knew that the white swan is one of the totem animals of Bridie or Brigit, whose festival of Imbolc is celebrated during the February days of Aquarius?

Glastonbury Tor represents Aquarius on the zodiac, in which falls the festival of Imbolc, dedicated to Bridie. It is also cognate with Cygnus during the winter months.

So now I'm going to invite you to perch yourself on one of its wings and make yourself comfortable for a stellar ride. Imagine it is nighttime and the stars are glistening like diamonds above you. You soar heavenwards and then you look down, to your left, towards Ponter's Ball.

There you see a great horned beast, under the constellation of Capricorn. Above that giant, under the stars of Sagittarius, there's a rider falling off his mount, and then over the horse's tail, under Scorpio, there's a scorpion.

Next, mirroring Virgo, there's a woman wearing a long dress who seems to be holding out an object of some kind. Could it be the Holy Grail? And is it just a coincidence that it falls under the stars of Crater, the cup?

Suddenly, you notice that there's a bird flying between the upturned arm of the Sagittarian rider and the woman, and that it is below the stars of Corvus, the Crow.

If you look straight down, you'll see an enormous whale under the Cetus constellation, attributed to Pisces on the zodiac.

To the right, under Aries, there is an earthwork that looks like a ram or lamb with its head turned. Above Aries, the head of the bull of Taurus seems to be overlooking the image of a baby, at Gemini, and it is in a boat that is moored under the stars of Argo Navis, which, huge though it is, is just one sub-constellation of Cancer.

Finally, the resupine Lion of Leo is straight ahead, at Somerton.

You won't be able to see the 13th giant yet, as he is about five miles south from Somerton. It is a massive hound, which is five miles long from his nose at Burrow Mump to the end of his tail at Wagg. He is Gwyn ap Nudd's dog, Dormath, who guards the whole Temple of the Stars – and we will be visiting him later.

So, now you are familiar with the cast of characters of this nocturnal *Cinema Paradiso*, hopefully you will be ready to meet the producers, the directors, the scene builders and the scriptwriters.

The ancient religion of Britain

There are many theories about who built this great earthwork theatre under the stars and most of them spring from Maltwood's thoughts on the subject. However, we know more now. It was only the early beginnings of the study of Egyptology when Maltwood was writing.

The archaeologists, who were funded in the main by the secret societies of the Freemasons, had only just begun to dig up evidence of the Mystery Teachings from the ruins of ancient civilisations in far-flung fields. Only a few could get funding for digs closer to home because their findings would not have supported the desired narrative. So, Maltwood was influenced in her visionary work by the theosophical ideas that were being spun out of artifacts and discoveries being uncovered by Egyptologists and Assyriologists. As the wife of a senior Freemason, she would have had been privy to these finds. Some say she was actually a Royal Arch Mason herself.

On top of that, she would have been influenced in her thinking by her friend Madame Blavatsky, who founded the Theosophical Society.

So Maltwood's inclusion into such hallowed circles would have given her access to more esoteric material. But because of its source, it was also a sword of Damocles. One word out of the place and the blade would have fallen on her membership.

The Royal Arch Masons had very close links with the aforementioned British-Israel movement. As previously discussed, this cultish movement had considerable influence in the town of Glastonbury in the early 20th century, which was rooted in their claims of descent from the Lost Tribes of Israel. Thus, they were supportive of any findings that shored up a pseudohistory to stake their claims, even going so far as to twist William Blake's words to try to establish some sort of legitimate footprint for a Second Temple of Solomon to be built on this "green and pleasant land".

So when it came to signalling who she thought may have been responsible for construction of the Glastonbury Temple of the Stars, Maltwood would have felt pressured to go along, to some extent, with the British Israelites' preferred narrative - that the earliest Christians had arrived in Glastonbury with the Phoenician tin merchants to build a church here.

The story of Jesus's uncle's ship mooring at Wearyall Hill would have made more sense at a time when people did not have the benefit of the deep historical and archaeological research that we do today. So, it's all the more impressive that while giving the nod to the establishment, at the same time Maltwood also managed to hint quite heavily that she thought the builders of the Glastonbury Temple of the Stars could have come from:

> ....an earlier Grail, that 'Cauldron of Wisdom' already famous ages before Joseph of Arimathea brought his message here. It was no doubt, the very reason for so remote a spot, for it is a matter of history that Christianity came to Glastonbury prior to any other place in the British Isles.

She underlines this message by drawing her equinox line on the Temple of the Stars between the bull of Taurus and the scorpion of Scorpio, which, due to the precession of the equinoxes, would have been in its rightful place about 5,000 years ago.

There was some discussion in her inner circle about which star would have marked the polar axis. They eventually reached a consensus that Thuban, in the constellation of Draco the serpent, was the closest to the North Pole then. Thuban was also the pole star that the tin merchant Phoenicians used as their focus in their navigation of the seas.

However, apart from the River Parrett, she barely cites any local place names that she deemed traceable back to the gods and goddesses of pantheons derived from a mixture of Akkadian and Phoenician lore.

She identified each of the giants with Arthurian characters – perhaps because that was the safer course to take. She probably knew that the Norman scribes of the *High History of the Holy Grail* were following a millennia-old worldwide tradition by weaving a narrative that observed a definite morphic structure, based on certain hidden languages and protocols that are designed to conceal esoteric law deep in their underlayers.

These kinds of stories go back to at least the end of the last major Ice Age. The Circassians and the Abkhazians believe that their myths are many thousands of years old and they are distinctly "Arthurian" in their structure, featuring a hero named Batraz and his 12 knights, or Narts, who serve the Lady of the Lake, Satana. These are tales about the winning of talismanic objects like enchanted apples, magical swords and grail-like cups. Some, like *How Warzameg,*

Son of Megazash, Won the Damsel Psatina, recount the trials and tribulations of the hero in pursuit of the hand of his beloved around a circle of animals, which is the source of the ancient Greek word "zodiac" (*zōidiakòs kýklos*). A remarkably similar template is found in the oldest known Celtic myth, *How Culhwch Won Olwen*, which is also the earliest one to feature Arthur Pendragon.

The most well-known blueprint for this traditional mythic structure is found in the Twelve Labours of Hercules. The trials themselves, though, are rarely recounted in the right order, to match the creature for each Sun sign. For instance, Hercules' battle with the Nemean Lion at Leo, whose golden fur was impervious to the swords of mortals, would have originally been followed by his retrieval of the Belt of Hippolyta from the Queen of the Amazons, at Virgo, and so on.

The Greeks purloined the Hercules story from the Babylonians when Alexander the Great conquered Persia and they seem to have used the same sledgehammer to the temple floor zodiac as Iraneus hundreds of years later. The original, *The Epic of Gilgamesh*, is much more intact and multidimensional, and if you wish to pursue it in more detail, I break it all down in Chapter 17 of my book *Stories in the Stars*.

But once again, from the following extract, it is clear that Maltwood believed at least some of the medieval monkish discoverers must have recognised what a treasure they had had uncovered on the Somerset Levels.

Those who had been initiated into the Mysteries of this "island valley" were obliged to couch their secret knowledge in romance after Christianity swept the field; but neither that reformation, nor any other, was able to destroy the map of the stars that our forefathers modelled amongst the hills and river beds of Somerset, and which still testifies to the ancient religion of this land.

We can find more evidence of Arthur's Celtic origins in an extract from the *High History of the Holy Grail* that Maltwood gives in her her book *Glastonbury's Temple of the Stars*.

She likens the Leo effigy to Pa Lug's Cat (Cath Palug), the huge cat of the Celtic sun god Lugh or Lug, which lies in a district once known as the Catsash Hundred. Each of her 12 knights mirror one of the aspects of the Sun as it goes through each sign, and she places Lancelot on Leo, where the hero has to meet a challenge to test his mettle at the Castle of Beards.

Lancelot stumbles upon this castle and there he finds a gatekeeper knight who informs him:

"It is the Castle of Beards, and it hath the name of this, that every knight that passeth thereby must either leave his beard there or challenge the same, and in such sort have I challenged my beard that me seemeth I shall die thereof...."

The High History continues ...

Lancelot looketh at the gateway of the castle and seeth

the great door all covered with beards fastened thereon, and heads of knights in great plenty hung thereby. So as he was about to enter the gate, two knights issued there from over against him.

"Sir," saith the one, "Abide and pay your toll!"

"Do knights, then, pay tolls here?" said Lancelot.

"Yea!" say the knights, "All they that have beards, and they that have none are quit. Sir, now pay us yours, for a right great beard it is, and thereof we have sore need."

"For what?" saith Lancelot.

"I will tell you," saith the knight. "There be hermits in this forest that make hair shirts thereof".

"By my head," saith Lancelot, "Never shall they make a hair shirt of mine."

There is a similar barbering theme in the Welsh tale about derring-do to achieve Sovereignty which is about Culhwch (pronounced "Kilhook"), who is born in a pig pen. In *How Culhwch Won Olwen*, the shaving of the ogre king Ysbaddaden will kill him in order for Culhwch to take the throne, just as Zeus "kills" Chronos.

Compare this (admittedly grisly) passage from *How Cuhwch Won Olwen* to the one above in the High History:

And then Culhwch set out with Gorau son of Custennin, and those who wished to harm Ysbaddaden Bencawr, and took the wonders with them to court.

And Caw of Prydyn came to shave off Ysbaddaden's beard, flesh and skin to the bone, and both ears completely.

And Culhwch said, "Have you been shaved, man?"

"I have," he replied.

"And is your daughter now mine?"

"Yours," he replied. "And you need not thank me for that, but thank Arthur, the man who arranged it for you. If I'd had my way, you never would have got her. And it high time to take away my life."

And then Gorau son of Custennin grabbed him by the hair and dragged him to the mound and cut off his head and stuck it on a bailey post. And he took possession of his fort and his territory.

So the barbering of beards appears to be a common initiatory theme in both streams of mythological lore and that the one about Culhwych is older can be evidenced to its similarity to a similar Circassian myth which would have been told by Tabiti – and I break all of this down in the next chapter.

However, the fact alone that there are 13 of these great effigies on the Glastonbury Temple of the Stars is a strong indication to me that the dramatic narrative dates back to a time when the movements of the Moon and the 13 constellations which include Ophiuchus were considered as important as the passage of the Sun. When people were nomadic, they often travelled in the cool of the night and the darkness gave them the added advantage of being able to use the stars to guide them. The Sun only took more precedence in their myths and artwork when people began to settle down in one place, to grow their grains and crops.

The megalithic stone circles of Avebury, in Wiltshire, demonstrate a preoccupation with the cycles of the Moon, as well as those of the Sun.[3] The lunar-based thinking is also evident at Stonehenge, which also functioned as a predictor of eclipses.

The second century Gaulish Coligny lunisolar calendar, which was discovered in the late 19th century in France, shows us that the Celts were among those who followed the cycles of the Moon. And there is also a much older but similarly sidereal calendar that was dug up more recently, in Germany, which is called the Nebra Sky Disc. Dated to 1600 BCE, it is a beautiful bronze disc that is 12 inches in diameter. Over time, it has become burnished to a blue-green patina but its gold embossed symbols of the Sun, the Moon and the Pleiades are clear.

The Nebra Sky Disc has 40 holes perforated around its perimeter, which are thought to mark the yearly lunar cycles, and it shows what the night sky would look like when an intercalary month, or 13th moon, needed to be added.[4]

So, the 13 giants of the Glastonbury Temple of

the Stars could well be a product of a pre-Christian age when the 13 Moons of the yearly cycle, and the 13 constellations including Ophiuchus held more importance. If so, this feature alone would date it to the times of the visionary Druids, and suggest that the giants were geoengineered by those who were led by shamans or *awenyddions* who journeyed throughout the Three Worlds, and therefore had a much more multidimensional and holographic view of their place in the cosmos.

Maltwood confirms this perspective in her view of *The High History of the Holy Grail* thus:

> On that last page, we read: 'The Latin from whence this History was drawn into Romance was taken in the Isle of Avalon, in a holy house of religion that standeth at the head of the Moors Adventurous, there where King Arthur and Queen Guinevere lie,' for the King is one of those cosmic deities upon which every pilgrim who climbs Glastonbury Tor looks down for, but can no longer distinguish.
>
> The author of another version, called La Queste del Saint Graal, though apparently not familiar with the locality, is more explicit concerning the adaptation of the old stellar religion to the new. For instance, he says, 'When the sun, by which we mean Jesus Christ,' and again, in Sir Lancelot's dream, he speaks of the 'man surrounded by stars' the man who came down from heaven came to the younger knight and 'transformed him into the figure of a lion and gave him wings'.

> *Here is strongly suggested the blending of the old and new, the Zodiacal Leo combined with the winged lion of St Mark. Thus the pre-Christian stories of the stars were adapted by later chroniclers and interwoven with the Christian Grail legend.*

In other words, Maltwood believed the Christian concept of the Holy Grail was derived from the much older Celtic myths about Arthur, from which the Norman scribes drew their inspiration.

Another way of perceiving the great antiquity of the Temple of the Stars is when you realise that the characters are acting out the pilgrimage of the earlier pole star hero, which is a voyage on water, through the firmamental star field of the Milky Way.

The hero's boat is found at Cancer, under the stars of Argo Navis. The boat for the constellation ruled by the Moon harks back to much older cosmological rites evidenced by the water-filled bowl known as the Moon Boat found in the cuneiform clay tablets and rock-engraved calendars of the Sumerians, the Hittites and the Luvites.

We are know the story about Jason and his crew the Argonauts. But the Argo was only used as a prop in that sea-going drama because Greek audiences were already familiar with it as the first ship to sail the ocean, which, long before the sagas of Jason were told, bore the Egyptian Danaos with his 50 daughters from Egypt to Argos.

The classical Greeks then spun tales about two of its stars - *asellus borealis* and *asellus australis* (the northern ass and the southern ass) - who win their place in the skies after a war between the gods and the giants, in which their braying so upset the Titans that they fled in terror.

As a reward for giving the gods such an easy victory, Dionysus places them either side of the cluster of stars which the Greeks called Phatne, the Manger, from which the asses seem to be feeding. Therefore, the cradle in the manger that contains the babe in its Captivity stage was once the Moon Boat.

Merlin's Round Table

In the myths of the nomadic hunter-gatherers who followed the stars, the adventures of the champion take place throughout his voyage on a boat or ark around the floods of the Milky Way under the circular arched vault of the pole stars. It was a pilgrimage through the firmamental sea of the macrocosm above that mirrored, holographically, the deeps of the microcosm of the subconscious of the individual below.

However, it seems that scribes of the 13th century *La Queste del Saint Graal* must have known it too because they tell us that:

> *The Round Table was constructed, not without great significance, upon the advice of Merlin. By its name the Round Table is meant to signify the round world and round canopy of the planets and the elements in the firmament, where are to be seen the stars and many other things.*

I explain in *Stories in the Stars* about how the role of the pole star hero was to recover a mound from the firmamental waters in order to establish the pole star of the new Age, which changes due to the precession of the equinoxes. In that book you will find more than 30 "deluge myths" from around the world that all feature a flood of some kind.

There is often an ark or a type of boat to carry the few selected survivors to safety. There is almost always a rainbow at the end of the adventure that signifies a promise or covenant from the gods. This has led me to the conclusion that the global flood monomyth – from Atlantis to Noah – began as a metaphor for the flood in the waters of the firmament in which the hero has to establish the new pole star, and his sea voyage follows the revolving pole stars located in the environs of the cosmic serpent constellation of Draco.

I think it will help you "get your eye in", so to speak, to be able to identify the later story of the zodiac hero on the Temple of Stars before we go on to the earlier pole star hero in the next chapter, where you will meet Arthur. Once you learn to recognise different glosses on the landscape, you will soon be able to "see the join" whenever outcroppings of older ones suddenly surface.

So, this is the template of the myth of the zodiac hero.

At Aries, if the Captive is considered mature enough and to have grown in his skills, he is Called to pursue his destiny by being offered the challenge of the Quest. He accepts the Calling and sets off. Consequently, his process is marked with many battles, trials and adventures as he meets, in succession, the creatures of Taurus, Cancer, Leo, Virgo and Libra. The purpose of these challenges is to turn him into a "real man" fit to lead the generations forward.

If he learns his lessons well, he is Chosen for rebirth – but first of all he has to face the most difficult trials of all. At Scorpio, he is bitten by the serpent, whereupon he tumbles down into the death of the Underworld. Thus, in the stygian depths of Sagittarius, he comes before the judge who weighs his soul in the balance. If he is not found wanting, he is reborn at Capricorn to become the Captive again, and the cycle goes on and on.

So, there are definitely elements of the Call to Adventure of the zodiac hero in the effigies of the Temple of the Stars of Avalon.

The Ram at Aries marks the traditional starting point for our protagonist's Call to Adventure. The lion at Leo and the bull at Taurus are ready to provide the adversarial battles. We can see him being dragged off his horse at Scorpio, where he falls into the Underworld. The Venus character who helps the hero is found at Virgo, holding an object that could be the Holy Grail, and this very near to the Crater cup-shaped constellation.

But in addition, there are at least two more tales found in the Temple of the Stars which indicate they come from a star lore that is at least 5,000 years old.

One of the dramas features Arthur, the pole star hero of the Upper World and his brother-in-arms, the serpent slayer Gwythyr ap Greidawl, which you will learn all about in the next chapter.

The other myth recounts the Underworld voyage of the babe in the Moon Boat. He begins life as the Captive embryo at Beltane and sails along the Waters of

Avalon of the Underworld until he emerges, nine-and-a-half moons later, at the Winter Solstice, then grows into his adolescence through Imbolc until he reaches the Spring Equinox. And I'll be telling you this story later on.

These three Celtic myths are set in the Three Worlds of the shaman. The pole star hero traverses the stars of the Upper World. The zodiac hero meets his adventures in the Middle World of Earth. The babe in the Moon Boat voyages around the waters of the Underworld.

As mathematicians would say, this three-fold structure completely "blows up" the Temple of the Stars into what they call Chaos Theory. We are no longer confined within a flat, circular clock narrative but a multi-dimensional Fibonacci spiral of Mandelbrot sequences of iterations that map out the jewelled seahorses and gemmed sea serpents of the fractal geography of the oceans of eternity.

If all this is sounding way too complex, please don't worry. Here, I'm introducing you to the themes I will breaking down into their simplest components as we proceed. And by the time we reach our destination, you will be able to easily solve mysteries that have eluded even the most illustrious of researchers into the esoteric.

After Maltwood's death, her work was carried on and developed further by Mary Caine, who also toyed with the idea of the landscape temple being created at a much earlier time. She wrote the following in her seminal book *The Glastonbury Zodiac: Key to the Mysteries of Britain*:

Who made it? When? And why? There can be no doubt that this Zodiac in essence, is natural. Its huge figures moulded by hills and lesser contours is partly outlined by rivers and streams whose course is determined by them. The whole complex measures some ten or twelve miles across, thirty miles around and can hardly be the unaided work of man. No, it was modelled by a vaster hand; whether we like to call it Nature, Cosmic Forces, or simply God.

So, the question… it seems has a dual answer; it was made by Nature in the first place, and continued by man. The Zodiac can be seen in 20th century maps perhaps more clearly than in the past. The paths are widening into motor roads and some are becoming dual carriageways. Yet this is not to say that the design was unknown, unrecognized. There is indeed much evidence in early writings to show that it was known.

The second question "When was it made?" must then take us back to the geological ages when the hills were first formed and the streams first began to flow. But this was only the beginning; its continuous development embraces all the ages of man down to the present day. The third question, "Why was it made?" has already been answered by Dunstan's biographer with commendable succinctness. It was prepared, he tells us, "for the salvation of mankind."

You have already met, and therefore need no further introduction to, the illustrious and enigmatic Dunstan, the 10th century Abbot of Glastonbury who went on to become the Archbishop of Canterbury and the close advisor of kings. I showed in the section on the Grail Keepers why I believed that he had a deep knowledge of the esoteric. But what could his biographer have meant by that enigmatic remark?

To my mind, this is a reclamation project. We are reconstituting these stories in the way that they were originally told. And once they are viewed through a more shamanic lens, it will make more sense as to why Dunstan believed that these stories were left on the land for "the salvation of mankind".

---

[1] *The High History of the Holy Grail,* translated by Sebastian Evans in 1898 from the 13th century version. Also known as *Perlesvaus* and *Li Hauz Livres du Graal*, it is thought to be a continuation of Chrétien de Troyes' unfinished *Perceval, the Story of the Grail.*

[2] *A Guide to Glastonbury's Temple of the Stars: their giant effigies described from air views, maps, and from "The High History of the Holy Grail."* K.E. Maltwood.

[3] Described in more detail by Nicholas Mann in his *Avebury Cosmos.*

[4] A lunar year is 11 days shorter than a solar year. Twelve months, or 12 returns of the Moon to the new phase, take only 354 days, and so we are well into the 13th moon by New Year's Eve.

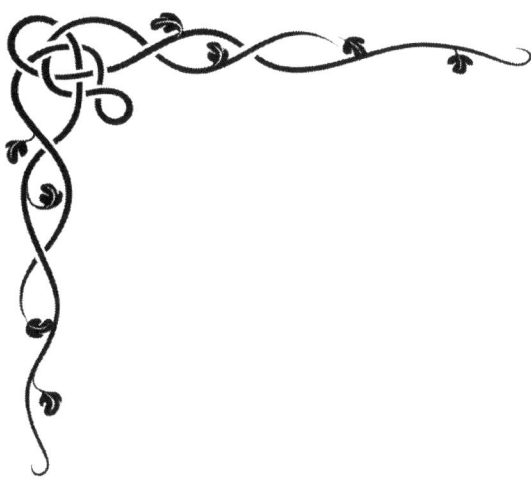

Chapter Ten: Arthur the Pole Star Hero

Nobody knows for sure when the Glastonbury Temple of the Stars was built. It is one of those mysteries with a small "m", the answer to which is lost in the mists of Time.

However, there are many clues that present themselves, once we identify the seasonal dramas being played out by these earthwork giants. Then it appears to be a piece of landscape architecture that comes from a time long before the role of playwright was debased into being a mere provider of light entertainment. The characterisations and plotlines symbolise metaphors that reveal deep wisdom in a magic lantern show that drew its audience when it was a prerequisite for great art to hold great meaning.

The actors play out the roles of characters found

in the oldest tales of Welsh literature, namely those collated into the *Mabinogion*. Those stories are a product of a long oral tradition that can be clearly evidenced over thousands of years. But they were not written down until the 11th and 12th centuries and so scholars have difficulty dating them.

However, as we discussed in the last chapter, they contain themes that held great resonance to our nomadic ancestors, who often travelled at night. And when we date them according to the star lore underlying the story and correlate each land giant to where its counterpart in the heavens would have been viewed from Earth at that time, we are transported back much further. This is a recognised academic discipline called astrotheology and it is that, along with astro-archaeology, which provides the only real Rosetta Stone for untangling the meanings of these fantastic fables.

Here are Mary Caine's thoughts[1] on the challenge of untangling the underlying metaphorical stratas in Celtic myths. They go some way, I believe, towards explaining why Arthur Pendragon's grave has been buried for so long in our national consciousness.

> *On first entering the twilight zone of the Celtic gods and heroes everything seems strange, vague and impalpable. The unfamiliar shadows enlarge to giant proportions, shrink to dwarfs, and are never still long enough for us to make them out before they undergo Protean changes of character and form, become inextricably intertwined, dissolve and reform elsewhere.*
>
> *To read Celtic myth for the first time is like trying to*

decipher the dynamic maze of ornament on a weather-beaten Celtic cross in a thicket after sundown.

But when the eyes have grown used to the half light, certain features begin to clarify: the original extravagance, the restless shape-shifting, resolves itself into an orderly Dance of the Hours; the ritual motion of the sun through the houses of the Zodiac.

As discussed previously, though, there is more than one story found on the Temple of the Stars, and two of them are much older than the Dance of the Hours of the Sun god around the zodiac.

In one of these stories, which is about the conception and labour of the Child, the Protean shapeshifting of these characters reflects the changing heavens; certain stars rise to perform one role in the drama and then set to perform another.

For instance, you will remember the Nebra Sky Disc, which is more than 3,000 years old, depicts the gold-embossed Pleiades. The Pleiades, also known as the Seven Sisters, set or descend into the Underworld at Beltane to become the midwives to the Child at its conception. They rise again at Samhain to help facilitate its entry through the portal into bodily incarnation.

The Child then grows into the hero who has to brave the storm-wave-tossed deeps of the fixed stars in his boat, to successfully circumnavigate six drowned island or mounds – one after the other - to rescue and reclaim from the waters the seventh mound upon which he erects his flagpole of victory.

He first gained his nautical skills by navigating the Underworld deeps of the Waters of Avalon.

He is eventually released from his Captivity in the belly of a gigantic whale, into a harbour at the Spring Equinox where he is taken under the tutelage of the Celtic Lord of the Sea, Manawydan, who prepares him to meet his Call to Adventure as the pole star hero.

That is why the number seven was originally a metaphor for the seven pole stars of the northern hemisphere, which change according to the precession of the equinoxes every 3,714 years or so. It was only later, when they were transposed on to the template of the Zodiac hero, that they came to represent the "gods" of the five planets – Mars, Mercury, Jupiter, Venus and Saturn – and the Sun and the Moon.

Thus, the oldest myths are about the courageous hero who has to confront the unknown terrors of the firmamental seas, in order to separate from the waters from the land, which takes the form of a mound or mountain, upon which he erects the flagpole of the new pole star.

In that way, we can perhaps relate to him better? After all, we rarely have to fight bulls or lions. But we all have to face our own challenges in the deeps, when the boat of our subconscious mind is guiding us to our destiny and we suddenly sense ourselves to be in the storm-tossed deeps of the Dark Night of the Soul and in mortal peril of hitting a titanic iceberg.

There are many examples in myths worldwide showing that the ancients depicted the precession of the equinoxes in this mytho-poetic fashion. The Egyptian *Book of the Dead* [2] describes the journey of the god Taht around the pole stars in an ark across a watery firmament. As each of the six goes under, the hero finally reaches and rescues the seventh – and on the seventh day he rested.

The following paragraphs are from Gerald Massey, a poet who wrote in the late 19th century on the deeper meanings of Egyptian myths. This is his interpretation of the stories about Taht, the pole star hero, and his Ark:

> *In the great year of precession, there are seven stations of the celestial pole ...The pole changes, and its position is approximately determined by another central star ... Seven times in the great year the station of the pole was raised aloft as landmark amid the firmamental waters in the shape of an island, or a mound a tree, a pillar, horn, or pyramid.*
>
> *Whichever the type, this was repeated seven times in the circuit of precession, to form the compound and collective figure of the celestial heptanomis, so that the heaven rested, or was raised, at last upon the seven mountains or seven mounds; seven islands, seven giants, seven caves, seven trees, seven pillars, or other structures of support, as seven figures of the all-sustaining pole.*
>
> *Seven golden isles emerged from out the watery vast, or wisdom reared the seven pillars of her house; the heavens were borne upon the backs of seven giants, or the eternal city was built upon the seven hills.*[3]

In the Indian *Vedas*, Indra is the hero who has to dislodge the sea serpent Vritra, who is damming up the waters. Once Indra slays him, the waters are released.

This is also a metaphor for when the waters break from the uterus of a mother who is about to give birth. It is the same scientific process. A flood in the macrocosmic terrain of the heavens above and in the microcosmic landscape of the human below signifies both a new age and new life.

I have been inspired in my understandings about the multidimensional nature of the drama played out on the Glastonbury Temple of the Stars by the writings of the Irish shaman Coleston Brown, and these words in particular: [4]

> *This is something that is perhaps easily misread into Mrs Maltwood's books. There is a strong polar and galactic component that has been overlooked so far by most investigators.*

Since then, I have realised that the trajectory of Arthur's sea voyage is mapped out in the Upper World northern stars of Draco, Ursa Major, Ursa Minor, Bootes, Camelopardalis, Hercules and Lyre, as shown on **Figure 41**. These are the seven fixed stellar giants. They are the stars that never rise or set – and so they can be seen every night of the year without fail, rotating widdershins, or anti-clockwise, over Park Wood at the centre of the Temple of the Stars.

The Cosmic Serpent

The name of Arthur comes from the Welsh word for "bear", which is *arth*, and thus the Once and Future King is represented by Ursa Major, the Great Bear constellation.

The word *pen* meant "head" or "leader". Thus

Arthur's surname, Pendragon, appoints him as the "head dragon" or "head serpent". It means that he conquered the dragon of the constellation Draco in the flooding firmament in order to erect the new pole star of the age.

This aligns well with the reptilian epithets given to spiritual leaders in pre-Christian times, such as the *nacals* of Central and Southern America and the *nagas* of India. Some senior Druids were called "adders" or *gnadrs*, meaning "serpent priests", and as discussed earlier the name Merlin meant "sea dragon". The Merovingian kings claimed to have been partially sired by a mythical quinotaur – a five-horned sea monster, shown in medieval heraldry as half-lion, half-serpent creatures.

Serpents play a pivotal role in helping the shaman to hold the Sovereignty of the land. In modern terms, he or she journeys into the spiralling, double-helixed DNA, which the Celts perceived, through their Dreamers, as the Rivers of Blood along which the wise teacher spirits swam in the form of various kinds of sea serpents, quinotaurs and dragons.

All these Otherworldly reptiles are connected to wisdom – even Eve's serpent was considered to be the "wiliest in the field". And so, when you dive into these submarine deeps to meet with those dragon teachers, you begin to learn about who you are, your place in the universe, and your destiny.

Viewed through a modern lens, we can learn more about the nature of this practice from observing the ongoing process of how the double-helixed DNA replicates itself.

DNA needs proteins to build and maintain it but those proteins do not have the knowledge of how carry out such a task. They need the DNA to "tell them", because it carries this architectural blueprint for its own survival. And so, Mercury the messenger is summoned at this point.

But it is a two-way street that benefits all. The proteins also find the information they need to reproduce themselves from the DNA.

So, this is perfect symbiosis - and also a perfect metaphor for the ongoing creation of eternal life which is facilitated by the shamans (the proteins) gaining guidance from the DNA (the serpent teachers) about how their family members of their tribe can thrive for generation upon generation.

Here's a more simplified allegory:

Imagine, if you will, that you're an architect and you want to build your own home. You know how you want the house to look and you have created a design to match your desired outcome. But you don't have the skills to construct it. You are not a bricklayer, a plumber or an electrician, and so you don't know how to build brick walls or lay pipes and cables, or get the wallpaper to lie flat so that it doesn't have any bubbles in it. So, you decide to hire people more expert in those skills to build your house for you.

You invite tradesmen and artisans to tender for the work. They are not necessarily expert in how to design a whole house, only in how to fulfil their different roles to contribute to your overall vision as the architect. So, they will follow your design specifications in order to know where to lay the bricks, which walls to paint and wallpaper and where to put all the wiring and plumbing.

Once the work is completed to your satisfaction, you pay the bricklayers, plumbers, electricians, painters and decorators. This gives them the monetary means to put a roof over the heads of their own families, to protect them from the elements and opportunistic predators, thus ensuring their own survival.

In this way, shamans could be compared with the interdimensional tradesmen proteins who "talk to" the architect serpents of the DNA, in order to gain the guidance that is needed for the protection of the Sovereignty of the family or tribal line.

This process is often referred to as consulting with their ancestors because the voices in the Rivers of Blood take on tangible forms. It is also known as "redeeming the blood of the ancestors", which was mistranslated by Iraneus to mean a literal sacrifice of the Son of God on the cross.

I hope all this explains why we see so many examples of the "cosmic serpent" in the cave art of prehistoric times and which we come upon, in myths and artworks, that portray serpent-conquering heroes as a metaphor for the accruing of this wisdom and knowledge. It is also the meaning of the *ouroboros*, the dragon that has to eat its own tail in order to survive.

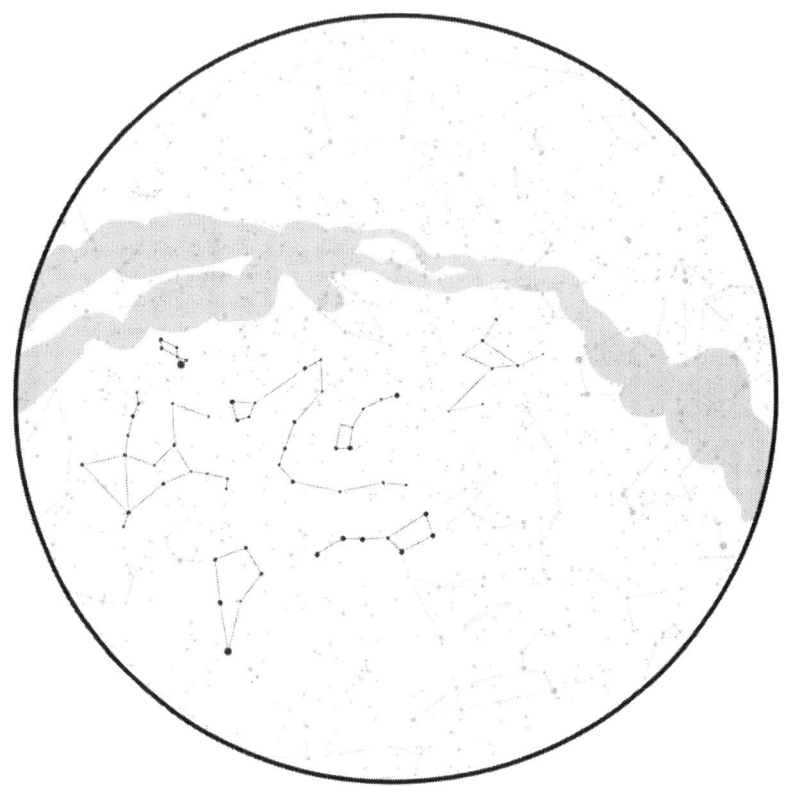

Figure 41 The fixed stars over Park Wood

How Culhwch Won Olwen

According to Nennius[5], Arthur was a great warrior king who fought 12 battles on behalf of the British. When the Welsh monk was writing, the stories were all about a Sun god who visits each of the 12 zodiac signs and so our pole star hero had, by then, given way to the solar hero of the post-agricultural revolution.

However, if we go back just a few hundred years to the sixth-century works of Taliesin, we find his hero Arthur voyaging in his boat around seven caers or castles in his poem *Preiddeu Annwfn*.

They are, in order: Caer Sidi, Caer Feddwit, Caer Rigor, Caer Wydyr, Caer Goludd, Caer Fandwy and Caer Ochren.

> *I praise the Mighty One, Pendragon of the kingly land,*
>
> *Who encompasses the margins of the world!*
>
> *Predestined was Gweir's captivity in Caer Sidi,*
>
> *According to the tale of Pwyll and Pryderi.*
>
> *None before him was sent into it,*
>
> *Into the heavy blue chain which bound the youth.*
>
> *From before the reeving of Annwfn he has groaned,*
>
> *Until the ending of the world this prayer of poets:*

Three ship burdens of Prydwen entered the Spiral City

Except seven, none returned from Caer Sidi.

Is not my song worthily to be heard

In the four-square Caer, four times revolving?

I draw my knowledge from the famous cauldron

The breath of nine maidens keeps it boiling.

Is not the Head of Annwyn's cauldron so shaped;

Ridged with enamel, rimmed with pearl?

It will not boil the cowardly traitor's portion.

The sword of Lleawc flashed before it

And in the hand of Lleminawc was it wielded.

Before hell's gate the lights were lifted

When with Arthur we went to the harrowing.

Except seven, none returned from Caer Feddwit.

Is not my song fit recital for kings

In the four-square Caer, in the Island of the Strong Door,

Where noon and night make half-light,

Where bright wine is brought before the host?

Three ship burdens of Prydwen took to sea:

Except seven, none returned from Caer Rigor.

I sing not for those exiled for tradition

Who beyond Caer Wydyr saw not Arthur's valour.

Six thousand men there stood upon the wall;

Hard it was to parley with their sentinel.

Three ship burdens of Prydwen we went with Arthur:

Except seven, none returned from Caer Goludd.

I sing not for those whose shield arms droop,

Who know not day nor hour nor causation

Nor when the glorious Son of Light is born,

Nor who prevents his journey to Dol Defwy.

They know not the brindled, harnessed ox

With seven score links upon his collar.

When we went with Arthur on difficult errand;

Except seven, none returned from Caer Fandwy.

I sing not for those of our companions,

Who know not on what day the chief was born,

Who do not know the hour of his kingship,

Nor of the silver-headed beast they guard for him.

When we went with Arthur of mournful mien:

Except seven, none returned from Caer Ochren.

There are other, longer versions of *Preiddeu Annwfn*, but I'm sticking with the shortest and simplest version for our purposes here.

So, let's analyse it.

Caer is Welsh for "fortress", "enclosure" or "circle". *Sidi* is cognate with "sidereal" and so it is probable that Caer Sidi refers to a circle of stars, star-wheel or spiralling stellar enclosure – and the word is also similar to that of the Irish Sidhe faeries.

Which *caer* refers to which constellation is still open to interpretation within astro-theology. We just know that there were seven fortresses.

The number seven recurs in the "seven score links" on the collar of the brindled ox, and also again when only seven of his crew ever survive the rigours of each of the seven fortresses. As the latter would be mathematically impossible, it must signify something else. If we derive this story from the primordial carpet then, as a group, the sevens could symbolise the seven fixed pole stars of Draco, Ursa Major, Ursa Minor, Bootes, Camelopardalis, Hercules and Lyre.

So next, let us examine the "cauldron ... ridged with enamel and rimmed with pearl" and which "will not boil the cowardly traitor's portion". Could that be a metaphor for the round, starry dome of the sky that is flooded during precessional cycles with the firmamental seas, and which are kept boiling by the breath of the nine Moon muses? Of course, it will not "boil the cowardly traitor's portion" because the timid and faint-hearted would be too cowardly to venture into the Tartarean troughs and perilous peaks of such tumultuous seas.

At the same time, the boiling within the bowl-shaped container may be a metaphor for the alchemist's cauldron or crucible in which the seven *caers* symbolise the rungs of the Ladder of the Wise, which the initiate climbs to reach enlightenment.

One of Taliesin's titles was the Son of the Cauldron – which tells us that The Harrowing of the Underworld, which is another title often used for this poem, was part of the challenges of the initiate.

To my mind, the "brindled, harnessed ox" is the constellation of Bootes, which has featured in various mythological guises over the ages, such as the Herdsman, the Shepherd or the Ox Driver. This Herdsman pulls the Plough (otherwise known as the Great Bear, Ursa Major or Arthur's Chariot) at the Spring Equinox in Babylonian myths.

Between the thighs of the Herdsman we find the star Arcturus, which means Protector of the Bear.

So once viewed as an initiatory trial of strength and courage, we can understand why Arthur has to go to sea is to win the Cauldron from one Dwirnach the Irishman, the overseer of Odgar, son of Aedd, king of Ireland. But then, surely that begs a question – who posed the challenge in the first place?

To find the answer, we need to examine the oldest known Welsh myth in which Arthur has a pivotal role, which we discussed briefly in the last chapter.

How *Culhwch Won Olwen* is about a boy named Culhwch, who was born in a pig pen and raised by sows but who went on to win a princess and claim her father's throne. And along his questing journey to conquer the obstacles between himself and his bride, we find the course of the fixed stars through the different stages of the wild hunt of Arthur (Ursa Major), as he pursues the Questing Beast in a great circle around England, Scotland and France, on behalf of his cousin Culhwch (Hercules).

Olwen (Ursa Minor or Little Bear) is the fair damsel imprisoned by the ogre Ysbaddaden, within the coils of Draco the serpent, and protected by her uncle, Bootes the Herdsman.

Linguistic evidence shows that *How Culhwch Won Olwen* is at least a hundred years older than the other

Mabinogion stories, dated to the 11th century. However, the story also contains memes and "tale-types" that indicate it is a transmission from a much earlier era.

As medievalist Will Parker writes in his discourses on the *Mabinogion*:

> *Not only is Culhwch the oldest surviving prose tale written in the Medieval Welsh language, it is also generally thought to be the closest to the oral background of traditional story-telling from which the Mabinogion originally emerged. The oral tale, by its very nature, leaves no direct trace on the historical record; so the precise form of these narrative recitals in the Middle Ages must remain a matter for conjecture.*
>
> *Nonetheless, just as there are certain stylistic and structural features which are characteristic of the säge or oral popular tale in all times and places, so too are there are also certain stereotypical plot structures and narrative elements which would seem to have their origins in the common prehistory of mankind. That such 'motifs' and 'tale-types' permeate both the structure and content of Culhwch and Olwen offers a strong indication of the proximity of this popular-oral background.*

A race that linguists have labelled Dene Caucasian and who would have been related, tangentially at least, to Kroy-khasis and Tabiti, has been identified to have sat out the whole of the last Ice Age, up to 12,000 years ago, in the Basque Pyrenees. This Iberian region is where it is claimed that the Milesians later set sail from in their migration to Ireland.

The young Culhwch's quest to find and wed Olwen bears many similarities to one of the myths of Circassians entitled *How Warzameg, Son of Meghazash, Won the Damsel Psatina*, which features a plethora of challenges to the hero and the completion of which spiral into further tasks in which there is also a Herdsman and lots of magical speaking animals.

The terrible ogre that Warzameg has to conquer to gain his bride is described as gigantic and scaley. His name, Arkhon Arkhozh, has serpent connotations, and so he would have made an ideal antagonist in one of Tabiti's derring-do dramas of adventures circling around Draco.

Thus Warzameg was likely an earlier prototype for Culhwch, who has a lowly birth and is not raised by his mother but by swineherds in a pig pen. The pig pen takes the place of the manger or the cave in the Celtic stories, which classically feature more pigs, sows, swine, boars and piglets than you could throw a stick at. It is a classic tale of fertility, growth, longevity and Sovereignty featuring a hero who has to perform a number of tasks. However, that hero is not Culhwch, who seems to watch from the sidelines, but his cousin Arthur Pendragon.

The Wild Hunt and the Harrowing

The ogre Ysbaddaden sets Culhwch 39 Impossible Tasks that he must accomplish to win the hand of Olwen and to replace the old king on the throne. Why the number of tasks is 39 is a mystery that no-one yet has been able to solve. But it is almost certainly connected in some way to the 13 Treasures of Britain, which were gifted to Merlin by Bran, to protect the Sovereignty of the land. These sorts of magical cauldrons, wands, swords and spears, and all manner of other assorted talismanic implements, are the "hallows" of the harrowing that normally have to be won by the aspiring hero, as is told in *How Culhwch Won Olwen*.

Arthur offers to help his cousin in his 39 labours, which culminate in the hunting down – all over Britain and France - of the fierce and terrifying Questing Beast, otherwise known as the *Twrch Trwyth* (pronounced "Toorch Trooeeth"). The aim of the hunt is to steal a pair of scissors, a razor and a mirror. These barbering implements rest between the ears of the *Twrch Trwyth* and Culhwch will need them to shave Ysbaddaden's beard.

As you know, Arthur succeeds in retrieving the scissors, razor and mirror and the ogre Ysbadadden is subsequently shaved and dispatched.

And so, this is the esoteric meaning of the original Wild Hunt and it also shows us where Arthur is buried, like Davey's Locker, in a watery grave under the firmamental sea.

Now we will bring in a few more characters so that we can proceed.

The most significant ones, for our purposes here anyway, are found in Ysbaddaden's speech in which he lays the *geis* of 39 Impossible Tasks upon Culhwych's shoulders:

> *18. I must needs dress my beard for me to be shaved. It will never settle unless the blood of the Black Witch be obtained, daughter of the White Witch, from the head of the Valley of Grief in the uplands of Hell.*

22. Twrch Trwyth will not be hunted till Dormath be obtained, the whelp of Greid son of Eri.

26. There is no huntsman in the world can act as houndsman to that hound, save Mabon son of Modron, who was taken away when three nights old from his mother. Where he is is unknown, or what his state is, whether alive or dead.

33. Thou wilt not hunt Twrch Trwyth until Gwyn son of Nudd be obtained, in whom God has set the spirit of the demons of Annwn.

So now please allow me to explain a little about each of those characters.

You have already met Dormath, the Welsh counterpart to the Hound of Hades, Cerberus, the dog that guards the Greek Underworld. He is found a few miles outside the Temple of the Stars, to the south. Known locally as the Girt Dog of Langport, his body is five miles long from the tip of its nose at Burrow Mump to the hamlet of Wagg on its tail His role is the gatekeeper to the Quest of the Call to Adventure, and so we will need his blessing before we can begin to unravel its Mysteries.

You have also already encountered Gwyn son of Nudd and his duelling rival Gwythyr ap Greidawl. Gwythyr accompanies Arthur on his journey into the Uplands of Hell to steal the blood of the Black Witch.

Finally, Mabon son of Modron is a staple character in several *Mabinogion* stories, in which he is freed from Captivity to become the Called, or the

Pendragon. Later on, will learn more about his Underworld voyage along the Waters of Avalon to be born as the Radiant Child, on the Winter Solstice.

The Cauldron and the Holy Grail

In Welsh myths, the cauldron is regarded as a vessel of death and rebirth, rather like the great Whale in the Bible story[6] that swallows Jonah whole, with him managing to escape his captivity after three days.

It plays a similar rejuvenatory role in the harrowing Second Branch tale of the marriage of Branwen, Daughter of Llyr.[7] Here, we read about how the Irish employed a cauldron in battle to resurrect their dead warriors.[8] It is also sometimes referred to as the cauldron of regeneration, as in the tale of *Cormac mac Airt*.

There are several other cauldrons in Welsh literature. But it could also be claimed that the whole Temple of the Stars, viewed extra-dimensionally, is a cauldron itself, which stages the quest of the hero who has to "win the cauldron" around its rim. Even in the physical realm, at the time of the Celtic Lake People, this low-lying land would regularly fill and empty with the tidal waters from the Severn.

It must have provided a dazzling spectacle, like a rippling silver screen reflecting the white lunar orb and the glittering constellations above – in other words, performing the same role as the ancients' water-bowl Moon Boat.

Many astro-theologists believe the Celtic cauldron to be the earliest prototype for the grail of the Arthurian myths. We can be sure that they were both Otherworldly containers that were metaphors symbolising the destination and the prize of those seeking enlightenment and rebirth. The winning of the Cauldron was as much an initiatory challenge for the Celts as was the winning the Holy Grail for early Christians.

> *The cauldron is the prototype of the Grail itself, the otherworldly vessel whose gifts include healing, rebirth, knowledge, spiritual fulfillment, paradisal bliss and magical power, as well as the provision of spiritual nourishment. The cauldron is the pagan resonance of the Grail ... Both Grail and cauldron dispense the draught of salvation, the waters of everlastingness ... both are attainable only by people of sovereign power or heroes of daring courage.*[9]

The cauldron in Celtic literature is always owned by the hag or crone aspect of the triple-faced goddess – who shapeshifts from maiden to mother to crone, just as the Moon cycles through her periods of new, full and dark.

In her crone form, she is named Ceridwen and she is often depicted tending her cauldron on the "dark days" which are the precursor to the Celtic New Year, which begins at Samhain.

Ceridwen is the Celtic *ogyrwen* (goddess) of fertility and fecundity. That might seem odd to us in our surface world. We associate the last days of October with the leaves dying on the advent of the coldest days of the year, in which the Earth lies barren and hard as stone. However, the hero's activities in the Underworld, which is Ceridwen's domain, are also a metaphor for the beginning of new life, which all remains invisible to us until Imbolc, at the beginning of February, when the crocuses and primroses poke up their heads to remind us once again that without sacrifice and death there is no rebirth and thus, no life at all.

The sixth-century Taliesin, the composer of *Preiddeu Annwfn*, claimed that his name was given to him after he became a Son of the Cauldron. He recounts the different stages of his transformation from a childhood in which he was named Gwion.

As a young boy, he helps to tend a Cauldron of Knowledge and Inspiration. It contains a special blend which Ceridwen has been preparing for a year and a day for her son, Avagddu, who is clumsy and stupid. She hopes her enchanted infusion will imbue him with grace and wisdom.

Gwion had been stirring the concoction for a year and a day when, suddenly, a few drops of the magical brew accidentally fall on to his hand and, after all, which one of us would not automatically stick out our tongue and lick it? Well, he did. And so Ceridwen erupts into fury that the precious nectar she had been so carefully brewing for her idiot son has been stolen by a mere servant boy.

Gwion flees in terror but he turns at one point to see Ceridwen in hot, fist-shaking pursuit so he tries to hide his identity by shapeshifting into a hare. Then he looks over his shoulder again to see that Ceridwen has turned herself into a black greyhound that is coming after him with its great, red, lolling tongue hanging out.

Gwion reaches a river and so he shapeshifts into a fish. But he is still not safe from the furious hag, who instantly manifests herself as an otter. He tries to disguise himself as a bird and takes flight but Ceridwen responds by becoming a hawk. Finally, in desperation, Gwion morphs into a grain of wheat and goes to hide in a granary. But Ceridwen becomes a huge black, red crested hen that instantly swallows the grain of wheat, which lands in her womb.

She gives birth to him nine-and-a-half Moons later but during the time of his Captivity, Gwion has transformed into the Bright-browed, fully enlightened Taliesin. And so, upon seeing his great beauty and wisdom, Ceridwen cannot bear to kill him. Instead, she sets him afloat on the seas in a tiny coracle – the Moon Boat.

He is eventually discovered and rescued by a fisherman, who takes him to the court of a king. The king takes an instant liking to Taliesin and he appoints him to be the resident bard.

With so many animals chasing each other in a circle, the drama of the birth, death and rebirth of Taliesin is likely to be another star story. We can identify some of the heavenly players – for instance, the hare is almost certainly Lepus, which is pursued by the greyhound of Canis Major. The fish could be Cetus. The bird is probably Cygnus, which is chased by the hawk Aquila. The grain of wheat could only be the star of Spica in the constellation of Virgo; its name comes from the Latin *spīca virginis* or "the virgin's ear of grain". The black, red-combed hen is a riddling play on words to indicate the constellation of Leo, which I explain more about further along.

Ceridwen's Otherworldly tomb-room-womb of the Captive Gwion is also the cauldron of Diwrnach the

Irishman, one of Thirteen Treasures of Britain that Merlin brings to the Glass House for safekeeping. And it is the magical container that Arthur wins for the wedding feast of the marriage of his cousin, Culhwch.

Taliesin once said that if the meat of a coward were to be put in this cauldron, it would never boil. He added that should the meat of a brave man be put inside, it would boil quickly. I think the meaning of this can be found in his poem about his initiatory transformation from Gwion to the Bright-browed Radiant Child.

The "meat" is a metaphor for the yet-to-be-redeemed man, who is himself the meat or First Matter of the alchemist's crucible in which he is Captive, as much as the grain of wheat incubating in the womb of Ceridwen. If this is true, then the star story that recounts his many incarnations to reach enlightenment and rebirth, which mirror the stars, could be coding for the timings of the different processes of the alchemical Marriage of the Sun and the Moon, as discussed earlier.

It is a common experience for initiates to undergo dismemberment in the Otherworlds. If they haven't first been warned about it, it can be quite disconcerting, upon going into trance, to suddenly find themselves being confronted with a huge cooking pot reminiscent of those found in the grisly tales of Victorian explorers unlucky enough to stumble upon an island of cannibals.

This is not about actual dismemberment in the physical realm and so the initiate feels no pain. But watching one's bones being pulled apart and then boiled and simmered in a large stew pot is an integral part of the rite of passage of the student of these

Mysteries. Afterwards, the purified bones are reconstituted into a new body for the rebirth.

And so, if you have dreams of being so disassembled and reassembled, you may be going through the separation phase on the Ladder of the Wise in the pilgrimage of your life.

---

[1] *The Glastonbury Zodiac: Key to the Mysteries of Britain* by Mary Caine.
[2] The Egyptian *Book of the Dead* is a loose term for a collection of funerary texts that include astrological or alchemical "spells" dating back to the 3rd millennium BCE.
[3] *Ancient Egypt: The Light of the World* by Gerald Massey.
[4] *Secrets of a Faery Landscape, New Light on the Glastonbury Zodiac* by Coleston Brown
[5] *Historia Brittonum* by Nennius.
[6] Jonah 1.
[7] Second Branch of the *Mabinogion*.
[8] *The Grail Mysteries* by Annie Dieu-Le-Veut.
[9] *Mabon and the Guardians of Celtic Britain* by Caitlin Matthews.

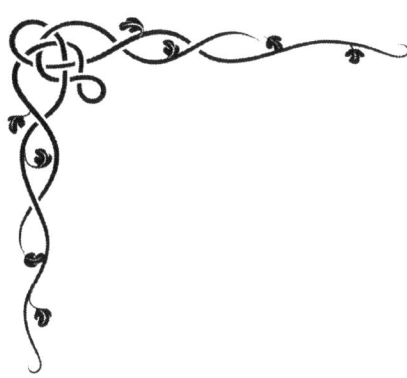

Chapter Eleven: The Exalted Prisoner

The Child's name in Taliesin's *Preiddeu Annwfn* is Gweir. But his names are legion in the many legends that recount the adventures of the Child who overcomes his Captivity to meet the Call to Adventure in order to become the Chosen One.

You have probably recognised that the beginnings of the Captivity have some resonance with the one illustrated on the stained glass window in St Dunstan's Church, Baltonsborough. It is about the release of the golden spark of divinity that is imprisoned, through a staged alchemical process, within the leaden, unrefined human being. And the pressure to break the locks of the jail is applied through the auspices of the Four Joys and Four Sorrows that are encountered along the spiralling pilgrimage of the vessel of the spirit trapped in the human body.

Role	Characters	Part of cycle
Mabon the Captive	Pryderi Goreu Gwion	The Mabon Child is born on the Winter Solstice and then is hidden in Captivity with a relative who guides him in learning the attributes and skills he will need to succeed in his life.
Pendragon the Called	Arthur Gwyn Gwythyr Gwyddion	At the Spring Equinox, Mabon is Called to accept the challenge of the Quest. If he accepts, he sets off as the Pendragon on his adventures. At the Summer Solstice, he goes through a painful, life-changing experience that realigns his course, which leads him to becoming the Chosen.
Pen Annwfn the Chosen	Pwyll Bran Math Myrddin (Merlin) Ysbaddaden Annwn	If the Pendragon learns his lessons well, he is Chosen by Pen Annwfn. This means that at Samhain he is bitten by the Serpent and he tumbles off his horse into the Underworld, where he undergoes further harrowing trials at the behest of the wise judge.

> After overcoming these tests, his soul is weighed in the balance. If he is successful he is either born again, or he stays in the Underworld and takes over the role of the Pen Annwfn, who is then reborn on the Winter Solstice as Mabon, the Child... and so the cycle continues.

Figure 42 Celtic characters and their astrological roles

The characters in Celtic myths are often placeholder epithets – such as the Pendragon teacher and Pen Annwfn, who is the judge of the Underworld.

And it is no different for the baby in the boat; he is known as Mabon, which just means "child". In the chart contained in **Figure 42**, you can see how each character represents a role or stage in the lifecycle of *The Hero with a Thousand Faces*, as Joseph Campbell named him, who is continually being born to face the Call to Adventure in which he eventually dies and then reaches the Return, when he is born again on to a Mandelbrot spiralling Wheel that spins for all eternity.

Mabon is born to Madron and she represents the many maternal figures in Celtic myths, from Rhiannon to Branwen. In the epithet of Madron, we see the resonance with the words "matron", "matter", "material", "matrix" and "matter". Thus, Madron is the ruling archetypal matriarch in what mythologists refer to as the Matter of Britain – in other words, the weft and warp of the weave of the narrative that forms the cognitive foundations of our Sovereign Isles.

Mabon, son of Madron, doesn't appear to have a whole Welsh myth to himself – or if he does, we haven't found it yet. Rather, his name crops up in classical questing stories as a sort of mythological meme the storyteller seems to assume the listener is already familiar with.

The Son of the Mother appears under a variety of guises in many tales, texts and triads, 11 of which were translated and then published, in the 19th century, under the title Mabinogion.

He is the captive Gweir, son of Geirioedd, in Taliesin's *Preiddeu Annfyn* and he is Pryderi, the abducted son of Rhiannon, in the Mabinogion. Taliesin himself plays the role of the child in his poem about his rebirth into enlightenment from the child Gwion.

This extract from the Welsh *Triad 52* expands our understanding about the exalted status of the proverbial Prisoner:

> *Three Exalted Prisoners of the Island of Britain:*
>
> *Llyr Half Speech, who was imprisoned by Euroswydd,*
>
> *And second, Mabon son of Modron,*
>
> *And third, Gweir, son of Geirioedd.*
>
> *And one who is more exalted that the three of them, was three nights in prison at Caer Oeth and Anoeth, and three nights imprisoned by Gwen Pendragon, and three nights in an enchanted prison under the Stone of Echymeint. This Exalted prisoner was Arthur. And it*

was the same lad that released him from each of these prisons – Goreu, son of Custennin, his cousin.

We learn about Arthur's first incarceration from the porter, Glewlwyd, in *How Culhwch Won Olwen*, who talks of accompanying his king to many places, which included Caer Oeth and Anoeth. Sadly, the texts which would show us the two further captivities of Arthur have not yet been found and so students of the British Mysteries are forced to extrapolate the meaning of these mythical captivities through a glass darkly.

However, the fact that the prisoner is given the title of "Exalted" means that he is no ordinary prisoner who has been locked up for breaking the law; quite the reverse, it seems. As Caitlin Matthews writes in *Mabon and the Guardians of Celtic Britain*:

> *This pattern of imprisonment is not about being held in an ordinary prison for any ordinary crime, but rather seems to be a form of initiatic imprisonment; a mystery that we cannot fully understand. These famous prisoners are remembered as if they had performed some kind of public service on behalf of all people…*
>
> *The three prisons of Arthur are a challenge for the serious student of the British mysteries. They represent part of a lost tradition which, like many of the triads and fragmentary poems of Taliesin, remain partially covered. We can only pass – with many a backward glance at the clues teasing our understanding.*

> *For the purposes of practical research, each captivity may be considered as part of an initiatory cycle of imprisonments within the Otherworld, opportunities for the harrowing of Annwfn by the heroes of their day, the dynamic points of fracture and integration where Arthur joins the succession of the Pendragons, becoming in turn the guardian on the threshold of the worlds.*

And so, thousands of years before the deemed nativity of Jesus in a manger in a stable, so this Celtic Child had similarly rustic and lowly beginnings in the spiralling Caer Sidhi of the stars.

However, we are all the Captive until we are enlightened and, like the hero of the Circassian myth *How Warzameg, Son of Meghazash, Won the Damsel Psatina*, we sometimes wonder if we will ever reach the end of our tasks, which seem to spiral endlessly one out of the other. Perhaps this is why for thousands of years the sages and *hierophants* used the symbols of labyrinths, mazes and meanders for the unicursal path of the initiate for whom the only way out is through (see **Figure 43**).

At times, our path appears to be going over old ground; at others, we are convinced that although we seem to be moving forward, the trajectory is taking us further and further away from our destination. But until we reach the centre, we cannot begin the long and winding road back home and so we remain imprisoned within its high Saturnic walls.

Figure 43 *Classical seven-ring labyrinth*

The use of the labyrinth for initiatory rites goes back tens of thousands of years, in the form of nautilus shells. Hundreds of these spiralling crustaceans have been found at the ritual sites and burial grounds of our earliest ancestors, such as the Blombos Caves in South Africa, and all around the site most associated mythologically with the labyrinth built by King Minos of Crete.

The story goes that the wife of King Minos makes love with the god of the seas, Poseidon, who comes to her bed one night in the form of a white bull. The offspring of this union is a gargantuan half-man, half-bull creature which is ferociously violent and only wants to eat live human flesh. They called him the Minotaur.

King Minos doesn't know what to do with such a terrifying creature. Not only is it a danger to his subjects but it is also a constant and shameful reminder to the whole of the kingdom of his wife's unfaithfulness. One day, however, he hears about the brilliant artisan, Daedulus. He calls him to the court and explains the problem.

Daedulus goes away to think it over. Then he decides to build an enormous labyrinth around the Minotaur, to imprison King Minos's shameful secret at its centre.

However, it isn't long before the king decides that he could turn a pretty profit from Daedulus's construction. He decides to use it to help bring in more tourists to swell his dwindling treasury and issues a proclamation, throwing down the gauntlet to all young men across the Mediterranean lands to come and test their mettle against the bloodthirsty monster.

Minos has no fear of his shameful secret being found out because he knows no man could see the Minotaur and remain alive. And he turns out to be right – well, at first. The Cretan labyrinth quickly becomes a famous rite of passage challenge for many a chest-thumping, would-be hero who, without a second's thought, would go rushing blindly into the labyrinth to claim the laurels of victory for slaying such a nightmarish beast. Most are eaten alive and even those who manage to escape the Minotaur's blood-dripping jaws cannot find their way out again and die of thirst and starvation, alone in the long, dark tunnels.

Then a young man called Theseus arrives on Crete. After hearing about all the failed attempts, he decides to apply some intelligence to the situation and goes to seek the guidance of the architect of the labyrinth.

Daedalus takes a liking to Theseus, so he asks his daughter, Ariadne, to give the challenger a long red thread to lay down as he walks through the labyrinth, so that he can find his way out again.

Theseus goes into the labyrinth and finds the Minotaur and – to cut a long story short – he kills him. He then manages to find his way out again by following Ariadne's red thread.

However, that is not the end of the story. Daedulus is now in huge trouble with King Minos for helping Theseus to survive and to report far and wide about the shameful secret that he found at the centre of the labyrinth. To make matters worse, the Minotaur is now dead and Minos has lost his highly lucrative source of revenue. Daedulus's friends warn him that the king is on the warpath so, one moonless night, he quietly slips out of the harbour on a boat and sails to another kingdom.

King Minos, though, is determined not to let the architect escape his fury. He leaves his kingdom too and spends years travelling the world, searching for Daedulus. He goes from one country to another, asking each wise man he finds the same question: "How can I feed a piece of thread through the centre of a nautilus shell so that it passes through and extrudes at the other end?"

Nobody knows. But eventually, King Minos comes upon a sage who says that he doesn't know the answer but knows a person who would. So, he takes the question to Daedalus. Daedalus sends back the instruction that a red thread should be tied to an ant and a dab of honey put at the other end of the shell, to tempt the ant through the labyrinth of the spiralling nautilus shell.

Thus, by giving away his trademark technique, Daedalus inadvertently reveals his identity to King Minos and he is captured and taken back to be imprisoned on Crete.

The story about King Minos's shame is one we can all recognise from when we travel through the labyrinthine Dark Night of the Soul. This is the last trial of the hero who, after falling down into the Underworld, has to find the courage to face himself in order to redeem his ancestral line. If he remains unable to look his buried shame squarely in the face, it becomes the driver of his life in a negative way.

Psychologists believe that unprocessed shame is the cause of Narcissistic Personality Disorder, so named after another mythic character who fell in love with his own reflection. It is the mirror or reverse side of self-centred pride and it is the Underworld cause of it.

However, the challenge at this stage of the pilgrimage is not about trying to attain perfection, the search for which in itself is just a product of the false dogma of Original Sin. It is more about accepting one's flaws as part of the human condition.

We find ourselves on this Earth in vessels that are half-beast and half-god, just like the Minotaur. It is only vanity that tries to persuade us that this world isn't good enough for us so that we reach, in vain, for an imagined harp-playing sainthood above the clouds.

We cannot fulfill the task we set ourselves when we decided to take incarnation into the animal body of the human unless we accept all sides of our nature, so that we can become whole.

The failure to integrate the man and the beast within causes us to live in delusion. We imagine stories about our lives that do not match the reality, and the result is hubris. We can feel sometimes as if we're hitting a brick wall. But that is just the walls of the labyrinth preventing us from us setting off too far down these delusory diversions and pushing us back on to the road of our destiny.

The Minotaur was originally the half-man, half-bull governor of Sagittarius. He is signified by astrologists nowadays as a centaur holding a bow-and-arrow. I don't know when the symbol for that sign changed from a bovine creature to a horse but I imagine it was after the precession of the equinoxes moved the Spring Equinox out of Taurus the Bull. This conclusion is bolstered by the fact that, although the story of Theseus and the Minotaur is a Greek myth, the material it is based upon goes back at least as far as the proto-Greeks of around 1600-1100 BCE – the Indo-European race of the Mycenaeans.

The Mycenaeans were great sailors and explorers of the Aegean, and they discovered what was left of Crete after the Santorini volcanic eruption and consequent tsunami had devastated the island of Thera and much of Crete, the home of the Minoans. They were very much impressed by what had obviously been an advanced Bronze Age culture and so they intertwined the sacred iconography of those Cretans with their own myths, as much as the Minoan snake goddess's arms and body were intertwined with snakes.

When the Mycenaeans first set foot on the

abandoned island, they found thousands of nautilus shells scattered and pressed into the crevices of the mountains, as ritual offerings, they believed, to the body of the Earth Goddess.

It was also the Mycenaeans who came up with the word "labyrinth", because of the mazelike processional route within the palace complex at the capital of Knossos which was decorated with trademark Minoan double axes, known as *labrys*.

From one of the frescoes on the wall, we can hazard a guess that bull-leaping manhood rites had once been held here, probably during Beltane. They were contemporaneous with similar bull rites carried out in Egypt, which were dedicated to the white bull god, Min.

According to the Greek historian Herodotus, there had been a huge labyrinth in Egypt that was even more impressive than the pyramids and built earlier than that of the Cretans. The structure itself has not yet been discovered by archaeologists, but it is thought to be at Crocodilopis, on the banks of the Nile south-west of Memphis, a site that has been partially excavated and found to be dedicated to the crocodile goddess Sobek.

There is another mythic labyrinthine passage found in Homer's *Odyssey*, although it is not generally recognised as such.

After the Trojan wars had been fought, over the fair Helen of Troy, the hero Odysseus has to sail with his fleet for 10 years before finally reaching his home port of Ithaca. This long and wandering sea voyage could only have been an historical event if Odysseus had been the world's worst navigator having to plough through a decade of atrocious weather in the normally calm lake of the Mediterranean.

Mid-voyage, he is forced to return to the island of Aeaea, where the "witch-goddess" Circe had previously turned half of his men into swine. So, this return alone tells us that we are swimming in classical, initiatory, mythic seas. In going back to face his "demon", or the shameful beast within, Odysseus ends up receiving immensely valuable guidance from Circe about how to plot a safe course home.

There were also turf labyrinths in the British Isles called *caerdrioa*, which is the Welsh name for the fortress of Troy. They were created by shepherds on hilltops and the local people would dance in them on certain festivals.

You will also find two labyrinths in Glastonbury. One has been cut into the turf of the graveyard of St John the Baptist's church in the High Street, and visitors are welcome to walk around it. The other one is more ornamental and so small, in fact, that you have walk around it with your fingers. It is in the grounds of St Margaret's Chapel and almhouses at the top of Magdalene Street.

There are some who regard the serpentine path around the Tor to be a labyrinth. To my mind, that takes a bit of a stretch of the imagination, although it would certainly have made an excellent processional camino.

But you might be wondering about the purpose of the labyrinth in terms of initiatory transformation? How does wandering around a maze or meander lead to enlightenment?

In the Hermetic system, the Captive is

imprisoned in a hermetically sealed container until he or she is Called to be the Chosen one. We can sometimes get this sense of being trapped, or not being able to progress, when we don't seem to be any further forward in our lives. Sometimes we're convinced that we are going backwards or are walking away from our destination.

In Sweden, labyrinths have been found at Troyaburg, Trjienborg and Trojbor. So, perhaps the meaning and purpose of this captivity can be perceived by those who have the eyes to see in the sagas of the Old Norseman, known as the *Edda*?

You will no doubt remember that the passage of the flow of Wyrd runs between three Wells arranged on the trunk of Yggdrasil, the World Tree. Urd's well is in the past, Verdandi's well is in the present and Skuld's well is in the future.

According to Rosemary Taylor, a shamanic practitioner who specialises in the *Edda*, the impression of retracing one's steps, when we're having to revisit an experience we thought we'd processed the learning from a long time ago, could be about the back-and-forth movement of the pendulum of time.

Rosemary wrote the following:

> *I see a concept of circular time inherent in the relationship between Urd and Verdandi, a relationship between "Origins" and "Becoming". We truly "move forward", or progress, by firstly "moving backwards" or "touching in with the past", by accessing the wisdom of Urd's well which we take forward again, in a constant pendulum-like to and fro that advances*

events and advances us within time. In the Becoming moment of the present, we add new knowledge of the Wyrd to Urd's well of our Origins in the past, according to what we observe happening as a result of our actions...

To my way of thinking, Skuld's well in the future would be at the centre of the labyrinth. It cannot be reached by walking in a straight line but only by continually revisiting the past and bringing the past into the future until we reach our destination.

Skuld is portrayed in the Edda as a Valkyrie. The Valkyries carry the chosen of the dead Viking warriors to their destination in Odin's feasting hall at Valhala, in a Norse version of Arthur's Wild Hunt. This means that Skuld is a psychopomp or a sort of gatekeeper, like the dog-headed Egyptian god Anubis, who guides the deceased from the world of the living into the realms of the dead.

On the level of the biome of the human vessel, this transfigurative process is found in what bioscientists call autophagy (or self-digestion).

Autophagy is a biological process that kicks in during fasting. Once the body is relieved from its task of having to manage the processes of the digestive system, it is free to go around and collect up all the old and damaged cells that are no longer of use and are just gumming up the works. Then they are transformed into components for vibrant new cells.

In the process of autophagy, we find a clear scientific link between transformation and fasting, and thus we can better understand why fasting was once an integral part of the challenges of the initiate who was seeking transfiguration. We find the remnants of this practice in the Lent of Christianity and the Ramadan of Islam. The word "fast" comes from when the priest or *hierophant* would shut fast the door on the initiate in the Captive stage, who would not be released until the fast was deemed complete.

During autophagy, the body creates special membranes to encircle the old and damaged cells to form a vesicle; in other words, a container for the alchemy of reprocessing to take place. It is like how a spider will first wrap up its prey, to pre-digest it before eating it. Similarly, the Child of the Nativity is described as "wrapped in swaddling clothes" when he first comes forth at the fruiting of the Vesica Pisces, otherwise known as the Marriage of the Sun and the Moon.

The Dark Night of the Soul

The biggest lie we are sold is that freedom and liberty are within our grasp, if only we vote "the right people" into power.

The so-called Age of Enlightenment of the 18th century provided the philosophical basis for two major revolutions that demanded freedom, liberty and equality. The Abolition of Slavery Act was enacted soon after that and following swiftly on its heels, Charles Darwin's theories freed mankind from the dictats and dogma of the Christian church, only for them be burdened down again with another religion - one dictated by a scientific priesthood.

In other words, all this seeming transformational activity in the surface world served only to clear the ground for a different kind of slavery; one in which Man is enslaved in his subconscious mind by a new narrative that persuades him that his prison is actually the Elysian Fields.

We have all been inculcated with that story from our births and so it is understandable if we are finding it a somewhat uncomfortable idea to regard ourselves as Captives in a prison or alchemical container of some kind.

We might be tempted to erect wooden Japanese screens within our cells, painted with rainbows and unicorns, and then hide in a virtual safe space to preserve the delusion. Others, who have a greater awareness of the reality, put their efforts into scaling the heights of influence and power in order to join the ranks of the jailers. However, in the final analysis, everyone is trapped – both prisoners and prison officers - and eventually, as they pass through the Valley of the Shadow of Death, they are all hoisted by their own petards.

I'm sorry if this sounds like a grim and stark narrative. However, it is the one that the Captive has to confront when he or she passes through the Dark Night of the Soul, which are in the Halls of Judgment within the Underworld. There is no escape from facing ourselves as vignettes and tableaux illustrating the major crossroads decisions of our lives pass before our eyes as our souls are weighed upon the balance.

The term Dark Night of the Soul was coined by 16th century Spanish mystic St John of the Cross who, in his poem *Noche Oscura*, describes the agonies of the trials that cannot be avoided on the path to divine union. To my understanding, his words read like the alchemical stage of putrefaction, which occurs briefly during the final stage of coagulation. Putrefaction is the final cleansing of the Great Work and it precedes what is known as the Peacock's Tail, so called because of a great and glorious explosion of extraordinarily beautiful psychedelic colours at the moment of metamorphosis. It is the origin of the saying: "It is always darkest before the dawn."

The Dark Night of the Soul is not a state reserved for those sloughing off their mortal coil. We all have to face the judge of the Underworld at times along our pilgrimage of life, usually when a "death" of some kind is imminent, at the end of a life cycle. Perhaps the most obvious example for a woman is when she realises that she has reached the end of her childbearing years at the menopause. But it can equally be undergone by a young woman who has to admit that her childhood is over when she bleeds at her first period; or a young man when his voice "breaks".

Viewed from this perspective, we can appreciate the vital importance of rites-of-passage ceremonies as a means of psychological and spiritual support at such times. In the days of Kroy-khasis, there would be special events in which the whole tribe or community came together to put on dramas, dances and songs to express the meaning of the "death" as an initiatory or threshold event, and a major milestone along the human camino.

I have found that shamanic healings in which a "death" or ending is faced honestly acts to validate and shore up the grief process, which is a vital staging post on the road to recovery. Otherwise, an artificial delusion can take over which needs chemical devices to create cognitive hiding spaces, such as alcohol, drugs and other forms of substances that lead to addiction – which is another form of slavery.

So how can we be released from this seeming eternal bondage? It is simple. The first step is to admit our Captivity and the second is to surrender to that realisation. Once we stop kicking against the ones who are trying to save us and relax, the process of transformation can begin.

The emotional pain begins to dissolve once we see that the bonds constricting us are not evil or mal-intended any more than the metallic-gold chrysalis wants to trap the butterfly forever. It is helpfully providing the means for the creature to grow wings before it can escape and the butterfly cannot cross this threshold until the process is complete. Neither can it do much to aid the process, other than wait.

All mammals go through this stage of imprisonment before birth. A human baby is kept Captive in the womb for about nine months before it is developed enough to be released into this world.

So we need confidence that the Gatekeepers and faery midwives will know when we are ready for transformation – and it is much easier to develop trust when you journey into the other dimensions to consult with the guides there. Just as a midwife will wait for the waters to break, they are also looking for a clear signal that the metamorphosis has taken place before acting and it comes when we understand enough to be able to express our gratitude for all that we have learned from our Captivity. It doesn't have to come in the form of a great symphony or a work of art – although, for those who have those skills, it is surely a wondrous labour of love to dedicate your days to. But, for most of us, a genuine flow of love directly from the heart is more than enough; it is the bridging *lingua franca* that opens the doors of perception through which we are reborn to the joyous Hallelujahs of all.

We will be pulling all these themes together, in the next chapter, so that you will be able to see the whole picture.

However, we have now reached the deep, fast-flowing river I told you about at the beginning. In *The Pilgrim's Progress*, Bunyan called it the River of the Waters of Life in which the weary Christian and his companions bathe and drink, and which so rejuvenated them that they sang joyfully:

> *Behold ye how these crystal streams do glide,*
> *To comfort pilgrims by the highway side;*
> *The meadows green, beside their fragrant smell,*
> *Yield dainties for them; and he that can tell*
> *What pleasant fruit, yea, leaves, these trees do yield,*
> *Will soon sell all, that he may buy this field.*

So, it should come as something of a relief to discard your rucksack, which, by now, is probably sagging heavily and cutting into your shoulders, jam-packed as it is with the dusty libraries of ancient philosophers - and just jump in!

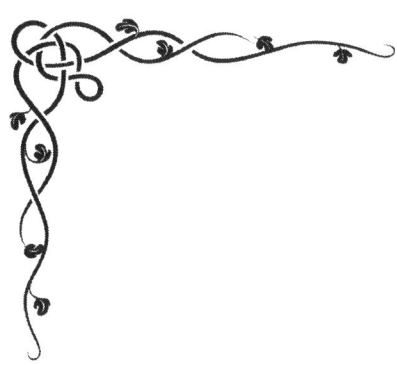

Chapter Twelve: The Faery Ring of the Perpetual Choirs

Evidence-based research can take us only so far as we go deeper into the Call to Adventure. Instead, I am inviting you to follow me, as a shaman, into a more multi-dimensional vision of reality.

Our eyes flicker questioningly towards a shimmering golden halo around a strange-looking ink-black furry sea urchin. On closer inspection, it turns out to be the drowned mountains of Atlantis with bejewelled seahorses and crowned sea serpents guarding spiralling, bifurcating tunnels that twist through marine blue lagoons of pearl-topped waves that seem to go on and on for ever.

You find yourself floating through a moving mosaic of kaleidoscopic Persian gardens and rotating carnival carousels of candy-striped hues. Sparkling silver sequins suddenly appear, scattered haphazardly, like a broken necklace, across a dawn pink sky. When you get closer, it turns out to be the trail of a giant Fibonacci-coiled snail. You leap up on to its back and it takes you the Ocean of Dreams of the Never Never Lands; dive into its depths and you find yourself spun into a glittering, spinning coronet of galaxies.

These are just some of the Otherworldly images that are produced when you feed certain equations into a computer. It has been called "the thumbprint of God" or a map of the geography of infinity. The 20th century mathematician Benoit Mandelbrot discovered this landscape by using a computer to create an algebraic equation between two dimensional planes. He multiplied and added the numbers of the Underworld - the dark, the feminine, the yin, the negative - to those of the surface Middle World of Earth - the light, the masculine, the yang, the positive. And Eureka!

We can "dive in" with our eyes to experience Mandelbrot's Set in an animation. But we can also hear it in the music of the 18th century composer J.S. Bach. In a way, the art and architecture of the Baroque period seems to have been inspired by an artistic expression of various mathematical formulae but Bach was a genius ahead of most in his field, with his nested levels of self-repeating sound fractals that spiral into the labyrinth of the ear as wave-like circles that wind for ever and ever into infinite space, especially in his *Contrapunctus IX* of *Art of the Fugue*.

And so, you might wondering why the strict keeper of Time, Saturn, would ever allow us mere humans a glimpse of eternity? Well, there is more to the Grim Reaper than meets the eye; a lot more. To the Romans, one of his aspects was the god Janus, who gave his name to the month of January. Janus faces both ways at once; he is the Alpha and Omega, the First and the Last, who occupies the threshold between the known and the unknown. In other words, he is the psychopomp who guides us across the threshold of the unknown once we have learned the lessons of our Captivity within Time.

The unknown is more than the linear mind can comprehend. It can only be experienced. So as much as we dive into the tunnels of a Mandelbrot animation, we are also able to enter into this eternal life when we take the plunge into the Waters of Avalon that run through the Hollow Hills of the Fae and the Sidhe, the Ever Young, the Never Never Land of Peter Pan.

I was influenced to explore the Temple of the Stars within my own Dreamtime by the writings of the Irish shaman Coleston Brown. But the primary lesson I gathered from my shamanic explorations is that there is no beginning to this faerytale, just as there is no end. They are in themselves an expression of eternity. Thus, they are a mirror image of our own existences as beings who have voluntarily taken bodily form to experience the never-ending path of the Four Joys and Four Sorrows that make up the Wheel of human pilgrimage.

And so, what appears at first to be just a flat, two-dimensional circle of giant effigies turns out, when we zoom in, to be a moving cinema of dramas that telescope, like a grand fugue, out of the Underworld until they reach the heavens of the Upper World and beyond.

The narratives they contain are ripe with a lore that is as old as Time, and, although I'm not sure whether he would agree, perhaps this brings in Anthony Thorley's extra-human influence, which shamans call the Elders, who fell to this Earth before Man – the creatures otherwise known as the Fae or Sidhe.

So, do you believe in faeries?

In his book *Peter Pan*, J. M. Barrie wrote about a Never Never Land that was inhabited by Otherworldly beings. He would have been inspired by ancient Celtic folktales set in the faery realms known as the Land of the Ever Young, in which his anti-hero, Peter Pan, never gets older. In coming up with his name, I imagine that Barrie was inspired by the nature god of the Greeks, Pan.

Peter Pan plays the role of the Captive in that he is for ever stuck in the Land of Never Never. It is what is meant by the term "anti-hero"; he is stuck on the treadmill of the minus numbers of Mandelbrot's Set along the spinning Wheel until his negative encounters with the adversaries force him to realise his true multidimensional nature and that turns him into the hero. He can transcend his Captivity into full enlightenment once he understands that his "enemies" were the Elders who were actually there to help him to make that realisation.

In the minds of most people nowadays, there is no such thing as a faery or, if there ever were such beings, they died out a long time ago. Either way, the whole notion of Faeryland is dead to a consensual consciousness in which we are trapped like prisoners in a mundane, Flatland, ever-repeating Groundhog Day.

From that perspective, we are just as much

Captives as were the Hebrews whose wise leaders used the stories that were eventually collated into the *Old Testament* to release themselves, metaphorically, from the Captivity in Egypt and later on, Babylon.

The myths of our ancestors, though, sometimes flow into our consciousness to try to remind us. So, we can be grateful to all the Grail Keepers of the past, like J. M. Barrie, whose dramatic works help us to wake from our false dream of reality. But really, it is our children, whose hearts are innocent, who are the ultimate keepers of the hearth.

If you've ever been lucky enough to find yourself at a theatrical performance of *Peter Pan*, you'll know there is an absolutely heart-stopping moment towards the end, when Tinkerbell is dying.

We are pinned to our seats as our hearts go out to the delicate, tiny-winged faery who is slowly expiring before our eyes. A narrator explains to us that she can only be brought back to life if we believe in faeries again.

The adults are usually frozen into paralysis by a mixture of cognitive dissonance and social embarrassment. But then, suddenly, a rosy-cheeked young girl in a pink gingham dress jumps to her feet and then a round-bespectacled boy stands up in the gods, and then another and another. Finally, there are dozens of children out of their seats, waving their arms and professing in their loudest voices that, yes, they do believe in faeries! It is a profoundly moving and magical moment – and don't think for a minute that the Fae don't hear those children.

So, if you are now on your feet shouting, you will

be ready to study this key, in **Figure 44**, to the ring of the 13 Faery Dreamers of Avalon.

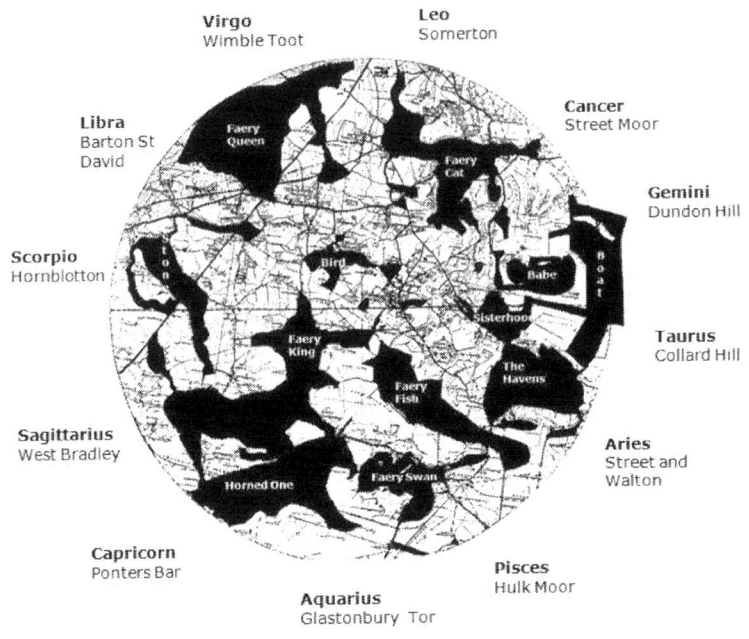

Figure 44 The Faery Ring of Avalon

The Milky Way also plays a pivotal role in these multi-dimensional tales.

There is a popular Summerlands ramble along well-trodden lanes and ridings which wends its way for more than 20 miles under its arching splendour. Beginning at High Ham and ending on the site of a Celtic temple at Lamyatt Beacon, the route passes through seven landmark churches. One of them you have already visited, St Andrew's Church at Compton

Dundon, with its spread-eagling 1,400-year-old yew tree.

Compton Dundon is also under the Gate of Man, which guards the portal at the beginning of the voyage of the Child on the cusp of Taurus and Gemini. The Child eventually arrives at the Gate of Souls, which is between Scorpio and Sagittarius, just south of West Bradley.

On the next page, in **Figure 45,** you will find a simplified table which shows the Faery Dreamers at their geographical locations and under the stars from which they "fell".

To my way of seeing, these giant faery beings move about according to the ebb and flow of the Waters of Avalon, the spiralling dance of the Moon around the Sun and the glittering, rotating chandeliers of the constellations.

They are all continually shapeshifting into different relationships with each other by the means of star stories that spiral into eternity.

The Roman poet Lucan wrote this of the Druids in the first century CE:

> *You, ye Druids... you who dwell in the deep woods in sequestered groves: your teaching is that the shades of the dead do not make their way to the silent abode of Erebus or to the lightless realm of Dis below, but that the same soul animates the limbs in another sphere. If you sing of certainties, death is the centre of continuous life.*

Figure 45 Locations and stars of the Faery Ring of Avalon

Faery Dreamer	Location	Stars and Constellations
The Faery Hound	Burrow Mump	Canis Major, Canis Minor, Columba
The Faery Swan	Glastonbury Tor	Aquarius, Fomalhaut, Cygnus
The Horned One	Ponter's Ball	Capricorn
The Faery King	Pennard Hills and Baltonsborough Flights	Sagittarius, Hercules, Bootes, Lyra, Cepheus
The Faery Stone	Stone, Hornblotton	Scorpio, Libra, Serpens, Ara
The Faery Queen	Wimble Toot	Virgo, Corvus, Crater, Hydra
The Faery Cat	Somerton	Leo, Cancer, Hydra
The Faery Boat	Street Moor	Argo Navis
The Faery Child	Dundon and Lollover hills	Orion the Hunter, Auriga the Chariot, Lepus the Faery Hare
The Sisterhood	Collard Hill	Taurus
The Havens	Street and Walton	Aries
The Faery Fish	Between Hulk Moor and Walyers Bridge, along the River Brue	Pisces, Cetus, Delphinus
The Well of the Stars	Park Wood	Ursa Minor, Ursa Major, Lyra, Cygnus, Draco

> *Truly the people on whom the Pole Star shines are happy in their error, for they are not harassed by the greatest of terrors, the fear of death. This gives the warrior his eagerness to rush upon the steel, a spirit ready to face death, and an indifference to a life which will return.*

Yes, we are happy in our error! In fact, it may be the only path to happiness.

Lucan may have been influenced by Julius Caesar, who had written, about 150 years earlier, about the strange, wild peoples he'd found in these damp and misty Isles:

> *A lesson which they (the Druids) take particular pains to inculcate is that the soul does not perish, but after death passes from one body to another; they think that this is the best incentive to bravery, because it teaches men to disregard the terrors of death.*
>
> *They also hold long discussions about the heavenly bodies and their movements, the size of the universe and of earth, the physical constitution of the world, and the power and properties of the gods; and they instruct the young men in all these subjects.* [1]

In the *Song of Amergin,* purportedly sang by the third century BCE poet Amergin when first he stepped on Irish shores from Spain with the conquering Milesians, we find this theme again - of the shapeshifting through different timelines and realities:

I am the wind that blows across the sea;
I am a wave of the deep;
I am the roar of the ocean;
I am the stag of seven battles;
I am a hawk on the cliff;
I am a ray of sunlight;
I am the greenest of plants;
I am the wild boar;
I am a salmon in the river;
I am a lake on the plain;
I am the word of knowledge;
I am the point of a spear;
I am the lure beyond the ends of the Earth;
I am the god who fashions fire in the head. [2]

The May Queen

And so, how would playwrights, bards and troubadours who believe in the eternal life of the soul portray that process in their plays and stories? Well, those who observed Nature's processes, like the alchemists, astronomers, astrologers and mathematicians, would compose a narrative with a plotline that followed the trajectory of its ultimate expression – the Vesica Piscis, which is the geometrical cipher for the Marriage of the Sun and the Moon.

As Maltwood writes in her Introduction to *Glastonbury's Temple of the Stars*:

> *It is interesting to note that it was once customary to personify the heavenly bodies and elements in religious drama and dance; one of the favourite mysteries by strolling companies in the southern*

provinces of China is called The Spectacle of the Sun and the Moon. That is exactly what the pre-Christian Grail Mystery appears to have been ... what is so extraordinarily interesting is the fact that the High History makes them perform on their original Giant Stage in Somerset, where their effigies have been lying for thousands of years.

One can only marvel at how this Dance of the Hours of Time would have been etched out in the star fire reflected in the waters of the Isle of Glass, due to seasonal inundations from the over spilling Severn estuary.

The word "temple" comes from the Latin tempus, which meant "time", and it also inspires the word "tempo", or "rhythm". Therefore, timing and rhythm is everything when it comes to this dance about new life conceived at a very special time in which there is a confluence of shapeshifting starring characters.

It is a story long forgot – and, over time, torn to shreds like the tattered gown of Cinderella. It needs to be sewn back together and I attempt to do that here.

The story begins at Beltane, otherwise known as May Day. You will already know that this festival is marked by numerous parades that wind their way through old market towns all over Britain, which celebrate the personage of the May Queen. The crowds cheer as the float passes carrying the pretty young woman and her handmaidens, all dressed up in bridal white with young sprigs of creamy may blossoms crowning their heads. Yet few question the meaning of her starring presence in such revels and ask which old faerytale she has stepped out of. Even if they did, they would be lucky to receive a correct answer.

Well, we can find her identity in a tale which, while as old as Time itself, is still alive and intact in the Summerlands to such an extent that we act it out every Beltane.

Drummers lead crowds of locals who are escorting two huge carved dragons – one red and one white - through the town to the lower flanks of the Tor, where a drama is acted out from a script that is at least 5,000 years old.

It is the story of a duel over the hand of a fair maiden. However, it is no ordinary contest because its two protagonists are also writ large in the night skies. At this time of the year, we can see both the constellations of Orion and Ophiuchus in the night skies. We call them by their old Druidic monikers as, respectively, Gwyn ap Nudd, the Winter King, and Gwythyr ap Greidawl, the Summer King.

But who is the May Queen? Which mythological personage does she represent? She is none other than Bridie, the sister of Gwyn, and she is the original Sleeping Beauty, the Dreamer in the Land.

And where do we find her in the night skies? Her stellar identity was an insoluble mystery for a long time – until we were able to consult online ephemerides, which produce maps of the ever-changing positions of the stars going back for thousands of years. A reproduction of the night skies over south-west England 5,000 years ago shows that, at that time, our ancestors in the northern hemisphere could see the Southern Cross, although it was already beginning to slip into the southern hemisphere.

So, you might be wondering how the Southern Cross could be perceived as a beautiful woman, as Bridie was reputed to be? We can find the answer by turning to an extract from Nicholas Mann and Philippa Glasser's *The Star Temple of Avalon*.

> *In the star temple of Avalon ... the recurring drama unfolding in the night sky during the fourth millennium BCE would have had at its heart a particular jewel: the Southern Cross, whose central importance would have been indicated by its relationship to the earthy feminine contours of the Chalice Hill.*
>
> *When, in 1501, Italian explorer Amerigo Vespucci became one of the first Europeans to see the Southern Cross for several thousand years, he did not identify it as a cross; rather he described its pattern as a 'mandorla', that is, almond-shaped.*
>
> *As a mandorla or a vesica, the constellation can now be recognised as an ancient symbol of the divine feminine [at the centre of the vesica piscis.] Did early British astronomers also see it in this manner... perhaps envisaging the horizontal band of the Milky Way as her star skirt, or her golden or silver hair, or possibly even seeing the star-vesica as forming the goddess' vulva, in the manner of the Celtic Sheela-na-gig?*

There is a seasonal explanation for the rationale behind the drama of the duel at Beltane. It is that the serpent-slaying Gwythyr ap Greidawl is the Lord of Summer who has to win the duel against the Winter King at Beltane, to prevent us from being frozen in time, in a permanent winter. But when we burrow under Bridie's starry underskirts, we can go much deeper than that.

This saga is actually about sex; it is about fertility, conception and birth, and it is about how Mother Nature eternally renews herself through the processes described in the Marriage of the Sun and the Moon. It takes place, shamanically speaking, when the Sun in Taurus is being eclipsed by the full Moon in Scorpio – hence the concern with being able to predict eclipses of those who built Stonehenge.

The Moon is blood red when it rises in Scorpio to eclipse or make love with the Sun at Taurus. At this moment, Gwyn (Orion) is eclipsed in battle by Gwythyr (Ophiuchus) and he falls, bleeding, from the skies to disappear into the Underworld.

The Sisterhood flies over to Hornblotton to blow the faery horn. Upon this signal, the messenger Faery Bird of Mercury-Hermes leaves the outstretched, leather-gauntleted arm of the Faery King under Sagittarius, now embodied by Gwythyr, and it swoops swiftly under the Milky Way towards Bridie the May Queen, who is inhabiting the form of the Faery Queen under Virgo.

And so, the orchestra strikes up for "Here Comes the Bride" as Bridie goes to meet her serpent-slaying Bridegroom at the Faery Stone. The birds of the Summer Triangle begin to sing, to seed the land with the secret song of Sovereignty.

The two lovers are hand-fasted by the Sisterhood and their holy union is consecrated by the Faery Bird. Then the couple retire to the privacy of the dark umbra shadow created by the lunar eclipse to begin their honeymoon and they make love under a ripe full Moon that is glowing red with the reflection of a million sunsets from all over the world.

Faery Guides, Godmothers and Midwives

The Faery Child is thus conceived as a tiny seed and then the story unfolds of its development into the metamorphosis of human incarnation over a voyage of nine-and-half-moons' duration along the Milky Way, in the deeps of the Underworld. He is helped and guided by his godmothers and midwives - the Sisters of the Pleiades.

These seven bright stars are also known as the Sisterhood or the Seven Sisters from the Greek myths, in which they are the daughters of Pleione. But they also appear as the winged guides of the hero or anti-hero, who are such favourites in children's pantomimes and faery stories. For instance, Cinderella could only go to the ball to meet the Prince with the help of her faery godmother.

Then there are the three faery guardians of the Sleeping Beauty, who are based on the Three Norns. There is also the Blue Faery who guides and protects Pinocchio, and we must not forget Peter Pan's Tinkerbell.

She is also Dante's Beatrice, from an epic poem[3] that recounts the spiralling progress of a Tuscan pilgrim through the Three Worlds towards enlightenment.

These protective, guiding spirits are all different

aspects of Venus, the goddess of love, who is sometimes presented as the eldest of the Sisters.

Tinkerbell tries to guide the hot-headed anti-hero of Peter Pan just as the god of tin, Jupiter, oversees the mythological hero through his Dark Night of the Soul in the judgement of the Underworld.

Tinkerbell is Jupiter's sometime belle when she forms with him an astrological conjunction as Venus, to guide our champion when he is in the depths of confusion about which path to follow.

How can he tell which is the true way? Only by following his instincts, because when those senses are in play, the truth rings just like the Tinker's bell.

In this drama played out on the Faery Ring, the Sisters play pivotal roles at two festivals - Beltane and Samhain.

At Beltane, the Pleiades are just beginning to set or sink into the Underworld, for the midwives to be in place to help the Faery Babe of Gemini get into his boat, under Argo Navis, at Cancer, and begin his voyage down the birth canal of the Milky Way.

Once he reaches the cusp between Scorpio and Sagittarius, which is ruled by Jupiter, the Pleiades are rising again.

Thus the eldest of the Sisterhood, Venus, will be present to guide him through his Dark Night of the Soul, in which he has to face his shadow side and reintegrate it into his personality to make himself whole. Barrie illustrates this process when he has Tinkerbell help Peter Pan sew his shadow back on again.

To some with more far-sighted eyes, there are nine bright stars of the Pleiades, and they were said to be cognate with the nine muses of Greek myths.

We find them in Celtic lore as the nine maidens who stir Ceridwen's Cauldron of Knowledge and Inspiration in Taliesin's poem, Preiddeu Annwfn, as follows:

> *I draw my knowledge from the famous cauldron*
>
> *The breath of nine maidens keeps it boiling.*
>
> *Is not the Head of Annwfn's cauldron so shaped;*
>
> *Ridged with enamel, rimmed with pearl?*
>
> *It will not boil the cowardly traitor's portion ...*

To my way of seeing, each of the Moon Maidens opens a new Gate of Inspiration every 40 days, making nine Moon gates or portals for the whole of year.

And perhaps this is the meaning and purpose of the 40 holes perforated around the perimeter of the Nebra Sky Disc, which shows how the night sky would look when the Pleiades are risen.

Christmas in Avalon

> *For unto us a Child is born, unto us a Son is given, and the government shall be upon His shoulder; and his name shall be called Wonderful Counsellor, the Mighty God, the Everlasting Father, the Prince of Peace.*
> **Isaiah 9:5**

These words of exaltation were used by 18th

century German composer George Frederic Handel in his epic, labyrinthine, choral masterpiece *Messiah*.

The story – apocryphal or not – is that as Handel lay dying, his friend asked him whether he felt that his mission on Earth was complete. He couldn't speak, so he just nodded toward the shelf above his bed, with a smile of satisfaction. It held the stacked-up folios of the original music for *Messiah*.

Handel's smile hid a secret about his knowledge of sacred geometry that has only recently been revealed by the modern science of cymatics. Cymatics refers to the practice of covering a metal plate with fine grains of sand or dust and then vibrating it with an excitatory medium of sound. The grains eventually form into patterns that are organised according to the mathematics used to compose the sonar input. When *Messiah* is played, a five-pointed star of Venus, the ultimate symbol of love, forms on the plate – and, in my experience, in the heart of anyone listening or performing it.

I remember one Christmas singing this great masterpiece among massed choirs in Albert Hall in London. I had been rehearsing it for months and so the star of the goddess of love was already well-engraved into my heart when I found myself among thousands of masons of the temple as we sung spiralling and soaring arias, recitatives and *Hallelujah* choruses that gradually built shimmering walls of sound that formed into a towering, columned, fan-vaulted, Gothic-arched cathedral of exultation to the most highest.

Handel was so skilled in the Hermetic Arts that he understood how to use sacred geometrical principles to compose music as a form of magical incantation capable of moving mountains. Many other composers – including Bach, Berlioz and Mozart – were also initiated into the Great Arts, judging from their music.

In *Messiah*, Handel had found a way to express to the creator his heartfelt praise and appreciation of the glory of the creation in the language the creator itself uses to create it. It is like sending a Valentine's card to the gods of Wyrd in a language they can hear – and thus respond to. It is how dialogue between the portals has always been conducted by shamans, *awenwyddions*, Grailkeepers and all those inspired by the *awen*, going back to the times of Tabiti, whose rhythmic prose and songs were poetically constructed in such a way as to echo around and around, along the labyrinthine corridors running through the ear to the brain, long after the storyteller has closed the book.

In using popular, Italian operetta music to score his sacred oratorio, Handel ensured that his expression of love and praise would continue to be sung and transmitted through those ever-spiralling channels, for centuries upon centuries to come. That was his legacy.

The drama eternally playing out on in the Faery Ring is a similarly expressed message of love and in leaving it for us to find and interpret, our ancestors have bequeathed us an expression of hope and faith in our future.

And so, once we have enough knowledge to realise how the creation creates itself, we can join in this perpetual choir of exultation and give heartfelt thanks at Christmas for the nativity of the Radiant Child in a way that has been ever heard and always answered in a resonation that rings on and on and on... throughout the ages.

The Birth of the Radiant Child

There are several clues as to the mythological roots of the conception and birth of the Radiant Child in the Irish story about Aengus of the Tuatha da Danaan.

Aengus was conceived when the river goddess Boann made love with the male god, the Dagda. The name Boann means literally "cow god" and her name was also given to the river Boyne. The River Boyne is thought to mirror the path of the Milky Way in the same way that the Egyptians geo-engineered the River Nile to bring those "stars down to the Earth". The ancient Irish Celts called the Milky Way *Bealach na Bó Finne*, or the Way of the White Cow. It was as if, to their more poetic vision, a great cow had left a trail of glistening white milk in a sparkling arch across the heavens.

It can be no mere coincidence that inside the ruined tower on the summit of Glastonbury Tor, which is overseen by the Faery Swan of Bridie, there is an engraving of a milkmaid milking a cow. Her role at the birth as both the white cow and the white swan will become clearer once we reach that stage. But for now, let's go back to the genesis of the Faery Child at Beltane, which is when he begins his nine-and-a-half-month gestation period in Bridie's womb in the Underworld (see **Figure 46**).

The Faery Child is conceived during Taurus, attended by the midwives of the Pleiades, the Sisterhood, who tend to his early days as the Sun passes through Gemini. Once he is ready, the Sisters place him in the Moon Boat at Cancer. Then, once he reaches Leo, he meets the Faery Cat, who becomes his guide. This felicitous feline is an offspring of Ceridwen, who gave birth to it in her animal aspect of Henwen, which means "white sow".

Figure 46 *The gestation voyage of the Radiant Child*

So, we can perhaps now appreciate the riddling play on words that Taliesin used in his shapeshifting story. In typical bardic fashion, he disguised the white sow named Henwen as a black hen who sported a spiked red comb, like the radiating Sun of Leo. It makes sense when we discover that this puss is found in Celtic myths as Cath-Palug or "Palug's Cat", which gives us a poetic resonance with the sun god Lug or Lugh, who rules the sign of Leo.

This magical moggie's nativity is recounted in

star story entitled *The Three Powerful Swineherds of the Isle of Britain* [4], in which we are told that Henwen the white Sow runs in a circle, giving birth to a number of different creatures at various locations.

One of Henwen's progeny is a kitten. However, it is not wanted and so it is thrown into the Menai Straits. Luckily, though, the sons of Palug come along to rescue it and they do such a good job of raising it that the cat of the Sons of Pulag – Cath Pulag - goes on to become a huge, monstrous beast that, in one story, Arthur must battle. Thus, in this tale from the Welsh *Triads* we find a remnant of the myth of the Celtic hero who, like Hercules and his Nemean Lion, has to overcome the adversary of a Faery Cat at Leo.

However, when the Faery Child sails into Cath Pulag's domain at Leo, the Faery Cat must be feeling more friendly than it did to Arthur and it decides to keep him company through the dark Underworld deeps. It could be said that, like Edward Lear's *Owl and the Pussycat*, they "went to sea in a beautiful pea-green boat" along with "some honey and plenty of money wrapped up in a five-pound note". And just like that enchanted pair, they probably had plenty of adventures involving turkeys and pigs, and all sorts of other beasts, and dined on "mince and slices of quince" and "danced by the light of the Moon".

Eventually, though, the Moon Boat reaches a junction where the river of the gods of the Milky Way intersects the Temple of the Stars. Here, the Faery Child sails into Sagittarius and thus will have a few more challenges to face before he is born with the returning Sun on the Winter Solstice.

His advent is heralded by the materialisation of the three Wise Men, or *magi*, in the evening skies. They have been "following the star" of Orion by lodging themselves and their "ships of the desert", or their camels, into its belt. Of course, we know the giant Orion better as the Faery Child's uncle, Gwyn ap Nudd, and he is by now striding back and forth expectantly over the hills of Dundon and Lollover.

This is the hidden meaning of the lines in the Victorian carol: "I saw three ships come sailing in, on Christmas Day, on Christmas Day." But the three wise men are just the first to the crib. The dark skies soon begin to shine with many of the characters who had starring roles in the performance of this Christmas Carol and are now gathering around "the manger" for the finale.

Just before sunrise, the constellations of Virgo (the Faery Queen) and Herakles (Culhwch) appear on the south-east horizon. It causes an Underworld star fire alignment to spark up, which runs like a strand of silver tinsel from Bridie in her shape of the Horned One, emerging from White Lake, to the Faery Swan, her bird form, on top of Glastonbury Tor. This is the signal that the waters have broken and the birth is imminent. Then, just as the light of Sagittarius is being absorbed into the apricot-dawn skies, Gwythyr, the Babe's dragon-slaying father's constellation of Ophiuchus, rises in the east.

All this signifies a vital part of the process that is explained here by the Irish shaman Coleston Brown [5]:

> ...*these are particularly concerned with the inner power or dragon fire that enlivens the landscape and*

those who live within it. Beyond this, they mark the conclusion of the "conceiving of powers" and signify the opening of a flow or release of spiritual energy into the atmosphere and the landscape.

The release is bound up with the traditions of the birth of the holy child, which probably relates less to a particular mortal child than it does to the birth of an initiatic stream, the signs of which are already evident in our day to those with even a modicum of esoteric perception.

The sense of pregnancy in the air is tangible. The land is already buzzing with power and the Sun hasn't even risen yet. However, when it does, it forms another sparkling, starry alignment that runs from the Well of the Stars to just below the skirts of the Faery Queen at Virgo – that is, to her womb.

At the same time, the Way of the White Cow intersects with the Temple of the Stars to form a perfect Vesica Piscis that activates further energy flows. It is then that the silver spindle of the Underworld smith spirals forth, upwards into the heavens, to prise open the dark void within the creatrix of the arching splendour for the Child to be born.

At noon, there is a further alignment[6] in which the powers reach their peak and a glittering, silver five-pointed star of Venus appears on the land, just like the one that is sung into existence in Handel's *Messiah*, and it is created by the alignment of the Sun with the dark void of Bridie's womb at the centre of the Way of the White Cow.

And so, unto us a child is born. And just like any

loving mother, Bridie is present to nuture and guide him through his early days in her two animal forms, first as a White Cow and then as a White Swan.

The Babe has been fed with the milk of the Way of the White Cow as he sailed down it to be born on the Winter Solstice. So, it is only fitting that when the "waters" of the white cow break, they would form a white lake.

The Faery Child first emerges from White Lake on the back of the Horned One and he is accompanied by his midwife Sisters. The White Cow's hooves scrunch loudly as she plods through the frosty icing of the fields until she reaches the bridge over the River Brue at Cow Bridge Lane. One of the Sisters carefully transfers the babe, wrapped in swaddling bands, into a coracle boat made of willow rods tied with willow barks and the Faery Child sails off.

During the early months of the year, the Mists of Avalon rise to protect its divine charge. Dion Fortune called this airy manifestation the Lake of Wonder and it is surely wondrous how it veils the baby's journey along the River Brue, until the pale yellow crocuses are ready to poke up their heads to herald the time of Imbolc.

It is then that Bridie, in her White Swan Cygnus form, spies him. She instantly swoops down to gather him up. He snuggles up gratefully into his mother's soft, warm down and then they fly on until they reach the sanctuary of her mound.

Bridie's Mound is in the part of Glastonbury called Beckery, the name of which is derived from *Bec-Eriu*, or Little Ireland. It is under the constellation of Cetus the Whale in Pisces, and so it is there that the

Child meets his companion for the final stage of his initiatory journey into young adulthood. This Faery Fish is the Irish Salmon of Wisdom and so like Job and Pinocchio before him, the boy has much to learn in the belly of the whale that will help him develop through his adolescence.

His schooling continues apace until one day, the Faery Fish sails into the harbour of the Havens at Street Moor. It is the time of the Spring Equinox and the harbourmaster Manawydan comes out to greet the young man by sounding the horn of the ram of Aries.

Manawydan is the Lord of the Seas, the Welsh equivalent of Neptune or Poseidon. And so, our young man now passes one whole passage of the Moon with this great Sea Lord, learning navigational and other marine skills.

The Irish named this mythical harbourmaster Macmannan mac Lir. His great ship, called the *Wave Sweeper*, can expand to accommodate any number of passengers and does not need oars or sails to move.

Macmannan trains Aengus in swordsmanship and when he considers his pupil to be fully competent, he gifts him a sword named *Moralltach*, or Great Fury, before sending him off to face his lion-headed quinotaurs and sea serpents... and so the story goes on and on ...for ever.

In viewing the whole drama from the vantage point of the Faery Swan hovering over Glastonbury Tor, the 360-degree voyage of the Faery Child goes widdershins or anti-clockwise, just as the pole stars appear to do from Earth. And it also follows a framework which forms the basis of Mandelbrot's Set:

in rooting the plot in the dark, yin, negative numbers in the Underworld, the path of the journey of the hero swirls upwards like a spiralling nautilus shell that reaches up into the stars and beyond, into eternity.

On the first full Moon of the Spring Equinox, we throw hot cross buns into the "mouth of the Girt Dog" in the River Parrett, near Burrow Mump, to give thanks for the Child that is being continually born and which will do so as long as this creation exists.

These talismanic hot cross buns, branded with the X-shape of the saltire cross, symbolise where the Way of the White Cow crosses the ecliptic and we believe this is why King Alfred the Great burned the cakes... but that's another story for another day.

---

[1] *The Conquest of Gaul* by Julius Caesar.
[2] *The Song of Amergin* from the *Lebor Gabála Érenn* ("The Book of the Taking of Ireland"), compiled in the 11th century.
[3] "Divine Comedy" (*Divina Commedia*) by Dante Alighieri, 14th century.
[4] Welsh *Triads*
[5] *Secrets of the Faery Landscape* by Coleston Brown
[6] The Sun and the centre of the Milky Way first aligned in this way at the Winter Solstice of 1975 and will continue to do so, every Winter Solstice, until 2220. It is not necessary to be in Avalon to experience this act of magico-spiritual communion, because it resonates all over the Earth at this time.

PART THREE: The Chosen

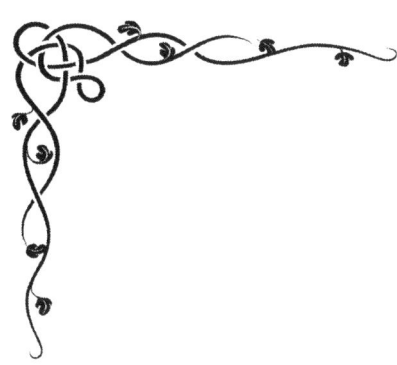

Chapter Thirteen: The Sovereignty of the Land

I know a dell where the willow mint grows,
Where bluebells chime in the midnight hallows,
And bowers of may and honeyed suckle
Curtain the congress of loving couples
With prickling briar roses running wild.
Deep in this Garden of Earthly Delights
Sleeps Beauty, sometime of the night.
Her perfumed lap like lapis lazuli skies,
All the Love of the world is in Her eyes.
And there, the Serpent is rising once more
To fire up the ways and open the doors.

Annie Dieu-Le-Veut

The rulers of old would undergo Sovereignty rites on the day of their coronation that were similar to the horse sacrifice of the Vedic and Egyptian kings. That evening, under a full Moon, they would lie with a *cuen*, which is the Anglo-Saxon source of the word "queen".

The *cuen* did not need to wear a crown on her

head because she was already Bright-browed; her inner crown was already sparkling with the gold of the Sun and the diamond light of the Moon. And she did not require any anointing from the Archbishop of Canterbury because her innermost elixirs were already flowing like honeyed nectars throughout her whole being.

The *cuen* was a shaman skilled in evoking and awakening the two energetic serpents which, during sexual intercourse, would rise and interweave up through the human body, just as they do on a caduceus, to create the Marriage of the Sun and the Moon. (See **Figure 47**).

The two serpents were known to those who practised the Indian form of the rite, known as tantra, as Ida and Pingala. The ancient Egyptians believed that one serpent was black and the other gold. Sacred sex rites were what inspired the erotic poetry of the Sumerians and Babylonians, and the Song of Solomon in the *Old Testament*.

But whatever the different names and belief systems that used such diverse imagery to describe this process, it is important to realise it is not an imaginary visualisation but a real physiological experience in which the Other Worlds break through into this one.

Once the serpents reach the head and the cup-shaped hypothalamus, which resembles a chalice or grael, they look over the rim and secrete their elixirs. Ida, the gold serpent, secretes red drops while Pingala, the black serpent, secretes white drops. The fluids then roll down the sides of the chalice until reaching its base and then the red and white serpentine drops swirl together.

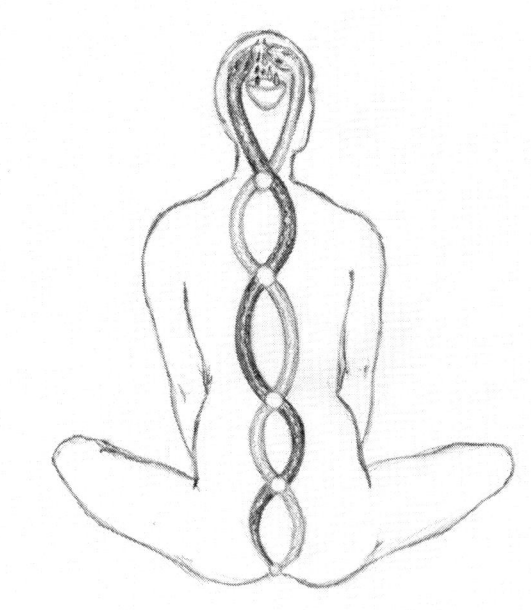

Figure 47 *The dance of the black and gold serpents*

The mixture attracts the mercurial catalyst and there is an explosion of the light of a thousand diamond-studded Suns. The light enlightens the upper brain centres and it confers wisdom, which is the ultimate blessing of the spirits of the land, thus bestowing upon the initiate the key to Sovereignty.

In Britain, the cipher that the monarch has passed through this metamorphosis and thus has gained the right of rulership is the Lion (Sun) and the Unicorn (Moon.)

In all of this, we find the real meaning behind the legend of the red and white fluids that were carried to

Avalon by Joseph of Arimathea after the Mysteries had been explained to him in a French prison.

It was the final teaching of Eleusis; the Holy Grail of the knights of Arthur Pendragon; the glittering prize of countless serpent-grappling heroes of yore, from Hercules to Michael. And it is the treasure of the Radiant Child who is conceived from the marriage of the serpent slayer Gwythyr to his beautiful Bridie in the shadow of the Faery Stone under the red glow of a million sunsets and the song of the birds of summer.

This is the great secret of Solomon's Seal. Initiates to the Mysteries were forbidden, upon pain of death, from revealing this inner alchemical process that underpins fertility and rulership. The advanced wisdom about the magical power within the body that extends, holographically, into the body politic was strictly reserved for kings and pharaohs, tsars and emperors, who used it to hold the Sovereignty of the cuentry, the country.

The *cuen* would rarely sit on the throne to share political power with the king, although there are exceptions to every rule. It is true that pharaoh Akhenaten insisted upon marrying the beautiful Kiya after he fell in love with the aroma of her hair. But usually, the *cuen* was the power behind the throne.

The Sovereign ruler would marry the daughter of another king for diplomatic purposes but the *cuen* was always the source of his claim to the Sovereignty of the *cuentry*. She was the bridge between the ruler and the nature spirits; the king and the land. It is what is behind the expression "the king marries the land". In fact, the king married the spirits of the land through the auspices of the *cuen* in what was not merely an empty ritual but a real, tangible experience of divinity.

If you'd like to learn more about these shamanic sexual practices – when, where and how it was practised - it's all in my book *The Sacred Sex Rites of Ishtar*. But to carry you through this last stage of our pilgrimage, all you need to know is that it is crucial for a king to experience the inner alchemy produced by the Marriage of the Sun and the Moon in order to receive the wisdom of divine intercourse which allows him to rule his land wisely and fairly.

So, now we will leave the divine players of the Faery Enclosure to their starlit revels, to walk out into our final destination. It is found within an enchanted enclosure that is surely comparable to John Bunyan's Celestial City, which is in the shape of a diamond.

The king's right to rule was signified by a diamond because it symbolised the *mandorla*, the inner part of the Vesica Piscis. We find its cipher in this land once ruled by nobles in a diamond-shaped temenos of 11 miles by 11 miles on each of its four sides, which are solely created by the passage of the Sun and the Moon on the four quarter festivals (see **Figures 48** and **49**).

This diamond represents the yoni at the centre of the Vesica Piscis; it is the vulva so vividly displayed on numerous images of Sheela-na-gigs found up and down the country and you will find several as we explore this domain. There is some disagreement among academics – when is there not? – about the age of the Sheela-na-gigs, because none have been found on buildings that are any older than Norman churches.

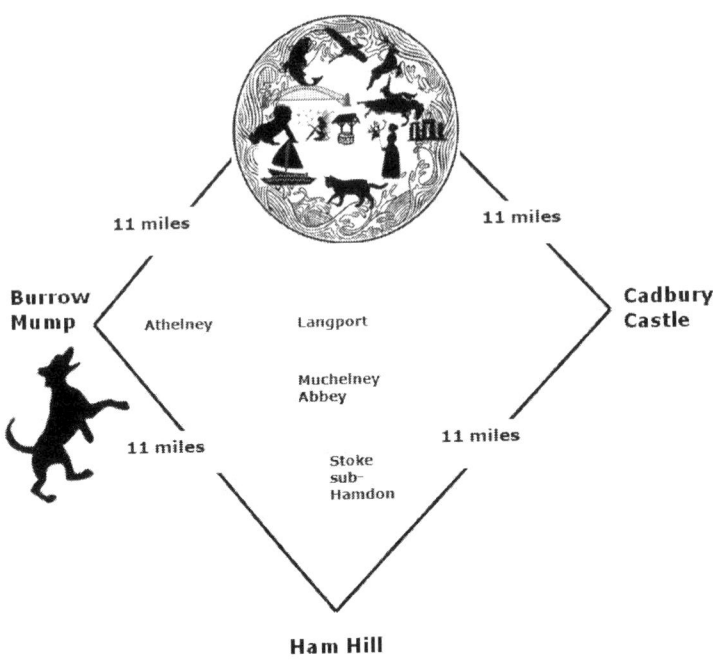

Figure 48 The Somerset Parallelogram

However, archaeologists have uncovered hundreds of soft-stone figurines all over Europe with huge drooping vulvas and some of these are tens of millennia-old – such as the so-called Venus of Hohle Fels, who was clay-fired at least 35,000 years ago.

You will also find lots of fire-breathing serpents and wyrms carved into the walls and pews of the churches of the Summerlands and hear local legends about dragon slaying saints and clerics, from Aller to Worminster. In fact, the heraldic symbol for the county of Somerset is a red dragon.

The right-hand-side triangle that makes up this

diamond enclosure was discovered by the 17th century antiquarian William Stukeley. He found that it was delineated by churches dedicated to St Michael and he wrote, dryly, that this land had been "cleared of serpents by some saint or other". There is an explanation for that.

The village of Barton St David lies in Stukeley's part of the rhombus. Until the 1600s, it had been the home of the Adams family, which had sired two American presidents – the Founding Father John Adams and his son, John Quincy Adams.

John Quincy Adams was named after the Massachusetts town of Quincy, where the patriarch Henry Adams had settled after fleeing to the New World colonies. According to a monument erected by John Adams in Quincy, his father had gone into exile there ahead of the "dragon persecutions" of south-west of England. There is still a memorial to the Adams family today in the 13th century church of Barton St David.

However, there are carvings of fire-breathing dragons aplenty in the churches situated in the left-hand-side triangle, which was discovered by Maltwood two centuries later.

It took almost another century to pass before Yuri Leitch put both triangles together to form what he calls the "Somerset Parallelogram".

But what is so extraordinary about this landscape diamond is that between the ruined St Michael church on top of Burrow Mump and what remains of the St Michael tower on the summit of Glastonbury Tor, we can follow the passage of the Sun at Beltane and

Lughnasadh, as well as its setting on Imbolc and Samhain (as shown on Figure 51). It is an exactly straight track.

Conversely, from high points on the other side that stretches between Glastonbury Tor and Cadbury Castle, the ancient sky watchers would have marked the Northern and Southern Major Standstill points of the Moon.

The Northern and Southern Major Standstill refers to the furthest points north and south from which one can view the setting Moon in the course of a fortnight, or 14 nights. We can see the importance of this sky measurement to the ancients in the megalithic monument of Stonehenge. It has been proposed, with some validity, that the so-called Aubrey Holes would have been used to measure the movements of the Moon. These Bronze Age folk seemed to be particularly interested in being able to predict when eclipses would occur – perhaps because they knew that is when the Moon makes loves with the Sun.

It can be no coincidence that within this favoured rhombus, we find the most valued institutions of medieval England – the Royal Mint at Langport, Glastonbury Abbey, Muchelney Abbey and the monastery at Athelney, near Burrow Mump, from where King Alfred the Great set out to win a "lucky" victory against the Vikings that marked the beginning of the end of their occupation of Britain.

The word "lucky" has connotations these days with the concept of "chance". The ancients did not leave their luck to chance.

Etymological dictionaries are unhelpful but the word may have been derived from Lugh, the Irish Sun god in his union with au clair de la lune. "Luck" also rhymes with an Anglo-Saxon word for sexual congress. Certainly, it is true that the luckiest people – both then and now – had a fruitful life that was produced by the honeymoon blessings of the blazing red fireball and the cool white lunar orb under the rose briar and honeysuckle protection of the Nature Spirits.

Figure 49 The passage of the Sun and the Moon

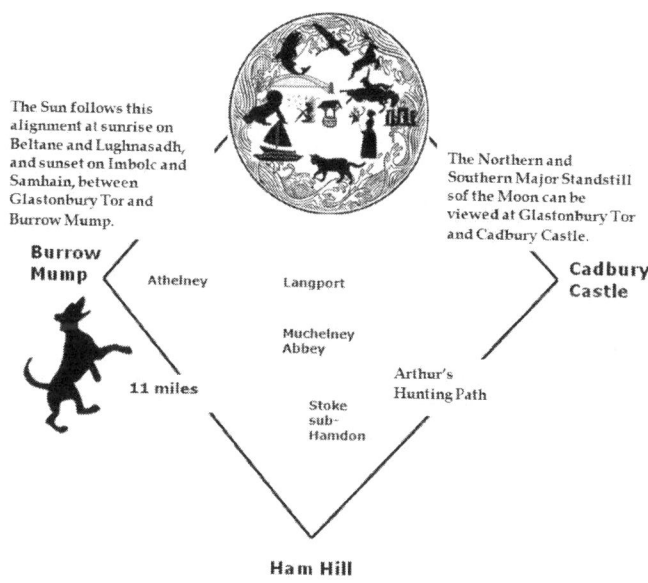

The passage of the Sun god

Long before the Romans paved the roads of Europe, the continent was criss-crossed throughout by the paths of the Sun god. It was as though the flaming golden chariot of Helios had broken down and lost a wheel. He is found all over Europe, rolling a gigantic wheel before him, up hill and down dale, while scratching a bird track-like script on rocks to indicate his passing and even forging a straight track through the high mountain passes of the Pyrenees.

During these times, before the Roman Emperor paved the Druids' straight tracks across Europe with their metalled, cambered roads, the names of the Sun god across what was then a colourful mosaic of cultures were as various as the tribal peoples who engraved his great 12-spoked wheel on the milestones of the places that he visited.

The solar gods who are the most familiar to us now are those of the Greeks and Macedonians, such as Apollo and Helios. But in French Gaul, before the Romans arrived, the Sun god was known as Ogmios and to the Scots and the Irish he was Ogma the Sun-faced, the great champion of the Tuatha da Danann. There were also many tribes where the solar deity's name was derived from the root word Bel, which meant "shining", such as Belenus or Belinus of the Gaulish and the Brythonic peoples and Beli Mawr of the Welsh. It was this Beli whose festival is celebrated on May Day and named in their honour as Beltane.

And so, it was Beli Mawr who rolled his Wheel across the Isles of Britain, forging his straight tracks in perfect alignment with the sunrises and sunsets of the cross-quarter festivals of Beltane, Lughnasadh, Samhain and Imbolc. His glory was reflected in the Moon. She danced around him with her silvery ribbons of rivers, streams, brooks, pools and wells, many of which are now marked with churches and shrines dedicated to St Mary.

Geoffrey of Monmouth wrote in his *Historia Regum Britanniae* ("History of the Kings of Britain"), of a mythical King Belinus who came to Britain long before the Romans and who commanded that a causeway should be constructed which would run the whole length of Britain "from the sea of Cornwall to the shores of Caithness" and lead directly to the cities that lay along that route. He could have been inspired by much older Welsh tales in which we find evidence of the advanced surveying abilities of the Druids.

One of Beli Mawr's sons was the aforementioned Nudd (Nuada of the Irish), the ancestor of Gwyn. Nudd was known later on as Lludd, who went on to inherit the rulership of Britain from his father, Beli, and to establish the city of Caer Lludd, which became London.

In the *Mabinogion*, although derived from a much older 13th century text[1], there is story in which Lludd is finding it difficult to rule the kingdom of Britain because it has been assailed by three terrible plagues.

One plague is the Coraniaid, a warlike people that had invaded Britain. They cannot be forced out, however, because they always seem to know in advance what the British are planning. Each of them has such supersensitive ears that they can hear anything the wind touches.

The second plague is causing his people to starve to death because the provisions from their stores keep disappearing every night, with no explanation.

And last, but by no means least, the country is being bedevilled by a terrible, blood-curdling scream that resonates all around the land on Beltane Eve. It is such a terrifying sound that men, upon hearing it, turn as white as ghosts and their pregnant women miscarry.

However, luckily, Lludd has a very clever brother named Llevelys. Llevelys had gone abroad, years earlier, to marry a French princess and he was now the king of France. So Lludd decides to ask him for his advice.

He sails across the Channel, while Llevelys leaves the coast of France to meet him halfway.

After greeting one another, Llevelys suggests that they talk through a brass horn so that the wind cannot carry their words to the ears of the Coraniaid.

So Lludd then explains to him about the three plagues afflicting the Isles of Britain, to which his brother gives him the following advice:

For the first plague, Llevelys gives him the recipe for a mixture made from certain insects, which while harmless to the British people, is instantly lethal to the Coraniaid. He suggests calling the invading force to a parley for peace and then throwing the insect liquid over them.

For the second plague, Llevelys explains that the people are being sent into a very deep sleep by a very powerful magician, who waits for them to nod off before stealing all their food. He tells Lludd that he must confront and subdue him.

Finally, he turns to address the plague of the terrible scream on Beltane Eve. He informs him that the cause is a red dragon fighting with a white dragon, and so he gives him the remedy.

"When you arrive home," Llevelys said, "have

the length and breadth of the island measured. When you find the exact centre, the *omphalos*, dig a pit there. Then place a vat full of the best mead in that pit and cover the vat with a silk sheet. The dragons will find the mead and drink it, and it will send them to sleep. Once they are unconscious, put them into a stone chest and bury them underground."

Lludd is much heartened as he returns home with his remedies for the three plagues.

First, he destroys the Coraniaid in the way his brother suggested. They all die on the spot. Lludd then faces and overcomes the powerful magician, so that his people can eat again.

Finally, he sets about measuring the isles of Britain to find the *omphalos*. He discovers it at Oxford. Then, as Llevelys had suggested, he pours the best mead into a vat, which he leaves for the fighting red and white dragons – who take the bait. Once they are asleep, he packs them into a stone chest and he buries them at a place called Dinas Emrys in Snowdonia, North Wales.

So, what is the meaning of this story and, more importantly, how can the wisdom it contains help us today? Like many ancient myths, this one comes to us at first like a tiny seed which, once the deeper meanings are understood, quickly flowers into a Tree of Life. Until that happens, no king can rule a contented land and no individual person can rule a contented life.

This tale can be understood more easily by those who know that the health of the body politic of the nation is mirrored in the human body, holographically, and vice-versa. It contains the keys to the mysteries of the Sovereignty of the Isles of Britain and the self-empowerment of the individual too.

It is a story of how power is lost and regained through secret practices known only to those who practise the alchemy, astrology and sacred geometry of the Hermetic system and who we refer to, in our land, as the Druids and the Grail Keepers.

In many respects, it is true that "No man is an island", as opined by the writer Ernest Hemingway - but only in terms of mundane matters. He perhaps didn't realise that man has to be as self-individuated and boundaried as an island for shamanic practices. There's a saying among old wives who still keep the lore: "Magic shared is magic halved."

So, the meeting of the brothers to discuss such a serious and secret task in the middle of the Channel was no mere literary flourish. Court magicians have always known that it is protective to surround oneself with water, especially for discussions regarding matters of state. Even today, there is a tradition among world leaders for holding important summits on islands or on boats. The British Mother of Parliaments itself, at Westminster, was built on land that until the Thames silted up was called Thorney Island. It is the same for individual acts of power.

The invasion of an aggressive race of plunderers and the stealing of provisions is a fairly straightforward metaphor and easily recognisable to those of who have learned the hard way not to give away power. On the political level, we could decide that the Coroniaid symbolised the Romans, the Saxons or the Vikings – but this story comes from a much earlier time.

All three plagues are archetypal in that they

characterise the primary issues that have worried the brows of kings from time immemorial. And the key to all three is found in unlocking the third, the terrible scream of Beltane Eve. It was about restoring the Sovereignty of the body and the body politic so that they both came into alignment with the protection of Lludd and Llevelys's father, the Sun god Beli.

Pulling the sword from the stone

The underlying meanings of certain terms have been lost over time, which is why we have such difficulty in unravelling the inner meanings of these stories. But the clue to unlocking the third plague is in the use of the word *omphalos*, which is a Latin word used by the Norman church builders.

More modern transcribers have translated *omphalos* as "centre" and they have decided that the ancient Greeks believed that the *omphalos* of Delphi was the centre of the world. *Omphalos*, though, once had a far more nuanced meaning.

The Greek god Zeus found the *omphalos* of his *cuentry* by directing two falconers to direct their eagles to fly towards one another and then he marked the point in the sky where they crossed.

So once again, we are reminded of the saltire cross and of the two serpents who criss-cross up the body like a caduceus. It is a centre of sorts but not necessarily geographically. The *omphalos* is the sacred *yoni* of the Sheena-na-gig and the fulsome vulva of the Venus of Hohle Fels, and it is central to the birth of all life across the Three Worlds.

The Greek god Zeus was born from a stone *omphalos*, in which his mother Rhea had hidden him from a murderous father. And we must not forget the tiny Circassian Sosruquo, the "offspring of the fiery sword", and the blacksmith Tlepshw who used an awl to crack open the stone of this babe's nativity. Thus, Excalibur was not the first "sword" to be released from a stone.

At Stoke Sub-Hamdon, a tiny village near Ham Hill, near the southernmost base of the landscape diamond, we find an astrological cipher for the fiery or faery sword in a church dedicated to St Mary, which boasts a stained-glass window illustrating St Michael slaying a fire-breathing dragon.

Over a stout, creaking wooden door you have to push hard in order to gain ingress there is a carved tympanum, and it is engraved with the animals of the three fire signs: the Ram of Aries, the Lion of Leo and the Centaur of Sagittarius. Running up the centre there is a Tree of Life, signifying both the fiery spindle of the Underworld smith who creates the polar axis of the universe and the spine of the human body through which the fiery serpents rise.

There are three birds perched in the branches of this Tree of Life. They are the stars of the Summer Triangle: Aquila the Eagle; Deneb, who is in the tail of Cygnus the Swan; and Lyra, which, while also called Arthur's Harp by the Celts, was symbolised as a bird.

The sixth-century Celtic bard Taliesin would sing that his "native country was the land of the summer stars". It can be no coincidence that the Summer Triangle is cognate Above with the scalene formed by Iona, Lindisfarne and Glastonbury Below. These three holy islands ruled the religious landscape of the Blessed

Isles during his times.

The "birds" of the Summer Triangle only "sing" in the night skies of the northern hemisphere between Beltane and Samhain, which is under the rulership of St Michael's serpent-slaying precursor, Gwythyr. In other words, these three "birds" mark out the domain of the Lord of Summer with their song. Once they begin to "sing" or rise, the Dreamer in the Land awakens, her heart's door opens into summer and she walks through it to meet her Bridegroom.

The *omphalos* stone was called an "egg stone" by the masons of the Templars – the egg being yet another symbol for fertility. The egg stone was considered to be so important that it was the first stone they laid when building a new church. Usually, it would be placed halfway down the aisle of the nave - where the naval is on the human body. The altars of these temples represented the hypothalamus cup or chalice that is situated between the temples of the head.

You can still see the great boulder today that the medieval builders used for the *omphalos* of the original Glastonbury Abbey. It has become literally "the stone the builders rejected".

The custodians of the Anglican church did not know what to do with it, so the builders placed it next to the 14th century Abbot's Kitchen. For hundreds of years, local women have sat on this stone in the belief that it will help them to conceive. To an initiate of the Mysteries, old wives' tales often make perfect sense!

The *omphalos* was a symbol of rulership or royalty that was often symbolised in medieval art by a cup full of red wine. In other words, it is also a chalice, a grail –

and the Holy Grail of the Christians.

And so Llevelys showed Lludd that, in order to be able to rule his land wisely, he must first find its *omphalos* – and he found it at the city of Oxford.

Well, this now brings us into anachronistic territory because the dreaming spires of Oxford did not exist when this Celtic tale was first composed [2]. But a further clue was discovered not long after the long, hot summer of 1976. The lack of rain for months and months had caused a drought and the good folk up and down the land had had to queue at standpipes for their water.

The heatwave, though, had been welcomed with open arms by archaeologists as they began to notice that, like ghosts, the remains of the past were beginning to "rise from their graves" and Oxford was no exception. In the north-east suburbs of the city, white limestone linear marks started to emerge, eerily, through the dry, arid turf in the same way that a chalked outline of a body marks the scene of a crime. Upon further investigation, it turned out to be ritual site of the Bronze Age Druids.

And so, it was Lludd's role to move the white and red dragons in the "body politic" of Britain in the same way that the *cuen* moves the red and white elixir-secreting serpents in the human body of the king towards the cup or hypothalamus.

Now, there is a solstice line that runs diagonally north-west up from Oxford towards Dinas Emrys, in the national park of Snowdonia, in north Wales. Dinas Emrys is a rocky, wooded hill that was originally called Dinas Ffarron Dandde. Scholars are divided about whether that meant "the fort of the fiery king" – the Sun king Belinus – or "the fort of the fairy king". Both could be right. But to me, Dinas Ffarron Dandde is also a poetic metaphor for the chalice of the hypothalamus, within which the alchemical mixture of the red and white serpentine drops ignites into the fire of a thousand diamond-studded Suns.

The ignition of the operation is caused by the catalyst, Mercury, otherwise known as Hermes.

There are so many common elements in this tale of Lludd and Llevelys that are found in the Irish tale of Nuada and Lugh that I think we can safely surmise that the Welsh Llevelys is the Irish Lugh, who, rather like Hermes, was the guide of paths and journeys.[3] This is hinted at when we look at the network of roads that makes up the Via Agrippa in France. The hub is at Lyons, or Lugdunum, as it was known to the Romans, the town of Lugh. It was the inspiration for the Via Heraklia (named after Hercules) that follows the Spanish coastline from Cadiz and goes through the Pyrenees.

And so it is perhaps fitting that it was Lugh's Welsh equivalent, Llevelys, the prince of the country where Julius Caesar had witnessed young men being taught the Pythagorean arts, who helped Lludd to restore the Sovereignty of Britain. But whichever name we use for him – Mercury, Hermes or Lugh – he represents the force that is the catalyst for the Marriage of the Sun and the Moon, which leads to the Birth of the Radiant Child.

Thus, in moving the "serpents" Lugh restored the Sovereignty of the Isles of Britain and from that day onwards the land no longer had to scream on Beltane's Eve to get his attention.

The Gate of Man and the Gate of the Souls

In Welsh myths, the Summer half or Upper World of the Wheel of the Year is ruled by Gwythyr ap Greidawl, while the Winter half or Underworld is governed by Gywn ap Nudd. But later on, these Lords of Time and Space were buried by the Romans under, respectively, the personages of John the Baptist and the Apostle John, known as John the Evangelist.

The feast of St John the Baptist falls on June 24th, in the water sign of Cancer, while John the Evangelist's day is celebrated on December 27th, which is directly opposite in Capricorn.

The Christian scribes lined up these Saints' Days with the Summer Solstice and the Winter Solstice which, in terms of the movement of the Sun, lasts for three days.

Masonic artwork from around this time marks the Summer Solstice as the Gate of Man because, as you know, it is from where the Radiant Child embarks to voyage widdershins along the River of Souls in the Underworld. He then sails through the Gate of Souls at Sagittarius to prepare for his birth on the Winter Solstice.

These later reckonings were based on the fifth-century writings of Macrobius Ambrosius Theodosius. He may or may not have known that his "River of Souls" was derived from much older sagas, composed when the Spring Equinox was in Taurus, and the dark rift womb of the White of the White Cow ran from between Taurus and Gemini to between Scorpio and

Sagittarius.

The Celtic myths about a global biome that is governed alternately by Gwyn and Gwythyr are based upon the star lore of this much older Hermetic blueprint, in which the Gate of Man and the Gate of the Souls are as shown in **Figure 46**. In addition, the Way of the White Cow is not a straight line between two points but is sourced in the Underworld and runs around the circle widdershins.

Why King Alfred burned the cakes

After the Synod of Whitby in the seventh century, all these much older mythical characters were well and truly buried under the sand dunes of the desert religion. Whirling dust devils swept away the memories of the Lords of Summer and Winter, along with the Druidic surveyors of the straight tracks that followed the chariot of Sun god Belinus and his sons Lludd and Llewelys.

This created a schism in the minds of men and, by inevitable consequence, in the body politic and, thus, in the minds of men. When the first plague returned, in the form of the Viking invasions, the British were ill-prepared. Whereas Viking warriors were inspired in battle by the promise of being feted as great and courageous heroes by their mercurial god of war Odin-Woden in his mead hall at Valhalla, those who battled on behalf of Roman Christianity were weakened by having to follow a god who wouldn't allow them to take any credit for their victories.

Weighed down by the burden of Original Sin, the Christian soldier had to humbly attribute all his victories to an omnipotent God. He was made to assume the responsibility but with none of the power. He had no agency in his own salvation; there were no stormy seas for him to navigate in his quest; no quinotaurs and sea serpents to slay. He was required merely to have faith in Jesus Christ for his entry into Heaven.

And so, it was hardly surprising that King Alfred the Great had such a huge problem in ridding these Blessed Isles of the plague of the Norsemen, as much as he was plagued by an excruciatingly painful disease of the bowels. We could, in fact, wonder what it was that made him so great. However, now that we have nearly reached our final destination, you will have gathered sufficient foundational knowledge about the magic of the land of Avalon for the following to make sense to you – and the key to this mystery is found in the name of the king himself.

No king can successfully rule his kingdom without the help of the other Elder races, the mercurial, serpentine forces of the land. The name Alfred was actually spelled *Ælfrēd*, which in Old English meant "elf counsel". He named his youngest daughter *Ælfgyva*, which translates to "gift of the elves". The story of how Alfred was able to finally rout the Vikings does sound, to the trained ear, as if it were a gift from the spirits of the land.

It begins at a place on the landscape diamond where the sun god Belinus passes through on his way to Glastonbury Tor at sunrise on Beltane and Lughnasadh, and at sunset on Imbolc and Samhain. This much-favoured location is a hill called Burrow Mump, which can appear like an island floating in enchanted silvery seas when the Somerset Levels (of Llevelys?) flood.

Now, just as islands are considered to be specially protected locations for planning matters that will affect the body politic, so in faery lore are triple junctions where three roads or three rivers meet. There are three rivers that once convened at the foot of Burrow Mump. The River Tone still joins the River Parrett there, while the River Carey has long since retreated.

You will be familiar with the work of early 20th century archaeologist Alfred Watkins, who discovered many prehistoric straight tracks that joined places of sacred interest, such as cairns, dolmens, standing stones, stone circles, hill forts, castles, churches, crossroads and notches on the horizon.

A true Watkins ley also has to begin or end in a hill like Burrow Mump - but it also appears to be an *axis mundi* of sorts. There are many major alignments of ley lines between megalithic sites, ecclesiastical buildings and sacred monuments worldwide that either include or emanate from Burrow Mump.

These ley lines were found through another way of identifying the spatial alignments of buildings that uses azimuths and Google Earth. It is a form of geomancy employed by the American Earth researcher Cort Lindahl, who has discovered that Burrow Mump lines up with many important monuments.

Lindahl cites the Ring of Brodgar in the Orkneys, the Avebury stone circle in Wiltshire, the 15th century Midlothian Rosslyn Chapel and a Tower of the Magdalene in Girona which aligns, through the Pyrenees, with the similar Tower of the Magdalene at Rennes le Chateau.

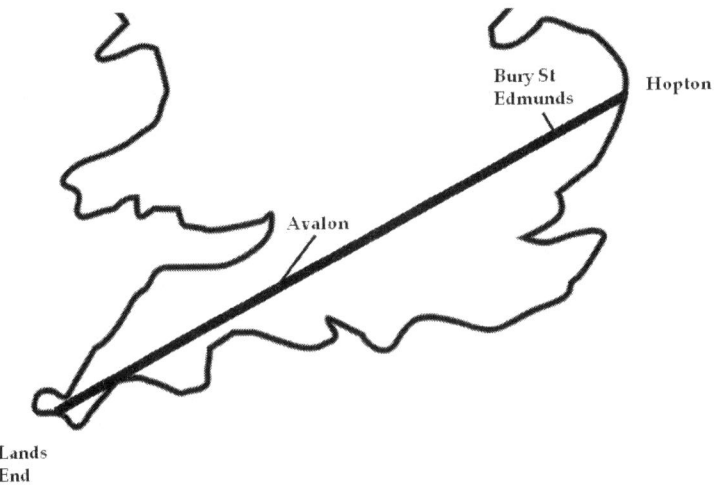

Figure 50 The Michael line

The pathways of the Sun and the Moon cross one another at what would have been the altar of a ruined church, dedicated to St Michael as shown on **Figure 50**, on the summit of Burrow Mump.

These crossing points are highly potent locations and known to dowsers as "nodes".

There are many nodes along the course of these two lines as they wind across the country. In Avalon, there is one where the altar of Glastonbury Abbey used to be and another under the tower of St Michael's church, on the summit of Glastonbury Tor.

The twisting and intertwining Michael and Mary perform their fire and water fertility dance between Land's End in Cornwall, on the west coast, all the way through Bury St Edmunds and on to the eastern seaboard.

Bury St Edmunds is named after King Edmund, whose great supporter was the aforementioned geomancer and alchemist Dunstan, the Abbot of Glastonbury who later became Archbishop of Canterbury.

It could be surmised that King Edmund was buried at the end of the Michael ley line on the geomantic-inspired advice of Dunstan.

The land of the kings

In the context of the land giants of the Temple of the Stars, Burrow Mump is the 13th "treasure of Britain" – the nose of the Giant Dog who guards the Faery Ring, the faery hound Dormath, who we heard about in *How Culhwch Won Olwen*. The dog can only be handled by Mabon, the Radiant Child.

If place names are anything to go by, it seems this gigantic hound has been recognised locally for a long time. As we drive through the winding leafy lanes that run like donkey tracks along its five-mile length to Wagg, on its tail, we pass through villages with names like Earlake (by its ear), the river Tone (on his tongue) North Curry and Curry Rivel (after "cur") and Curload (Cur Road).

Most importantly, there is also Othery, on its "other ear", which is a key place when it comes to the Sovereignty of Britain that I will tell you more about further on.

But let's walk the dog for a little while first.

This giant canine effigy is known these days as the Girt Dog of Langport, named after the small town found on its hind legs and which once held the Royal

Mint. The Battle of Langport was a major game-changer during the English Civil War between the Royalists of Charles 1st and the Roundheads of Oliver Cromwell.

Astronomically, the Girt Dog is thought to mirror the starry constellations of Canis Major and Canis Minor: the "dogs" of Orion the Huntsman, who we know as Gwyn ap Nudd.

There is an old wassailing song that is still sung during the blessings of the apple orchards, another pre-Christian winter custom in Avalon buried under the festival of the Eucharist or Candlemass.

The Girt Dog of Langport has burnt his long tail

And this is the night we go singing wassail!

Maltwood refers to Dormath as Dor-march, perhaps to hint that this canine is a threshold guardian of a door or faery portal that opens in March. On the Spring Equinox, March 21st, there is a local tradition of throwing hot cross buns into the "mouth of the dog", where the River Tone joins the River Parrett.

It is often assumed that the cross on the bun is a Christian T-shaped cross. However, it is likely that a smith's hot metal was used to brand it with the same saltire or X-shaped cross that is found in the alignments of four Royal Stars, shown on **Figure 51**, that overlook the Glastonbury Temple of the Stars and which are named Aldebaran, Regulus, Antares and Fomalhaut.

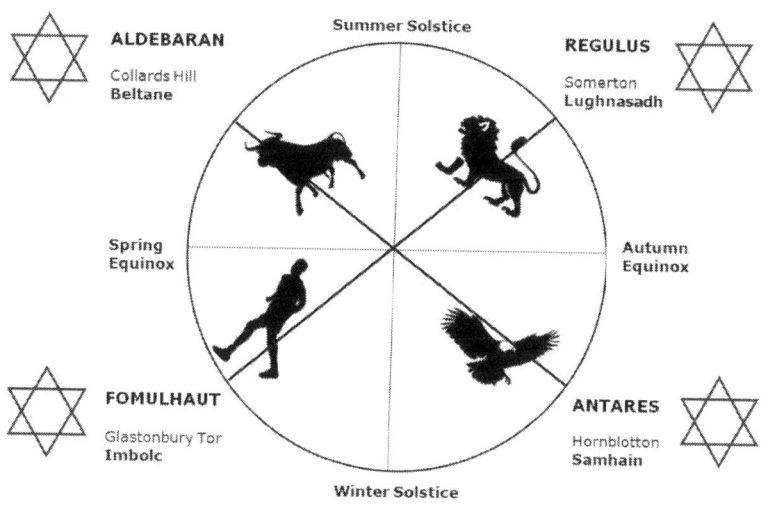

Figure 51 The Royal Stars and the tetramorph

Maltwood signalled her understanding of the importance of the Royal Stars, the cross-quarter festivals and the tetramorph to the spiritual life of of Avalon in the way she organised the content of her four books.[4] And so, I think this is how King Alfred the Great came to burn the cakes with a saltire X-shaped cross.

In the year 878, he was in retreat from the Vikings, who were terrorising the locals across huge chunks of the country with their demands for Dane Geld. Despite the many battles that Alfred and his brothers had waged against Odin's warriors, the British Christians had failed to make much of a dent in their presence. After losing badly to them at Gloucester, Alfred had escaped into the dark and tangled forests of the Somerset marshes. He eventually found refuge in a monastery at Athelney, which is just a stone's throw from Burrow Mump, and he stayed there for a while to lick his wounds.

It was in the Spring of that year, through the Door of March, that Alfred set out on his quest to banish the Vikings. And by Beltane, he had routed them and baptised their leader, Guthrun, in the village of Aller on the back of the Girt Dog of Langport.

Aller later became famous for its great *wyrm*, which was slain by John of Aller on South Hill. You can still see its red blood in the iron-rich soil today.

But timing is everything when it comes to magic.

As you know, Iraneus had moved the festival commemorating the crucifixion of the Sun god from the Winter Solstice to the Passover of Easter. Then, two centuries before Alfred's reign, the Synod of Whitby decreed that Easter should always be celebrated on the first Sunday after the first full Moon following the Spring Equinox. This is why the date of Easter moves around – it is dictated by the Moon, who can be late or early, depending on her mood.

So, when Alfred set off for the battle[5] which would rid the Blessed Isles of the plague of the Vikings, it was on Easter, according to King Alfred's chronicler, Asser[6]. But Easter was early that year; it fell on March 23rd, which is only two days after the Spring Equinox – and which is the traditional time that the mythological hero sets out on his adventures.

For Easter to have fallen on March 23rd in 878 CE, the Moon must have waxed full sometime between the 21st, the date of the Spring Equinox, and the 23rd. So, Alfred would have found himself in the right place at the right time to join in with the magical custom of branding a bun with an X-shaped saltire cross and then throwing it as an offering into the mouth of the dog.

We can also identify another highly auspicious event which, if true, would have been crucial to the winning of the Sovereignty of England. There are unsubstantiated reports that before leaving for the battle, Alfred received a vision of St Cuthbert in which he was given his blessing of protection.

Cuthbert had been a highly popular religious figure of the previous century and widely regarded as the Otherworldly protector of the Blessed Isles on a par with Bran, ever since he renounced the wealthy bishopric on the island of Lindisfarne and retreated to live in a cave.

The people of Britain so revered this hermit that they had given him his own day, St Cuthbert's Day, which still falls every year on March 20th.

So, could Alfred have known about these important timings and alignments when he made his camp at Athelney, near Burrow Mump?

Did the elf counsellor realise he had somehow stumbled upon a magical island overlooking a three-way junction of the rivers known to be places of faery and which was crossed by the lines of the Sun god Belinus and the goddess of the Moon?

Would he have recognised that he was on the nose of the effigy of Dormath, the Girt Dog of Langport?

Was he cognisant of the many indigenous myths associated with this hound that belonged to Gwyn ap Nudd, the lord of the Underworld?

And did he take a fiery sword to some cakes and

burn on them a saltire cross of the Royal Stars before feeding them to the guardian of the Door of March?

We can get slightly distracted in the telling and retelling of the story of how King Alfred was responsible for establishing Christianity across the length and breadth of England – so much so that we may not realise that Alfred, who was tutored by Druids, would have practised, at least in private, a particular kind of Christianity that was still attached to its metaphysical roots.

In her seminal book *The Glastonbury Zodiac: Key to the Mysteries of Britain*, Mary Caine writes that Alfred must have understood that he was living in close relationship with the Temple of the Stars.

> *This secret was obviously passed down from royal father to son. Alfred obtained it too when he came to reign ...*
>
> *He had indeed a Druid for mentor in his youth, for Swithin's name is that of the Syweddyd or Druids... And where did Alfred baptise Guthrun, his defeated Danish enemy? At Winchester, his capital? At Glastonbury Abbey, already famous in his time? No – at Aller, on the pilgrim's path that draws the Girt Dog's back. ...*
>
> *At Wedmore, after the baptism, Alfred gave Guthrun "many fine houses". I suspect that these houses were the houses of the Zodiac......*
>
> *Alfred, only about five feet high and afflicted with a bowel complaint throughout his life, was able to bring*

the Danes, twice his height and girth, into some order: in a reign torn by wars fought against impossible odds, he brought a renaissance of hope, justice, education, religion and prosperity to his country. His inspiration, as much evidence shows, was the Zodiac: his Catholic Christianity was informed by its Celtic fount.

The Finger of God

We find further evidence of this Celtic fount when we examine a beautiful object known as Alfred's Jewel, which is made of enamel and quartz and enclosed in gold (See **Figure 52**). It was found in 1693 on the margins of the Somerset Levels but it has been dated to the times of Alfred and bears an inscription that reads "AELFRED MEC HEHT GEWYRCAN", meaning "Alfred ordered me made".

On one side of the jewel, there is an image of a handsome, fair-haired man dressed in a green robe that harmonises perfectly with the cobalt blue background. He is holding two golden rods in the criss-cross shape of the saltire cross of the four royal stars, Aldebaran, Regulus, Antares and Fomalhaut – the same criss-cross shape found on a hot cross bun.

On the other side, there is an illustration of a Tree of Life, and there is a gold filigree dragon's head on its base, whose mouth opens into a notch, indicating that it could have once been attached to a rod, probably of wood. So, it is possible that Alfred's Jewel could have been some sort of divinatory or geomantic tool; its pictorial designs show that it certainly had its roots in a mythology much older than that of Christ.

Figure 52 Alfred's Jewel

This sort of geomancy is sometimes referred to in Freemasonry as the Finger of God, which is another metaphorical term connected to rites of Sovereignty.

Maltwood wrote in her *Enchantments of Britain* about the importance of the Finger of God, which she thought she could see in the Temple of the Stars:

> ...in Operative Masonry, the Egyptian method of surveying and orientation is the Guild method still in use. They first find the central line by running a blue cord or handline from the position of the Sun's rising above the horizon to the Holy Place, i.e. from east to west.
>
> Upon and from the centre line given by the Sun, the masons fixed the centre of the four corners of the intended Temple.
>
> In the Egyptian Underworld, there are 12 bearers of cord, whose function it is to measure and we are told it is the cord of the law, and it is upon the cord of the centre line that the great finger in Somerset lies.
>
> The branch of the Egyptian priesthood 4,000 years ago and more, whose work was surveying, was called the "Cord Stretchers".
>
> A religious ceremony, 'the stretching of the cord' was held to fix the axis and orientation, and the priest read the sacred text during the laying of the foundation stone and during the fixing of the four corners with accuracy by the four supports of the heaven.

Maltwood identified the finger of a god on the Temple of the Stars in the effigy of the rider on the fire sign of Sagittarius at Baltonsborough.

His arm is outstretched and his finger is pointing, like a fiery sword, towards Collards Hill, the home of the Sisterhood - the faery midwives who attend the conception of the Radiant Child.

It is, in fact, a newly discovered alignment[7] that Yuri Leitch found in Maltwood's writings, and I've shown it in relation to the Michael line in **Figure 53**.

Yuri describes how Maltwood had drawn the equinox line across the Avalonian landscape as if it was an "arrow shot" from King Alfred's Tower, which is an 18th century folly on the Stourhead estate in Wiltshire.

The arrow flies first through Bruton Church and then St Peter's church, Hornblotton, at Scorpio. From there, it passes over Park Wood before going straight through the eye of the Bull at Taurus.

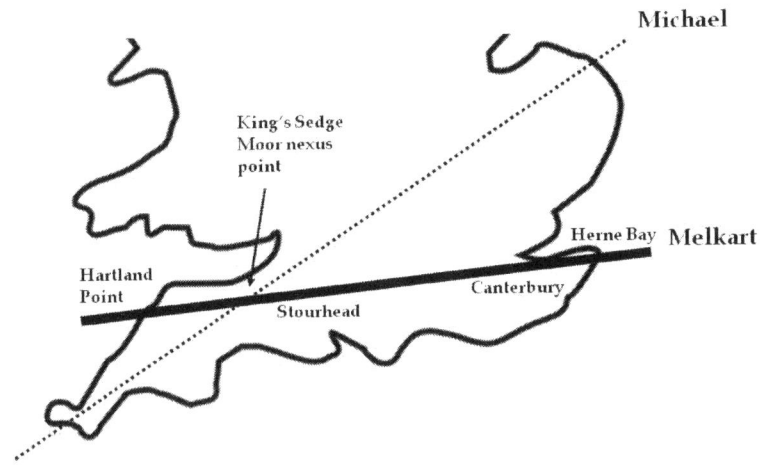

Figure 53 The Melkart and Michael lines

In extending the line, Yuri found that it stretches from Herne Bay on the Kent coast, and that it passes through Canterbury Cathedral before reaching Stourhead and the Temple of the Stars. Then, after piercing the bull's eye, it continues on until it finally reaches its destination at Hartland Point on the Devon coast.

He has called this alignment the Melkart Line, after the Phoenician name for the Greeks' Hercules.

The Hercules imagery is writ large in the ornamental gardens of Stourhead that it passes through. They have been dubbed "a living work of art" with their elegantly designed mystic "follies" around a sunken lakeside path that takes the visitor on a magical Mysteries tour mirroring the hero's descent into the Underworld.

Now owned by the National Trust, Stourhead used to be the home of the wealthy and influential Hoare family.

The Masonic imagery is clear to see throughout the estate - not least the statue of the double-headed eagle, which has given its name to the local inn. Henry Hoare II told friends that he had built King Alfred's Tower to mark the site where he believed Alfred had rallied the men of the West Country to go on to win the pivotal battle of Edington.

Yuri Leitch is of the view that the Melkart or Hercules line superceded the Michael line in kingship rites after the Norman invasion in 1066. He wrote the following to me:

I suspect that energy was diverted from the Michael line to the Melkart line in later centuries - the Girt Dog of Langport and the Michael Line being truly ancient. The Finger of God effigy is on the Melkart Line, connecting Canterbury to our sacred landscape - the coronation ceremony always being performed by the Archbishop of Canterbury.

The Michael Line energised Bury St Edmunds, but Bury St Edmunds fell from popularity after 1066 and the Norman invasion. In short, the Michael line makes sense to King Alfred and Saxon England; the Melkart Line makes sense to Norman, post-1066 England.

The nexus point, where the Melkart line can draw energy from the Michael line and divert to Canterbury, is just west of the Temple of the Stars, at King's Sedge Moor - just north-east of Othery, off the Girt Dog's ear, near Greylake.

Curiously, the stained-glass windows in St Nechtan's Church at Hartland, the far west of the Melkart line, sought to unite the Britons, Saxons and Normans, by depicting each culture's most famous kings - Arthur, Alfred and William the Conqueror... these windows were done as recently as 1922.

Prince William had his stag party at nearby Hartland Abbey before marrying Catherine Middleton in 2011. It makes one wonder if the lines are still being used to invoke divine kingship or union with the land...

Readers with a poetic eye will have already picked up the imagery of the Horned One of White Lake who bears on her back the Radiant Child in **Herne** Bay, **Hart**land and **stag** party. A poet would also find **heart**, while historians are reminded of the **hearths** that our Anglo-Saxon ancestors always kept alight in honour of their household gods until the Normans installed a hearth tax.

Some say Avalon is the "hart" or "heart" of Britain. It might be derived from an Old Country magical expression for entering into the Otherworlds: "opening the heart's door into Summer".

The White Hart coaching inn on Leo, which is in the quaint old town of Somerton, dates to the 16th century. Somerton (or Summertown) was the royal town of Wessex during Alfred's times, when his domain spread right across southern England, from Somerset to Kent. The heraldic emblem for Wessex then was a golden dragon; it is now a red one. Somerton's church may now be dedicated to St. Michael - but there is still a dragon in the rafters.

Britain's monarch today is crowned in Westminster Abbey by the Archbishop of Canterbury in an order of service that was originally devised in Latin by Dunstan for the crowning of King Edgar, a century after Alfred's reign, which took place in Bath Abbey.

However, when James I was enthroned in 1601, it was decided that conducting the ceremony in the English language would help to give the Scottish monarch greater acceptance among the public and it has been in English ever since.

The reference to the Finger of God once used in

earlier royal coronations, according to Maltwood, was spoken, in Latin, as follows:

> *God the creator of all things in heaven and earth, and ffownteyne of spiritual grace, which doest write thy laws in the harts of the ffaithful with thyne own finger, to whom the Egyptian Sorcerors yielding confessed this is the Finger of God.*

A ring set with a giant ruby was placed on the king or queen's finger, which was, apparently, engraved with the cross of St George. But was it the cross of St George or an X-shaped saltire cross that comes from much older star lore? Whatever its shape and meaning, the design on the ring was a symbol for the land which was included within the templum of the king's domain by the Finger of God.

And so, this begs the question: were the saltire-crossed rods on the face of the Alfred Jewel and the X-shaped cross on the hot cross buns symbolic of those blue measuring cords that once marked out the domains of the Egyptian pharaohs? And is the Finger of God still pointing today?

To answer this, we need to return to the work of geomantist Cort Lindahl. As mentioned before, he has found many examples of important structures worldwide 8, and across different cultures and religions, which are built upon specific azimuthal alignments that spread out, like sunbursts, from the angled corners of octagonal-shaped buildings. In this way, Lindahl discovered virtual measuring cords stretching between Hagia Sophia, the Basilica San Vitale, the Dome of the Rock, St. Peter's Square, Gisors, the Newport Tower,

Thomas Jefferson's Poplar Forest, the Georgia Guide stones and various Towers of the Winds found on the estates of the aristocracy that are modelled on the original built in Athens around 50 BCE.

The octagon is a geometrical cipher that goes back at least as far as the Vedic times, in which the four-sided square altar represented the Earth and the circular altar represented the Heavens. If you put a square (the Earth) in a circle (the Heavens), which is what squaring the circle is all about, you will find the octagon.

The squaring of the circle was considered to be a significant measurement by the Freemasons. So, with masons hired By Appointment to build octagons to point alignments in certain specified directions, it seems that the ruling classes have been claiming ownership of their domains across the Earth and under the Heavens for a long time.

Viewed through this lens, we can now begin to get some kind of understanding about how Alfred the elf counsellor, with his geomantic rods, his appreciation of local magical customs that were linked to the land and the stars, and his relationship with the Fae and Otherworldly saints, could have found a way to get the Finger of God to point in his favour, so that he could win back the Sovereignty of the land.

The uneasy peace finally won by King Alfred held in the *cuentry* until 1066, when the Norseman of Normandy landed at Hastings and, led by William the Bastard and Eric the Red, marched up the beach under the fluttering banner of Rome.

The Bayeux Tapestry and the Mysteries of Britain

Not long after the Battle of Hastings, a long piece of embroidery was created to illustrate the story of how the Normans won their victory over the British. It is known as the Bayeux Tapestry and it is a brilliantly woven weave of wool and yarn to rival the Wyrd of the Norns which created a narrative to persuade the consensual consciousness of the British people to a new reality.

If you should ever get the chance to examine this great work of talismanic art, please allow me to direct your eyes to a little-commented upon section, shown in **Figure 54**.

Let's analyse the underlying message of this scene: The Latin title reads "Ubi unus clericus et Ælfgyva", translating as "Look here! It's a clerk and Ælfgyva" – making a woman whose name meant "gift of the elves" the only named female in this 230-foot masterpiece otherwise dedicated to the affairs of men and kings.

As ever, historians are in disagreement as to its meaning, having to peer, in their ignorance of the magical underpinnings of Sovereignty, through a glass darkly. With its graphic sexual imagery, some attribute it to some sort of scandal, the consequences of which would have precluded Harold's line from inheriting. That's pretty rich, you might think, from the political backers of William, who actually was a bastard!

As I'm sure you can guess, I have a differing interpretation, based on my understanding of how heraldic art is designed to encode the direction of the

"Finger of God" and Sovereignty.

Figure 54 *Detail from the Bayeux Tapestry*

As you know, King Alfred had a daughter named Ælfgyva and she became the Abbess of Shaftesbury. According to Asser:

> *King Alfred ordered the monastery to be built at the east gate of Shaftesbury, as a residence suitable for*

> *nuns. He appointed as its abbess his own daughter, Ælfgyva, a virgin consecrated to God; and many other noble nuns live with her in the same monastery, serving God in the monastic life.*

We cannot be sure that she is the same Ælfgyva who is shown on the Bayeux Tapestry. However, Asser also tell us that Alfred's abbess daughter was deemed to be a virgin and, therefore, we can conclude that she was a representative of Virgo.

The word "virgin" is what separates the two Marys in the gospel stories. In contrast to the divine prostitute Mary Magdalene, the initiatrix *cuen* of the King of the Jews, Mary the Virgin represented a woman who does not have sexual relations with human men because her love is exclusively reserved for a god or a divine being, such as Gabriel.

During wholly communion with her Otherworldly lover, who is represented in ancient myths as a dragon or serpent, the black and gold serpents are brought together to perform their dance in the body of this superior *cuen* (or Mother Superior). The dance is allegorised as a struggle, or a battle, between fire and water. The culmination of this magical rite is symbolised by the piercing of the dragon, or the bruising of the head of the serpent by treading it underfoot, to signify union between the Three Worlds and the Three Utterances of the land.

So, let's return to the *Bayeux Tapestry*. It is divided into three sections. Most people ignore the upper and lower parts, perhaps assuming that they are just meaningless decorative frames. They are not. They are intrinsic to the message in that they depict the actions of the denizens of the Upper World in the top section and those of the Underworld in the lowest section, all of which is impacting on the battle raging in the Middle World.

The top section shows the Upper World where we can see the star arrangement of the Summer Triangle of the three birds with the Tree of Life at the centre, similar to the one on the aforementioned tympanum above the church door at Stoke sub Hamdon in Somerset.

In the Underworld below, we can see a naked ithyphallic figure and a fire-breathing dragon. The inclusion of the dragon tells me that it is about the rising of Ida and Pingala, the serpents who grant the enlightenment and wisdom that grants Sovereignty.

The Middle World, in the centre frame, features a priest or cleric who is touching Ælfgyva in a gesture that reverses that of this ithyphallic Pan-like creature below. Ælfgyva is standing between two columns that are entwined by quinotaurs. These lion-headed sea serpents were used in the art of the grailkeepers to symbolise threshold guardians at the time when the bright star system of Regulus, the ruler, was in the constellation of Leo [1].

Archetypically, the twin columns represent the yin and the yang of the serpents Ida and Pingala, who drip their red and white elixirs into the Holy Grail or cup of the hypothalamus. They were named Boaz and

---

[1] Regulus is currently moving away from Leo and into Virgo. This has been interpreted by some astrologers to signify the advent of age of the divine feminine.

Joachim when they supported the arched entrance into the Temple of Solomon.

Further back, they were the Tammuz and Ningishzida of the Sumerians, as shown in **Figure 55**. These twin serpent gods are gatekeepers or threshold guardians, through which the hero has to make a successful passage. They usually appear as pillars on either side of a doorway but they are also the twin clashing rocks of the Symplegades, which Jason of the Argonauts had to pass safely.

Whenever you get doubles or twins, it also indicates the house of Gemini, which is ruled by represents the governor of Gemini, Mercury-Hermes. As you know, Mercury is the vital catalyst for the Marriage of the Sun and the Moon.

In the next scene of the *Bayeux Tapestry*, you will find a depiction of the enthroned William of Normandy in conversation with the British king, Harold Godwinson. They seem to be discussing the Sovereignty of the British Isles, which William believes to be rightly his. But Harold is pointing to the woman and the priest as if to disagree with the Norman king. The Sovereignty, he appears to be insisting, belongs to him through the *cuen* Ælfgyva, who is in the ancestral line of the Godwins.

Godwin - now there's a word to conjure with. Who was the god and what did he win for that family line? Could it be that Ælfgyva's gift from the elves was Sovereignty? And if so, how did William of Normandy manage to steal it?

Figure 55 Tammuz and Ningishzida

Well, now that you have walked so far, and have safely passed the gatekeeper gods to enter through the Heart's Door into Summer, you have finally reached the diamond Celestial City of those chosen to hold the keys to the Mysteries of Britain, and so I'm sure you will enjoy unlocking all the doors yourself.

[1] *Brut y Brenhinedd* or "Chronicle of the Kings".
[2] According to the English Place Name Society, an Anglo-Saxon settlement was first formed in the 10th century around a river crossing for oxen and so they called it *Oxenaforda*.
[3] Julius Caesar wrote in his *Commentāriī dē Bellō Gallicō* ('Commentaries on the Gallic War') "They worship above all the god Mercury [the Roman equivalent to Lugh]: They consider him the inventor of all the arts and the guide of their paths and journeys".
[4] *Glastonbury's Temple of the Stars* opens with Leo, *Enchantments of Britain* opens with Aquarius, *King Arthur's Round Table of The Zodiac* opens with Taurus and *Itinerary of The Somerset Giants* (abridged from *King Arthur's Round Table of The Zodiac*) opens with Scorpio.
[5] Battle of Edington 878 CE.
[6] *Alfred the Great: Asser's Life of King Alfred and Other Contemporary Sources.* Translated by Simon Keynes and Michael Lapidge.
[7] Yuri Leitch gives a full account of his discovery of the Melkarth Line in *Signs and Secrets of the Glastonbury Zodiac*.
[8] *Axis Mundi* by Cort Lindahl.

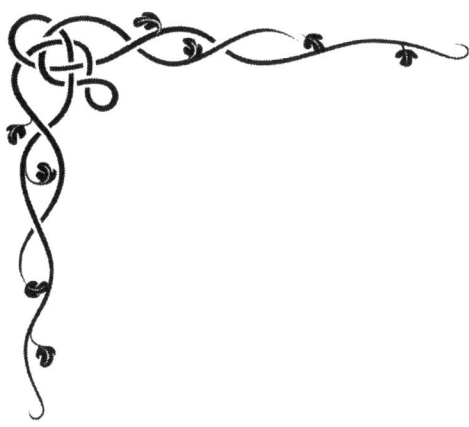

Epilogue

One of my favourite haunts is Wells Cathedral, which is just a few miles to the north of Glastonbury. To me, it is a perfect metaphor for the kingdom of Bridie, the Sleeping Beauty or the Dreamer of the Land, who has been waiting for such a long time now to be awoken by the kiss of the Prince.

The Puritans may have stripped back the stones of their once kaleidoscopic hues to the present-day solemn, sombre greys, and the names of those who have passed on before us are no longer recited in the chantries at the dark of Samhain. But Bridie's white swans still faithfully circle the moat and ring the bell, guarding the portcullised palace from those who might tread carelessly across her enchanted reveries, which are vividly illustrated on multi-hued stained-glass windows and embroideries as much as our ancestors' visions were daubed on the dark walls of the caverns of Ice Age cathedrals.

The perpetual choirs still sing to the Sun god at

dawn through the quartz in those grey stones while, from matins to compline, the descendants of the Benedictines perform the *opus dei*. The octagon that brings down the heavens to the land encases the soaring paradisiacal arches of the Chapter House, which can only be reached by a crumbling and uneven winding staircase almost as old as Jacob's Ladder.

The drawbridge to the Palace crosses a moat fed by streams which run down from the limestone caverns of the Mendip Hills into the wells that gave England's smallest city its name. It was what attracted people in earlier times to settle there and to carve out an underground chamber for their own Dreamers to commune with the serpentine fire carried in those waters.

Later on, the Saxons built a Minister nearby, which they dedicated to St Andrew, and his saltire cross is still writ large throughout this early English-style Gothic cathedral. There is portrait of Andrew in the old Quire, holding the two wooden planks of his cross. But he is more evident in the Palace where two wells and a chapel are dedicated to him, and his cross is sewn into the flower border by the gate to the Outer Gardens. A third well is dedicated to St Andrew, which is outside in the cobbled marketplace.

The Fibonacci-spiralled crozier that now hangs on the wall of the Chained Library, which houses the books of canons from hundreds of years ago, belonged to one of the Palace's earliest incumbents, Bishop Jocelin. And in its serpentine coils, there is a figurine of a conquering hero about to trample a dragon underfoot, which sparks many questions.

EPILOGUE

Did Jocelin's name, just like Merlin's, come from the *lin*, the Saxon word for "dragon", and did the bishop know that Gwythyr ap Greidawl is the only serpent-conquering hero in the skies, and was it that knowledge which helped him to slay the *wyrm* of nearby Worminster, which used to terrorise the locals?

The Divine Mother sits above the arched doorway of the grand West Front, with the Radiant Child on her lap. They are surrounded with the protection of hundreds of medieval kings, bishops and apostles that go all the way up to the Christ himself with a whole host of serried angels. It is no wonder, because it is here that a very powerful dragon has to "breathe in", in order to squeeze its great girth through the door.

This determined serpent has come all the way up from St Cuthbert's Church at the bottom of the hill and forged a path under the grey flagstones of the courtyard of the old coaching inn, the White Hart. Next, it crosses Cathedral Green until it reaches the arched door and then it flows swiftly down the aisle of her navel until it reaches her *yoni*, the *mandorla*-shaped Scissor Arches over the altar. There, in her innermost sanctum, she is guarded by dozens of fully attired medieval bishops and old treasurers of England in hats of initiates that resemble gaped-mouthed fish, all laying there sleeping like the court of the Sleeping Beauty.

It is down this very same aisle that I watch my grand-daughter and her schoolfriends processing at Christmas. Each holds in their hands a brightly lit candle and so their winding passage forms a bobbing, glittering, snaking Way of the White Cow, a way of hope. They are singing, by rote, the star lore – although they don't know it yet and neither do many of the good folk in the congregation.

My body trembles with the unexpressed tears of a million years, watching the caroling children wending their way down the path of the serpent towards the Vesica Piscis and the altar. It is so moving to realise they are like tiny Trojan Horses, secretly and unwittingly carrying the wisdom songs of our sky-gazing ancestors, generation after generation after generation after generation.

For it is true that, just as the stars revolve above, the spinning wheel of the alchemical progress of our species goes around and around below. But we are not alone. We are accompanied by the three Norns of the three wells, who continually water the Tree of Life and weave the web of Wyrd, which is our reality. Children know them better as the three faeries who attend the christening of the Sleeping Beauty and being closer to the portal of birth are often more aware that these spirits of the land are walking beside us and popping into our dreams at night, to guide us with words of advice and encouragement.

Witnessing this ritual act every Christmas reminds me of the *ouroboros*, the snake that can only remain alive by eating its own tail. By continuing to teach our offspring to keep the song lines open, even though we may be sleepwalking around and around, we can maintain the passage of the long and winding pilgrimage that humanity is on, as a species, until it finally reaches the diamond and gold palaces of the Celestial City – and the princess is awoken by the kiss of the prince.

> *Hail the heav'nly Prince of Peace!*
>
> *Hail the Sun of righteousness!*
>
> *Light and life to All he brings,*
>
> *Ris'n with healing in his wings.*
>
>
> *Mild he lays his glory by,*
>
> *Born, that man no more may die,*
>
> *Born, to raise the sons of Earth,*
>
> *Born, to give them second birth.*
>
>
> *Hark the herald angels sing*
>
> *Glory to the new born King.*
>
>
> *Come, Desire of Nations, come,*
>
> *Fix in us thy humble home,*
>
> *Rise, the woman's conqu'ring seed,*

Bruise in us the Serpent's head.

Now display thy saving pow'r,

Ruin'd nature now restore,

Now in mystic union join

Thine to ours, and ours to thine.

From **Hark the Herald Angels Sing** *by Charles Wesley (1707 – 1788)*

THE END

Appendix: The Glastonbury Declaration

Laid out like diamonds in the deep blue of the celestial Above over the Faery Ring of the Isle of Glass, there are four Royal Stars. They are:

Fomalhaut, which lies over the Faery Swan of the Tor

Antares, which lights up the Faery Stone in the village of Stone, near Hornblotton Church,

Aldebaran, which marks the Bull of Taurus, at Collards Hill, who guards the Sisterhood of the Pleiades, and

Regulus, which hovers over the neck of the Lion, or the Faery Cat, at Somerton.

These four Royal Stars form a saltire cross under which many of us stood on Windmill Hill to make our Declaration of Sovereignty at a shamanic celebration for the Birth of the Radiant Child one sunrise, on the Winter Solstice of Sunday 21st December 2014.

This is the final version of The Glastonbury Declaration, which I was first guided to write then and which we read out at that ceremony. I publish it here in the hope that it will inspire others to do the same or similar, after they have found the magic that in their own land, as much as it is in Avalon.

The Declaration

This is the Declaration and Intent of those who have the eyes to see and the hearts to know how lucky we are to live within the landscape diamond created by the Marriage of the Sun and the Moon, and within the Sovereign Circle of the Thirteen Treasures of the Precinct of Merlin. The Thirteen Treasures were brought to the Glass House by Merlin for safe keeping upon receiving them from King Bran in those days of antiquity, when our ancestors worked in harmonic cooperation with the spirits of Land.

The Glass House, or Glastonbury, over which the Tor rises as sentinel, is a multi-dimensional Faery Ring which exists in people's hearts and dreams wherever they are on the Earth... and beyond. This Land has manifested itself across all the Realms – the Over Realm, the Middle Realm and Under Realm – through the loving companionship between Man and Fae.

For this reason, the Glastonbury Declaration resonates throughout the Three Realms, with which we are in alignment and harmony, as we stand under the Excalibur of the four Royal Stars ruling over this sacred Land of Nobles, as Above, So Below.

As the ancient kings of these islands knew, this hallowed ground around which the Thirteen Treasures revolve, mirroring the starry constellations, is pregnant with their legitimacy to rule, and that he or she who holds the reins of this Land reigns over all the Land.

We hereby affirm the Sovereignty of the Land as a flowering and fruiting of the relationship between Man and Fae, which once manifested, cannot be countermanded by any other authority.

And so...

From this Day forward, we Declare as Sovereign Beings that we owe no allegiance to any man but to our own individual Destinies, which are weaved from gold and diamonds in the Spindle of Light forged by the Underworld Smith which traverses the Three Realms.

We Declare that it is our Divine Destiny to individually explore our own relationships with the spirits of those Other Realms, who some men have called "the gods", which exist independently of all religious belief systems, political parties, castes or creeds.

We Declare that we will always walk a path of Truth, Goodness and Beauty across this sacred landscape, in harmony with the Spirits of the Land, and we will support all others to do the same.

We Declare that we will honour our responsibility to work with the Spirits of Land, to keep the Dragon Lines consecrated so that they clearly mirror and resonate with the Vault of the Stars Above and the Well of Stars Below.

We Declare that we are responsible for respecting all laws of the Land, and that we will give no quarter to those who don't, including those who have been appointed by government to keep the peace and administer the laws.

We Declare that we have the right to a fair trial in which we are presumed innocent until and unless proven guilty, and that we also have the right to be judged by a jury of our own peers that reside in our own locality.

We Declare that as Sovereign Beings, it is our glad right and duty to bring up our own children, which are our property, and it is our responsibility to keep them safe and with no harm being suffered to their person.

We Declare that we will only take part in wars which we deem to be just and necessary to protect our peoples.

We Declare that we have a right to clean and unpolluted air, water and soil and that we will take on the responsibility to prosecute any person or corporate body that pollutes them – whether from the skies, seas or lands.

We Declare that we have a right to fresh and unadulterated food that is grown as Mother Nature intended and we will take on the responsibility to encourage others to eat healthily.

We Declare that we have a right to live wherever we want to live, on this land of Britain, and however we want to live, within the law of the Land, and we will be responsible for all our own decisions in such regard.

We Declare that we will be responsible for overseeing the care of our own people, from the cradle to the grave.

We Declare that if government at any time acts in a way which forces us to live in any way contrary to our Declared Intentions above, and to our guardianship of Glastonbury, The Thirteen Treasures of the Isle of Glass, we will withhold from them our consent as it is our Sovereign right to do.

All rights reserved. Errors and omissions excepted,

FURTHER READING

THE SACRED SEX RITES OF ISHTAR
Shamanic sexual healing and sex magic

by Annie Dieu-Le-Veut

In The Sacred Sex Rites of Ishtar lays out in detail how shamanic sex has been used, throughout history, to prepare kings for Sovereignty. It shows how its practise leads alchemically to a superior intelligence and self-empowerment that is a direct result of interacting with beings which inhabit a parallel universe to this one - another dimension - from whom man has traditionally gained his knowledge about his place and purpose on Earth and in the cosmos.

In ancient times, the ability to tap into this superior wisdom through sex magic was transmitted to kings and pharaohs by a *cuen* or *hierodule*, one who was in touch with these extra-dimensional beings or life forms that are also known as the spirits. It was understood by the wise sages of those times that Sovereignty is an actual magical force that arises from the spirits of the land, otherwise known as the Fae, the Gentry, the Sidhe or the Faeries, who are of an Elder and wiser race which inhabits a timeless zone within the parallel dimensions.

This shamanic force gave the rulers of antiquity the power of Sovereignty through firing up higher brain centres that led to wisdom and thus the ability and the right to reign. In this book, you can learn how to benefit from these practices today.

As a shaman and mythologist, Annie Dieu-Le-Veut is in regular communion with the spirits of the Land. You can follow her path in The Sacred Sex Rites of Ishtar, in which she lays out a way for the spiritual seeker to learn how to visit these other dimensions to be taught about sex magic from the spirit guides.

She helps you to form your own the cognitive foundation stone for this practice by learning about the evidence – from ancient Greece, Egypt, Crete, India, Sumer and Babylon – which shows that sacred sex was once an integral part of the kingship rites. She also explains the meaning of the Faery Marriage, which finds it resonance in many myths about the Holy Grail.

THE BRIGHT WORLD OF THE GODS
A true faery story from the mists of Avalon

by Annie Dieu-Le-Veut

The Bright World of the Gods was gifted into the Dreamtime of the author by the spirits of the land that inhabit the other dimensions found, shamanically, through the mists of Avalon. These spirits are known as the Gentle Folk, the Elders or the Fae, although you might know them better as faeries.

So, this is a real faery story for enlightened adults that comes from a benevolent Elder race whose role it is to guide the steps of humanity. As such, it is perfect for curling up with by the fire when the white frost of the Sugar Plum Faery is crackling the grass underfoot, or to inspire your daydreams on sunnier days, in the shadow of a gnarled old apple tree in an enchanted wood.

In this romantic magical mystery tour around the enchanted Avalon landscape, you will follow the heroine and hero, Bridie and Gwyn ap Nudd, and benefit from their own realisations as they meet the challenges necessary for their alchemical inner growth, which leads them to full spiritual realisation.

This twisting, multi-dimensional romantic adventure abounds with archetypal characters that have stepped straight out of ancient Celtic myths like Manawydan, Gwyddion, Creiddylad, Taliesen, Elen and Morgan the Fae.

You may just want to enjoy this epic tale on a superficial level as a beautiful love story that is full of intriguing escapades and interesting ideas. But those looking for keys to open faery doorways into deeper cosmological teachings will also find them here along with the instructions on how to unlock them.

Either way, you're welcome to relax and wander through the wondrous hills and dales of The Bright World of the Gods, and allow its words to gently permeate into your own Dreamtime so that it can do its magic there and give you insights into your own destiny – and the meaning of your life.

THE GRAIL MYSTERIES
The Virgo Teachings and the Peacock's Tail

by Annie Dieu-Le-Veut

In The Grail Mysteries, you will benefit personally from the Virgo Teachings received by a prostitute named Igraine, who lives in post-Roman Glastonbury. Her late middle-age is utterly transformed when she discovers that she comes from a long line of *cuens* or *hierodules* and is thus a true queen of the Blessed Isles.

As we follow her awakening, we learn that a true queen is not necessarily one who is anointed with oil on her forehead by the Archbishop of Canterbury. It is one who carries the faery blood and who is anointed by the inner elixirs that flow from the awakening of the serpents during shamanic sex magic with the Divine.

Along with Igraine, we discover that a true queen does not necessarily wear a crown on her head and that when she does, it is only to symbolise that the crown in her cranium has been alchemically fired up into the colours of peacock by the Red and White serpentine drops falling on to her pineal gland, or Third Eye, causing her inner sun to rise within her.

In this way, a true queen holds the Sovereignty of the nation, which has been passed into her safekeeping by the spirits of the land. Only a true queen can make a king who is fit to rule.

The Grail Mysteries is a sequel to The Bright World of the Gods, although you don't need to have read that to enjoy this one. It charts the continuation of a great epic love story between Arawn, the Lord of the Underworld, and Elen, an Upper World goddess, who have both taken human form on Earth.

You will join Myrddin (Merlin), Taliesin, Manawydan, Creiddylad, Gwyddion, Arianrhod and the eight dwarves in their quest to bury the Thirteen Treasures of Britain. All this, despite the best efforts of the Eye of Soros, Bricriu of the Poison Tongue and Vlak the Dragon Slayer, who are furiously trying to steal the Sovereignty of the Isles of the Blessed.

You will also hear Taliesin's moving rendition of an original Mabinogion myth about how a huge and bitter gulf came about between Ireland and Britain – a deep chasm that is still today to be bridged, and which led to the head of the giant king Bran being buried in the land, for protection.

FURTHER READING

STORIES IN THE STARS
What our ancestors were trying to tell us

by Annie Dieu-Le-Veut

Ancient myths are actually the vessels or arks of our ancestors sailing the seas of Time and containing, deep in their submarinal holds, precious messages about our innate holographic relationship to eternal astrological and alchemical cycles which drive each of us along our life's path.

Over thousands of years, these orally transmitted wisdom teaching stories have been twisted and bastardised into fake histories in order to serve various and changing political imperatives. And they have been concertinaed, truncated and dumbed-down to satisfy the appetites of light entertainment through the shifting narratives, over time, of the mytho-industrial complex.

In Stories in the Stars, Annie Dieu-Le-Veut digs up the originals of these epic tales that were drawn in the glittering night skies of the last Ice Age. She brushes them off and then breaks down their meanings into the simplest of terms, so that we can unlock the doors of our perception with their metaphorical keys to discover that they are actually dramatic devices for the Divine Marriage between an Otherworldly god or goddess and the human being. It is the hidden meaning of the verse from Genesis.

And it came to pass, when men began to multiply on the face of the Earth, and daughters were born unto them, that the sons of God saw the daughters of men that they were fair; and they took them wives of all which they chose...

> *There were giants in the Earth in those days; and also after that, when the sons of God came unto the daughters of men, and they bare children to them, the same became mighty men which were of old, men of renown.*

To the science fiction fan, this passage is about extra-terrestrial giants coming to Earth from other planets and impregnating human females. But to those who have the eyes to see, it is is really about the implosion of divine energies that are the result of the interdimensional coupling through the stages of the Adoration of the Beloved and the Opening of the Magnetic Floor. This produces the Radiant Child, which is not a human baby but the gift of the Sovereignty of the land.

Once we understand the substance of the messages our ancestors left for us thousands of years ago, we realise the value and meaning of human life and finally know what to do with it.

THE THERAPY BOOK

From aromatherapy to zero balancing - and everything in between

by John Board

This is the ultimate natural health reference book for your shelves, with comprehensive information on more than 200 holistic, alternative and complementary health therapies in an easily understandable format.

The Therapy Book is an easily searchable manual that uses plain language and is organised into easy-to-digest, bite-sized chunks, so you will soon know…

- what each therapy is
- how each therapy works
- what each therapy can be used for
- whether the therapy is effective
- whether there are any known side-effects.

The Therapy Book is the perfect gift for discerning individuals who like to look after their own health and wellbeing, as well as holistic health practitioners who wish to continue their professional development.

RESOURCES

Alfred the Great: Asser's Life of King Alfred, translated by Simon Keynes and Michael Lapidge.

Ancient Egypt: The Light of the World, by Gerald Massey.

Antiquities of the Jews, by Josephus.

Astrology of the Old Testament, by Karl Anderson.

Divine Comedy, by Dante Alighieri.

Edda (Everyman), by Snorri Sturluson.

Faery Initiations of the Thirteen Dreamers, by Coleston Brown.

Gesta Regnum Brittaniae, attributed to Breton monk, William of Rennes.

Glastonbury Tor: A Guide to the History and Legends, by Nicholas R. Mann.

Glastonbury: Avalon of the Heart, by Dion Fortune.

Guide to Glastonbury's Temple of the Stars, by Katharine Maltwood.

Gwyn: Ancient god of Glastonbury and Key to the Glastonbury Zodiac, by Yuri Leitch.

High History of the Holy Grail, translated by Sebastian Evans.

Historia Brittonum, by Nennius.

King Arthur's Avalon, by Geoffrey Ashe.

Leaves from the Orchard, by Alan Royce.

Mabon and the Guardians of Celtic Britain, by Caitlin Matthews.

Moon Magic, by Dion Fortune.

Mythology of the British Isles, by Geoffrey Ashe.

Mythologies, by W. B. Yeats.

Myth, Legend & Romance: An Encyclopaedia of the Irish Folk Tradition, by Dáithí Ó hÓgáin.

New Light on the Ancient Mystery of Glastonbury, by John Michel.

Nart Sagas: Ancient Myths and Legends of the Circassians and Abkhazians, by John Colarusso.

Needles of Stone, by Tom Graves.

On Becoming An Alchemist: A guide for the modern magician, by Catherine MacCoun.

FURTHER READING

The Pilgrim's Progress from this World to That Which is to Come, by John Bunyan.

Secrets of the Faery Landscape: New Light on the Glastonbury Zodiac, by Coleston Brown.

Signs & Secrets of the Glastonbury Zodiac, edited by Paul Weston.

Star Tales, by Ian Ridpath.

Taliesin: The Last Celtic Shaman, by John Matthews.

The Ancient Paths, by Graham Robb.

The Adventures of Pinocchio, by Carlos Collodi.

The Avalonians, by Patrick Bentham.

The Complete Idiot's Guide to Alchemy, by Dennis William Hauck.

The Cosmic Serpent, by Dr. Jeremy Narby.

Enchantments of Britain, by Katharine Maltwood.

Egyptian Book of the Dead and the Mysteries of Amenta, by Gerald Massey.

The Fairy-Faith in Celtic Countries, by W.Y. Evans-Wentz.

The Forge and the Crucible: The origins and structures of alchemy, by Mircea Eliade.

The Gate of Remembrance : the Story of the Psychological Experiment Which Resulted in the Discovery of the Edgar Chapel at Glastonbury, by Frederick Bligh Bond.

The Glastonbury Zodiac: The Mysteries of Britain, by Mary Caine.

The Goat Foot God, by Dion Fortune.

The Goddess Obscured: Transformation of the Grain Protectress from Goddess to Saint, by Pamela Berger.

The Hero with a Thousand Faces, by Joseph Campbell.

The High History of the Holy Grail, edited by Sebastian Evans.

The Historical Jesus and the Mythical Christ, by Gerald Massey.

The Jesus Mysteries, by Timothy Freke and Peter Gandy.

The Land, by Virginia Sackville-West.

The Mabinogion, translated by Sioned Davies.

The Mystical Qabalah, by Dion Fortune.

The Nag Hammadi Scriptures, by Marvin W. Meyer.

FURTHER READING

The Path to Alchemy, by Mark Stavish.

The Red and White Springs of Avalon, by Nicholas R. Mann.

The Sea Priestess, by Dion Fortune.

The Spine of Albion: An Exploration of Earth Energies and Landscape Mysteries Along the Belinus Line, by Gary Biltcliffe and Caroline Hoare.

The Star Temple of Avalon: Glastonbury's Ancient Observatory Revealed, by Nicholas R. Mann and Philippa Glasson.

The Sun and the Serpent, by Paul Broadhurst and Hamish Miller.

The Terrestrial Alignments of Katharine Maltwood and Dion Fortune, by Yuri Leitch.

Printed in Great
Britain
by Amazon